NORTHERN PASSAGE

John Hagan

Northern Passage
American Vietnam War Resisters
in Canada

HARVARD UNIVERSITY PRESS
Cambridge, Massachusetts, and London, England   2001

Library of Congress Cataloging-in-Publication Data

Hagan, John, 1946–
  Northern passage : American Vietnam war resisters in Canada / John Hagan.
    p. cm.
  Includes bibliographical references and index.
  ISBN 0-674-00471-X
    1. Vietnamese Conflict, 1961–1975—Draft resisters—United States. 2. Vietnamese
Conflict, 1961–1975—Desertions—United States. 3. Vietnamese Conflict, 1961–1975—Protest
movements—United States. 4. Americans—Canada. 5. Canada—Emigration and immigra-
tion. 6. United States—Emigration and immigration. 7. Amnesty—United States. I. Title.

DS559.8.D7 H33 2001
959.707'704'38   00-054012

Those who make the conscientious judgment that they must not participate in this war . . . have my complete sympathy, and indeed our political approach has been to give them access to Canada. Canada should be a refuge from militarism.

Prime Minister Pierre Trudeau speaking to Mennonite and United Church leaders, 1970 and 1971

He served honorably. True, he didn't go to Vietnam, but his unit wasn't sent. But there's another truth: He did not go to Canada. He did not burn his draft card. And he damn sure didn't burn the American flag.

Presidential candidate George Bush introducing Dan Quayle, 1988

In earlier immigrant booms we welcomed farmers, artisans, railway builders and construction workers. During the Vietnam war we also benefited from actors, poets, educators, writers, social workers, musicians, publishers, and urban planners. Most of all we got people who had social consciences that they refused to betray. Canada is immeasurably in their debt.

Historian Pierre Berton on American Vietnam war resisters, 1996

Contents

Preface: First Snow

Being born in a country is a different experience than becoming part of one. Before arriving in Canada we knew little about the nation we would gratefully come to call our home. When we arrived our lives stretched before us along paths as uncertain as the uncharted Canadian land mass that capped the Amerocentric television weather maps of our youth. Canada was not much more to us than a vague mental map of threatening winter storm systems: Alberta Clippers, thundering out of the frigid northwest and hurtling downward across the barren central plains before crashing like uninvited but predictable guests in the American heartland. Our new Canadian surroundings were a welcome alternative to the images of military service in war-torn Vietnamese villages and jungles. Nonetheless, we were in foreign territory.

Few of us realized how different this nation to the north was from our own. Some knew of, and even visited, Montreal's Expo in 1967, but most did not realize that this world fair celebrated Canada's coming of age in its centenary year, or that this bold look forward coincided with a rising nationalist sentiment that could hardly have been more out of synch with the rebellion and cynicism that preoccupied the United States in the midst of its undeclared war. Trudeaumania, the Quiet Revolution in Quebec, and new questions about the American domination of the Canadian economy were vague abstractions that gradually took on new and unanticipated meanings. Our understanding of our place in the world was changing. We were simultaneously new exiles and New Canadians. The world was changing with incredible speed around us.

I visited Toronto for the first time in the summer of 1968 and on returning to the United States spent an August evening listening to Phil Ochs sing in Chicago's Grant Park across from the Democratic Convention hotels the night before the infamous police riot. The brutal images of the Chicago convention are still familiar to most Americans, but it is less well known that Toronto was then also a city coming alive. The American ghetto, described in Chapter 3 of this book and in the *Manual for Draft-Age Immigrants* that led me there, was taking form in the Baldwin Street neighborhood just south of the University of Toronto. The first arrivals, the "draft dodgers," were soon joined in growing numbers by the "deserters." This area of the city was a benign but unruly communion of countercultural entrepreneurship and antiwar activism. We thought of ourselves as war resisters as well as draft and military resisters, but most of us still do not mind being called "dodgers," for this term still has a positive resonance in Canada. The mood then was a mixture of desperation and excitement; the atmosphere was electric.

My first visit to Toronto opened a new window in my limited view of the world, but I returned to my small Illinois town and to my unresolved relationship with my draft board. The next year was spent pursuing occupational deferments through substitute teaching on Jessie Jackson's south side of Chicago and doing community organization work with VISTA in small Oklahoma towns made famous in the songs of Woody Guthrie. By August 1969 the deferments were ending and I wanted to go to graduate school, for which deferments were no longer forthcoming. I was accepted at the University of Toronto and the University of Alberta. I flipped a coin. It came out Toronto, but I went to Alberta. During the week of Woodstock I headed north to Edmonton. It was a turning point in my life.

A friend of mine had gone to Edmonton the year before. Perhaps like many immigrants I chose a destination that promised a connection to someone I knew. I will always remember my father warning in a departing phone call that this was "the worst mistake I could ever make." My own thinking and the *Manual for Draft-Age Immigrants* persuaded me otherwise. Like most families, mine gradually resigned itself to my decision.

My friend fought a long battle with our draft board that ended with his renouncing his American citizenship in order to forestall criminal prosecution for draft evasion. A year later the Selective Service System was coming undone; our draft board seemed to realize I was following the same path of resistance, to what I assumed would be the same conclusion. To my astonishment, the board sent me a new occupational deferment in Alberta, dated the day before the U.S. government eliminated deferments. It made no difference: I already had decided to stay in Edmonton. Meanwhile, I wondered about those who went to Toronto, the eye in the storm of the Canadian resistance. This book is about the American draft and military resisters who were drawn to Toronto when this storm was in its full fury.

Who, why, how, and with what results were these young Americans drawn into the Canadian war resistance? The Vietnam war migration was the largest politically motivated exodus from the United States since the country's beginning. But what kind of exodus and exile was this? It began as individual acts of resistance against the draft and military laws of the United States. However, individual acts of law resistance do not in themselves make a social movement or produce long-lasting effects on the course of one's life. Chapter 1 of this book recounts the thinking behind decisions to resist the draft and military by emigrating and risking permanent exile in Canada. Chapter 2 presents previously unknown evidence of how and why Canada's Minister of Immigration at first secretly resisted this migration and then decided to support it. Canada's Immigration Act allowed young Americans to resist the Vietnam draft and military mobilization without the threat of going to jail. The rest of the book recounts what happened as this group of immigrants settled into their lives in Canada.

My own relationship to this movement was direct, but nonetheless somewhat remote. I participated in antiwar demonstrations in Edmonton while I was in graduate school; but Vancouver, Montreal, and Toronto, and to a lesser extent Ottawa and Winnipeg, were the focal points of resistance. I knew then that I would later write about this movement, but my involvement was from afar. In short, I observed more than I participated during my early years in Canada. It is obvious "whose side I was on," although I was on the distant sidelines of western Canada.

I did not arrive in Toronto until 1974, where I spent most of the next half of my life on faculty at the University of Toronto. Baldwin Street still had an American ambience. Amex, the most politically active of the Toronto resistance organizations, was preparing for its most dramatic role in the campaign for a universal and unconditional amnesty, which culminated in the nomination of a war resister for Vice-President at Jimmy Carter's 1976 Democratic Convention. The background of this climax to the Canadian war resistance, peripherally portrayed through the eyes of Ron Kovic in the film *Born on the Fourth of July*, is described in Chapter 5 of this book. There are still more than an estimated ten thousand American draft and military resisters living in Toronto. They remain an important, albeit now far less conspicuous, presence. The longer-term activism of this now middle-aged group is described and analyzed in Chapter 4.

At the core of the American Vietnam generation migration to Canada is the question of what kind of movement this was. Was it simply a marginal, short-lived, and highly individualized spin-off of the American antiwar movement? Or, despite its coming after that movement began and despite its roots in resistance of the draft and Vietnam military service, did the exile migration have its own original, organized, and lasting collective meaning as a turning point in the lives of the resisters and for Canada as well? Were the American draft and military resisters who came to Canada marginal, or were they instead marginalized by an American culture that did not appreciate the form of their war resistance and continuing activism?

As the epigraphs of this book suggest, there remain strong differences of opinion about the American war resisters. At the root of these differences is a debate about whether the Americans who came to Canada were wrong-minded or responsible in taking refuge there. Neither legal scholars nor analysts of social movements have put much effort into examining this issue or movement, choosing to focus instead on more central and better established forms of law resistance and social movements, most notably the U.S. civil rights movement. Yet studying lesser-known groups can be of vital social scientific as well as historical significance—especially as a means of expanding the scope of our understanding of the role of law resistance and social movements as turning points in the life course.

One hundred American Vietnam war resisters, most of whom still live in Toronto, helped to satisfy my curiosity about these issues. They patiently participated in my lengthy interviews and in so doing helped me put this story together. I originally assumed I would use pseudonyms for these people; but many individuals felt strongly that their names should appear, and only a few did not want their names used. Thus, Sandra Foster, Michele Sanders, and John Wolfson are the only pseudonyms used in this book. I have not included source citations for quotes from my own interviews, except where these interviews are with former government officials or involve establishing specific facts as part of a historical record of the Vietnam war resistance movement in Canada and the United States.

Robert Pritchard, president of the University of Toronto, helped me to arrange interviews with the Minister of Immigration, the Minister of External Affairs, and other key Canadian government ministers and advisers of this period. I also benefited from remarkable archival materials. The archives of the Toronto Anti-Draft Program are kept in the Thomas Fisher Rare Book Library of the University of Toronto and were opened for the first time for my research. I also used the detailed records of the organization and news magazine *Amex,* which were archived by Jack Colhoun, its longtime editor, at the State Historical Society at the University of Wisconsin in Madison. Unique insights were provided by oral histories recorded in the late 1970s by former residents of the American ghetto around Baldwin Street and maintained at the Multicultural Historical Society of Ontario in Toronto.

Doug Norris of the General Social Survey at Statistics Canada undertook special analyses of the Canadian census to assist me in estimating the numbers of American resisters who came to Canada during the Vietnam period and who stayed. The resourceful librarians of the National Archives of Canada in Ottawa assisted me in locating and declassifying previously restricted government and immigration department files. Jim Jasper, Glen Elder, and John Laub provided invaluable commentary on my work, along with several anonymous reviewers. Michael Aronson pushed and pulled me in the ways an exceptionally skillful editor can and must. Doug McAdam inspired this book with his *Freedom Summer,* provided invaluable input at crucial intervals, and pressed me to be clear about the issues on which we disagreed. This research was made possible by a Social Sciences and Humanities Research Council of Canada grant and a John Simon Guggenheim Fellowship.

Women are a crucial part of the story that follows. Karen Bays helped me decide to come to Canada and came with me; Patricia Parker organized and assisted me throughout the research, painstakingly transcribing every interview; Pam Erlichman helped edit the manuscript; and Linda Hagan listened and contributed to my ruminations about almost every interview and piece of archival material over the two years and more that I spent collecting data, writing, and rewriting. Linda and I became citizens of Canada together.

NORTHERN PASSAGE

CHAPTER 1

Laws of Resistance

A decade after arriving in Canada, Don Holman, who is today a well-known printmaker, recalled through an artist's eyes his crossing. He had been living in a commune and working in the war resistance while attending art college on a scholarship in Kansas City. Don had joined Students for a Democratic Society (SDS) and was speaking against the war to school and church groups. Shortly after graduation he was working in a studio when two FBI agents arrived at the door to deliver his induction notice, without the warning of a pre-induction physical. He decided then, in the spring of 1968, that he would leave the United States and come to Canada. Several members of his Kansas City commune came to Canada before and after him.

On the cusp of adulthood, Don Holman had already seen a dark side of life in the United States. Not long before he left Kansas City, the National Guard was called into the city in response to the disturbances that had followed the assassination of Martin Luther King, Jr. He remembers arriving in front of his home one evening to find soldiers in the middle of the road. The guardsmen were presumably protecting the neighborhood from post-King assassination rioting and looting. "There were three with rifles pointed one direction, and three with rifles pointed at me. A state trooper flagged me down. He didn't say 'Can I see your driver's license' or anything. He just ripped open the driver-side door and threw me up against the car and told me to freeze." Don vividly recalls a young guardsman trembling while holding a rifle on him. Don thought the guardsman looked crazed, really afraid, although Don also remembers feeling that he must have been the one who was more afraid, looking down the barrel of a gun. They didn't detain him long, but the experience made an impression. Within the month Don was on his way north—despite the reluctance of his father to discuss the issue and the suggestion of his mother that she didn't want him going to "some godforsaken country."

Don Holman didn't know much about Canada. A distant relative of his father's had discovered Holman Island in the Northwest Territories. Beyond this, he knew little more than what he had read in the *Manual for Draft-Age Immigrants*, published by the Toronto Anti-Draft Program. He had learned that Toronto was a big city, that he could drive there, and that he probably would not be sent back. His main concern was crossing the border. He packed his belongings into his battered red Triumph and headed north.

Don first tried to cross at Sarnia, Ontario. He nervously combed his hair back before approaching the Canadian border station by car. He told the immigration officer that he might be looking for a job in Canada and was politely told that it was illegal for an American to enter Canada for the purpose of seeking employment. Discouraged but undeterred, he returned to the American side and headed for Detroit, about an hour away. There he crossed over the bridge to Windsor and this time explained that he was coming to Canada to visit a friend. The officer waved him through, and he was on his way.

The first thing Don remembers is the color of the road. "The highway looked green," he recalls. He still insists thirty years later that the asphalt had a green appearance. "I remember it very, very clearly and distinctly . . . I look at colors. I would look at these roads . . . Each state has a different kind of color in the road; it's true . . . Right outside of Windsor . . . [was] the Macdonald-Cartier Freeway. I looked at the road, I had to stop the car, I had to get out and look at it, because it had a green cast . . . and I almost turned around and went back and crossed the bridge to look at the road on the other side to see if it was me or if it was really true."

He drove all the way to Toronto and remembers arriving on Dundas Street. It was the end of a long day, he was tired, and it was rush hour. He stopped at a gas station and asked directions to a downtown address where he was to meet friends who had preceded him from Kansas City. The gas station attendant found the address on a map and cringed, "Oh jeez, you're going down there. Oh, that's a rough neighborhood. You watch yourself, lad." This worried Don. What had he gotten himself into? Where was he headed? He drove, he found the address, but he couldn't see the problem. This didn't look like a dangerous neighborhood. This wasn't like any slum that he knew about. The area was off Yonge Street, close to Cabbagetown. If this was a problem neighborhood, Don knew that he had arrived in the right place.

A Remarkable Migration

The migration of Vietnam-era American draft and military resisters to Canada began as a trickle in the mid-1960s and grew into a fast-flowing stream by the end of the decade. Just over 100 resisters, known more commonly as "draft dodgers" and "deserters," came to Canada in 1964.[1] By 1965 the number was more than ten times that. Over 3,000 resisters came in 1967; from 5,000 to 8,000 came yearly from 1968 through 1973. These were just the men. More women than men came, most as partners and spouses, and some on their own.[2] This was the largest politically motivated migration from the United States since the United Empire Loyalists moved north to oppose the American Revolution. Americans formed about 20 percent of all immigrants to Canada during the period of the Vietnam war—more than any other immigrant group.

Altogether, more than an estimated 50,000 young Americans migrated to Canada in opposition to U.S. draft and military laws. If Americans of all ages are counted, the number is closer to 100,000. It will never be known exactly how many came or eventually stayed.[3] Neither government kept count. By the end of the war, Senator Edward Kennedy chaired Justice Committee hearings in the U.S. Senate and instructed Justice Department officials to come forward with lists of who they were pursuing for war-related infractions. This list included 4,500 names. The American government preferred to ignore the rest.[4]

The Canadian government required no information as to why individuals came to Canada, and this enforced ignorance helped keep some hostile immigration officials honest in their treatment of war resisters seeking to enter the country. These officials were the gatekeepers to Canada, and they used interpretations of immigration law and regulations to control entry, sometimes to the disadvantage of draft resisters and, in the early stages, usually to the disadvantage of military resisters. The border was the point where resistance to American selective service and military law intersected with Canadian immigration law. This migration had serious social and political consequences for the arriving Americans as well as for Canada as a whole.

Most American resisters initially came to Vancouver, Montreal, and Toronto. Many who entered elsewhere wound up in Toronto. Vancouver's labor force was tightly unionized, making jobs hard to find, and Montreal presented language problems. English-speaking and increasingly cosmopolitan Toronto became the place of settlement for the largest number of American resisters.[5] This book focuses on resisters who settled in Toronto, but considers broader implications of this migration for Canada as well.

Opportunity in Exile

The American resisters arrived with greater certainty about their reasons for coming than about the directions they expected their lives would take in Canada. Three decades later, with the resisters having lived more than half of their years in Canada, it is possible to assess how the move affected their lives. A number of questions now can be answered. How did they decide to come to Canada? How did the settlement process unfold? Did the legal and political events that brought the resisters to Canada continue to be important to them? How socially and politically active was this group once they settled in Canada? Are they still socially and politically active? Did their acts of resistance disrupt the likely trajectories of their lives? Or did their migration instead cause only short-term disorder and turbulence but with few lasting effects? If there were lasting effects, what are they? For example, are they reflected in career choices? Were there long-term occupational costs— for example, in reduced earnings? How did their migration shape the American resisters' feelings of national identity?

Note that each of these questions assumes that the American resisters made unusual and potentially transformative decisions to come to Canada. Their law resistance differed from situational tactics of civil disobedience such as destroying draft cards and records and blockading selective service offices as well as from more direct legal confrontations such as refusing military service and going to trial and to jail. The American exiles' draft and military resistance was a sustained strategy involving individual acts of legal noncompliance by leaving the country. Exile was not a choice commonly made by members of earlier generations.

Americans tend to be patriotic, and are apt to be unsympathetic to citizens who leave the country during wartime in acts of legal and political defiance against their government. Perhaps this is why neither Americans in general nor American social scientists in particular have given much attention to the exiles of the Vietnam generation. Also, like much else that happens outside of America's borders, exiles tend to be ignored and forgotten. Those both inside and outside the war resistance movement often saw the American war exiles as either making a self-serving "end run" around American law or withdrawing from the war resistance by going to Canada. To those in the

United States, the exiles remain a largely unknown and marginalized group. Yet exile was the end neither of the expatriates' life stories nor of their significance.

This is especially true if we want to learn more about the range of ways in which law resistance and social movements intersect and influence human lives. In an analysis of research on social movements, David Meyer has urged that we need more work on "marginal groups" as well as on "more established ones" because "the marginalized groups are also related to the political process." He observes that the dominant, political process theory of social movements, whose application I urge should be broadened, typically has encouraged researchers to pay greater attention to "more rational challengers" who are unambiguously engaged in turning political opportunities into social movements—for example, those who engineered the protests and demonstrations of the U.S. civil rights movement.[6] Meyer's analysis acknowledges that modern social movement theory draws implicit, if not explicit, distinctions in tacitly presuming that some activists and groups are more rational than others. Rather than leave this kind of presumption untested, Meyer urges the position adopted in this book: that marginalized individuals and groups be given new and greater attention for comparison with the more frequently studied "rational challengers" connected to the "more established groups."

Presumptions of wrong-mindedness if not irrationality subtly and persistently pervade American thoughts about the Canadian Vietnam migration, even though such presumptions about political movements typically have been discredited when they have been explicitly tested by social scientists. Furthermore, Canadian immigration law can be understood, in a straightforward extension of political process theory, as having offered a significant political opportunity for Americans rationally to resist the imposition of Vietnam-era draft and military laws. Yet we know little about whether or how such opportunities are mobilized by individuals and groups that are regarded as marginal, such as the American resisters. Meyer and others rightly worry that limiting attention to more "established" groups, as political process theory tends to do—in this case, by confining attention to groups resisting the Vietnam war in the United States—can restrict understanding of social movements.[7]

So the Americans who came to Canada as a means of refusing to serve in the Vietnam war are subjects of social scientific as well as historical significance. Use of Canadian immigration law to defy American selective service and military laws gave them a unique opportunity to continue their political protest against the military and the war without the impediment of imprisonment. Some observers, of course, argued that the Americans' leaving the country was more a matter of personal opportunism than political opportunity. Others countered with the argument that the act of going into exile was a significant form of resistance, even if it involved only an avoidance or evasion of draft and military laws and no further form of activism against the war or the military. The more active American war resisters in Canada frequently made the latter point on behalf of the less active resisters. Yet little is actually known about the movement participation and social activism of resisters in general following their migration.

Law resistance can be an important first step toward participation in social movements and longer-term social activism. In this book I examine law in the context of the life course as a means of exploring this linkage.[8] The 1960s was a time when the place of law in the life course became a more open question.

The Path Not Taken

To those coming of age in the 1960s, the normative life course of the 1950s was a straight and narrow path in need of liberation.[9] As the twentieth century progressed, the state had become increasingly involved in marking milestones along this path, beginning with one's birth and not necessarily ending with death.[10] For the presumed benefit of child and society, compulsory education established boundaries of legal transition from infancy to early childhood and mandated the minimum age for entering and leaving school. Laws were passed to monitor the timing of one's first consuming alcohol, consenting to sex, operating an automobile, entering into marriage, and working for paid remuneration. These and other laws demarcated the normative boundaries between adolescence and adulthood. They reflected societal expectations about preparation for and the onset of paid employment, marriage, and the responsibilities of adulthood.

In the United States of the mid-twentieth century, this all seemed normal. Laws specified punishments to enforce the age-graded expectations, but young people mostly were expected to comply without thought of penalties. Youths were socialized through family and school, by age and stage, with little official notice of alternative possibilities. Infancy gave way to early childhood education, secondary and postsecondary education gave way to work and marriage. This was the normative life course, legally demarcated. At midcentury, for most Americans, this was the way it was supposed to be. When adolescents, especially advantaged adolescents, challenged the normative expectations of the 1950s, they became cultural objects of curiosity, rebels without a cause.

Yet few lives actually were lived in such rigidly straight and narrow ways. Sex researchers found that precocious sexuality was common; delinquency researchers found that adolescent law violations were frequent.[11] The life course also brought twists and turns. Even in the 1950s many parents could recall the disruptions in their own life paths caused by World War II. Perhaps the disruptions of the war had produced a societal yearning for a more orderly life course. When the twists and turns of life trajectories were consequential, they often were regarded as turning points.[12] For example, World War II military service was unexpected, but it also was regarded as a formative turning point for many fathers of the postwar baby boom.

Some turning points, however, left less pleasant memories than others, and some were clearly damaging.[13] When these twists and turns were defined as disreputable, they were often occasions for legal intervention, and in retrospect some of these events foreshadowed bigger problems to come. For example, rates of selective service violations and desertion increased as the Korean war progressed.[14] Although Korea was officially a "military action" and not a war, draft and military violations were punished by law, with negative repercussions for those involved. In addition, there was growing concern that family breakdown and educational failure earlier in the life course could lead to conflict with the law, although some wondered whether the law might compound these problems. Indeed, implications of the law and its imposition began to loom more menacingly in the minds of some Americans. Sociologists in particular wondered if legal labels and punishments might often do more harm than good.[15]

Yet legal scholars and social scientists paid surprisingly little attention to the longer-term influence of law and unlawful behavior in shaping human lives. Analysts of social movements recognized the value of life-course data,[16] but without focusing on the biographical consequences of law resistance per se. A few early criminologists developed longitudinal data sets to allow analysis of the consequences of law violations in early adulthood,[17] but mostly these data were left to be more fully analyzed by others.[18] Those who study law and its effects are just beginning to realize the possibilities that longitudinal data collection presents for exploring the consequences of law violations and legal interventions in human lives. This is significant because the law itself is an important but neglected part of the life course, especially when the law becomes entwined with social movements and social change. This became apparent to young Americans during the buildup of the Vietnam war.

For many young American males confronted with the prospect of serving in the Vietnam war, the life path suddenly swerved out of control. The path that led from adolescence to adulthood now included having to participate in an unpopular war. A legal roadblock formed by selective service and military laws suddenly threatened to divert and redirect adolescents making the transition to adulthood. Young Americans protested by organizing demonstrations, burning draft cards, disrupting selective service operations, and interfering with the military buildup in various ways. Some went to jail for their protests, for resisting induction or for leaving the military, while a significant number stepped off the national path of military service altogether and crossed over a bridge that offered them refuge in Canada. This was a turning point in the life course that involved leaving behind one set of national roles and assuming another. It involved a form of dissent and resistance against American selective service and military laws that on the one hand made these young migrants into expatriates and exiles, and on the other, through the immigration laws of Canada, turned them into New Canadians.

Turning points are by definition consequential. This turning point was especially consequential because it combined a role exit involving legal dissent and resistance with a role entrance involving cross-national migration and the transition to adulthood. Dennis Hogan and Nan Marie Astone note that transitions into adulthood are of great interest to social scientists because they provide "entry ports" for subsequent familial and occupational careers.[19] The intention of some young Americans to resist service in the Vietnam war by migrating made their transition to adulthood unique. This was certainly not what the American Selective Service System envisioned when it set out its own conception of the normative transition from adolescence to adulthood.

The head of the Selective Service System, General Lewis Hershey, issued a document in 1965 under the title *Memorandum on Channeling* that spelled out an ambitiously detailed plan to influence the educational and occupational life course of young American males.[20] It did this by expanding the meaning of the word "service" and its implications for registrants for the draft: "The meaning of the word 'service,' with its former restricted application to the armed forces, is certain to become widened much more in the future. This brings with it the ever-increasing problem of how to control effectively the service of individuals who are not in the Armed Forces. It is in dealing with these other millions of registrants that the system is heavily occupied, developing more effective human beings in the national interest."[21] This sweeping memorandum went on to outline how the draft deferral and exemption system was intended to direct the life-course choices of young men.

A key point of the system was to encourage able registrants, who were usually of advantaged backgrounds, to pursue higher education and to select occupations deemed in the national interest. These jobs included teaching as well as work in national defense industries, public health, the Peace Corps, and VISTA. The incentives to pursue these occupations were educational followed by occupational deferments. The punishments for declining them were induction and military service. At first, this system rewarded socially and educationally advantaged young Americans by allowing them to delay or avoid military service; but delay and avoidance became increasingly problematic. As the military buildup in Vietnam increased, the legal escape routes from military service narrowed. The Selective Service System legally restructured the normative life course of young Americans until youthful American resistance against its tightening requirements made the system unworkable in the late 1960s. The migration to Canada was a significant part of this resistance and a turning point in the lives of those who were involved.

Disorder and Dissent in the Life Course

There was and still is a strong tendency among many Americans to see the northward migration of the American Vietnam war resisters as wrong-minded if not irrational, and irresponsible if not illegal. They saw this move as a disorderly departure from the normative life course established by and for earlier generations of Americans. This is reflected in the dramaturgical stereotypes found in recently popular fictionalized treatments of resisters. For example, Margaret Atwood in *The Robber Bride* introduces Billy as a self-centered and physically abusive draft dodger who leaves his penniless and pregnant partner on the Toronto Islands.[22] In *The Laws of Our Fathers*, Scott Turow describes Seth as an immature and ineffectual college dropout running from the draft who at the last minute before induction aborts a planned flight to Canada by going underground and participating in a plot to extort money from his own father.[23] In *A Prayer for Owen Meany,* John Irving creates a dyslexic narrator, John Wheelright, who loses his mother in a freak childhood accident; is raised by a widowed stepfather; eludes the draft through the nonaccidental loss of his trigger finger; and then, without apparent need or political purpose, migrates to Toronto to become a bachelor schoolteacher cloistered within the confines of a privileged private school.[24] Pat Conroy's *Beach Music* is narrated by a draft-dodging character who gets all the way to the Canadian border before guiltily turning back and features a character named Jordan who protests the Vietnam war by blowing up a plane and inadvertently killing two people before escaping to Europe to go underground in a monastery.[25] None of these characters is portrayed as rational or responsible in his war resistance.

Movies, too, have stigmatized resisters. After analyzing eighty-six Vietnam war films, Jerry Lembcke concluded that by the 1980s moviemakers commonly associated the antiwar movement with repugnantly irrational behavior and misrepresented antiwar Vietnam veterans as criminal, crippled, and crazy.[26] George Bush tapped into the popularity of such sentiments at the 1986 Republican Convention by getting applause with the line that his running mate, National Guard reservist Dan Quayle, "did not go to Canada." Even Todd Gitlin's landmark social history *The Sixties* dismissively characterized "draft dodging" by posing the stereotype-laden question "What if the logic of their individualist revolt led no further than sex, drugs, and rock 'n roll, and dodging the draft?"[27]

In a more generic way, early theoretical depictions of the life course, now discredited, used a related kind of imagery to portray individuals who strayed from the normative life path. Early researchers proposed that lifecycle transitions should occur at appropriate ages and in an appropriate sequence.[28] The usual order was to leave school, enter the labor force full time, get married, and then have a child. The place of military service was less certain.

Selective service provisions initially made it possible to delay military service until after one had left school and offered the further possibility of choosing an occupation that allowed one to avoid service altogether. Alternatively, one could either serve or find some ploy or ruse to minimize the interruption of the life course posed by military service. The war resisters who emigrated to Canada challenged normative expectations with a legally dubious and disruptive move. Researchers initially expected that variations from normative expectations would have a negative influence on later marriage and job experience.[29] An implication was that the nonnormative disorder and disruption caused by resisting the draft and military service and emigrating to Canada was wrong-minded and irresponsible to oneself as well as to one's family and country. Emigration added uncertainty to institutional arrangements already jeopardized by the need to negotiate a transition through military service.

Collective behavior theorists of the 1950s and early 1960s also depicted decisions to dissent and resist as irrational and irresponsible. Neil Smelser brought psychological attributions of irrationality and irresponsibility into the 1960s with his Freudian explanation of the protest movement, suggesting, for example, that "the striking feature of the protest movement is what Freud observed: it permits the expression of impulses that are normally repressed."[30] Lewis Feuer, who during the American war migration and toward the conclusion of his own career moved from Berkeley to the University of Toronto, emphasized the irrationality of 1960s student-led movements in his book *The Conflict of Generations*.[31] Smelser recently reintroduced a psychodynamic theme involving the role of ambivalence in social movements in his 1998 Presidential Address to the American Sociological Association.[32] Smelser now argues for the influential role of feelings of ambivalence, including powerful and extrarational if not irrational mixtures of love and hate, in political movements and other social phenomena such as cross-national migration.

Emigration decisions and social movement participation do often involve strong emotions, and Smelser's emphasis on the role of ambivalence is an interesting way of reintroducing this point. The challenge is to incorporate this kind of insight without continuing the erroneous and circular psychodynamics of the past. As Meyer concludes, "The basic tenets of collective behavior approaches (that is, irrational activity by atomized individuals lacking other means of pursuing their claims) did not stand empirical examination."[33] Equally troubling is the tendency of such "theories of the mind" to become what Charles Tilly has called a form of "phenomenological fundamentalism" in which "people do things because they have propensities to do those things."[34] In addition, this perspective tends to be applied only to protesters and emigrants rather than to the authorities, whose response to these dissenters is frequently intransigent, belligerent, or ambivalent. Despite these reservations, in the final chapter of this book I incorporate some of Smelser's thoughts about ambivalence by examining the role of legal developments in structuring the social psychology of the American resisters' long-term adjustments to Canada.

Reconceiving Disorder and Dissent

Contemporary researchers acknowledge that disorder and dissent often are rational expressions of human agency. Current life-course theory emphasizes that the time after high school is fluid and reversible[35] and that the 1950s normative life course no longer prevails.[36] This theory now suggests that alternative, nonnormative role choices may be beneficial, as judged by a variety of life-outcome measures, depending on what the roles themselves mean and how they are causally linked.[37] Newer perspectives also give greater attention to human agency in determining life outcomes in purposeful ways.[38] Law resistance can be an expression of agency and purpose, although researchers have not yet fully explored the implications of this possibility in the life course.

Meanwhile, social movement theory and research also have undergone a paradigmatic shift. Now emphasized is the role of rational action pursued through political opportunities, mobilizing structures, and culturally framed human agency. These newer resource-mobilization and political-process models of social movements share a common emphasis on rationally organized processes.[39] Doug McAdam writes that "social movements are seen, in both perspectives, as rational attempts by excluded groups to mobilize sufficient political leverage to advance collective interests through noninstitutionalized means."[40] However, this emphasis on rational action is neither universally nor unconditionally applied. Rather, this perspective has focused rather restrictively on more "central" and "established" social movements, such as the U.S. civil rights movement. But before we consider the scope of this theory, we must first establish its components.

The central thesis of the dominant political-process theory of social movements is that movement activity emerges in response to political opportunities. For example, Sidney Tarrow writes in *Power in Movement* that "people join in social movements in response to political opportunities and then, through collective action, create new ones." That is, "the 'when' of social movement mobilization—when political opportunities are opening up— goes a long way to explaining its 'why.'"[41] Although there is debate about what to include in the theoretical inventory of political opportunities, the first "consensual" inclusion in a taxonomy of political opportunities proposed by McAdam is "the relative openness or closure of the institution-alized political system."[42] Interestingly, relatively little attention has been given to law as a structure that opens such political opportunities. Canadian immigration law can be seen as a crucial opening of political opportunity for Americans who wished to resist U.S. draft and military laws without going to prison.

The second element in the political-process approach is the presence of mobilizing structures. Doug McAdam, John McCarthy, and Mayer Zald de-fine mobilizing structures as "collective vehicles, informal as well as formal, through which people mobilize and engage in collective action." The impor-tance of these structures is reflected in the premise that opportunity without organization usually does not take the form of a social movement. Thus po-tential movement participants must "have available to them 'mobilizing structures' of sufficient strength to get the movement off the ground."[43]

The mobilizing organizations that greeted most American resisters as they arrived in Toronto were the Toronto Anti-Draft Program and Amex. There was a basic body-mind division of labor between these organizations: the first looked after settlement needs and the second focused more on the polit-ical dimension of the newly arriving resisters. As we will see, there was an integrative, overlapping residential and organizational aspect to the rela-tionship between these mobilizing structures.[44] Social networks surround-ing such organizations are key parts of the political-process perspective, al-though their influence often comes later, as law resistance leads to more organized social movement activity.

The third distinctive feature of the political-process approach emphasizes the role of cultural framings in tying together political opportunities and mobilizing structures to form social movements. McAdam, McCarthy, and Zald describe these cultural framings as "mediating between the structural requirements of opportunity and organization" to provide "the emergent meanings and definitions—or frames—shared by the adherents of the bur-geoning movement."[45] As will become apparent, the American resisters struggled with the symbolic and cultural framing of their activities in Can-ada, and were often uncertain about what it meant to be exiles, expatriates, or New Canadians. This was further complicated as the American resisters became symbols of their new nation's autonomy and sovereignty in relation to the United States. This raised a question of how involved New Canadians should continue to be in American antiwar issues, and how persistent they might continue to be in their social activism.

These three factors of political-process theory are seen as shaping the rational and responsible organization of human efforts through collective initiatives directed at social change. McAdam argues for the emphasis on rationality in this framework by observing, "If movement participants are motivated only by the desire to express 'normally forbidden impulses,' or to manage 'feelings of anxiety and futility,' then we would hardly expect social movements to be effective as social change vehicles."[46] For political-process theorists, opportunity and reason replace the factors of impulse and anxiety in modern social-movements theory; however, as noted earlier, there are limits imposed on which social movements are thought to be understandable in terms of opportunity and reason.

That is, modern researchers suggest that law-linked dissent and disorder can be important turning points in the life paths of individuals and the environments in which they take place. Further, in conjunction with political opportunity and mediated by mobilizing structures and cultural framings, law resistance can be an important catalyst for social and political activism. However, the implications of these insights have been restricted not only because social scientists who study law have taken insufficient advantage of advances in longitudinal data collection, but also because political-process theorists have been hesitant to extend the scope of this perspective beyond established boundaries. A result is that many forms of law resistance are simply not seen by the public or by political-process theorists as rational responses to opportunities.

The Vietnam-generation migration to Canada is often seen by Americans as a marginal social movement, or as a collection of wrong-minded, individualized acts of personal opportunism, with the implication that this migration has little to tell us about law or social movements. For example, as discussed in Chapter 5, even President Carter, who conceded the racist consequences of the war, provided only a partial pardon for draft resisters, which included the idea of wrongdoing, rather than a more general amnesty, which would have better acknowledged a rightful resistance of American "dodgers" and "deserters." Contemporary statements of social-movement theory unintentionally reinforce this kind of characterization by advocating a limited application of the political-process perspective.

Doug McAdam is most explicit in his reluctance to assume that political-process theory can explain less established or more marginal social movements. The American Vietnam war migration to Canada falls into a category that McAdam calls a "spin-off movement"—a movement inspired by, yet separate from, an earlier "initiator movement." McAdam is doubtful that one could "document a significant expansion in political opportunities in the case of all—or even most—spin-off movements."[47] However, McAdam also is careful to emphasize that this doubt is based on speculation and that "only through empirical work will we be able to test this impressionistic hunch."[48]

In a recent critique of political-process theory, Jeff Goodwin and James Jasper suggest that theoretical speculation about spin-off movements raises serious questions. They reason that "if most movements arise in the wake of 'initiator' movements . . . and if most of these 'spin-off' movements are not the result of expanding political opportunities, then it follows that many, if not most, social movements are not the result of expanding political opportunities."[49] Since political opportunity is probably the most central concept in political-process theory, Goodwin and Jasper's critique raises serious doubts about the generality of the theory. Research clearly is needed on what many have regarded as marginal or spin-off social movements.

It is probably correct to say that the migration to Canada began as a spin-off of the American Vietnam war movement. Yet in contrast to McAdam's reservations I propose that the Canadian Immigration Act was a political opportunity that allowed the resistance involved in the migration of American war resisters to become the basis of a sustained antiwar movement and continuing social activism. That is, the extension of the political-process framework to this American migration anticipates a progression from law resistance through social-movement mobilization to lifelong social and political activism.

The question therefore follows whether political-process theory can account for significant consequences of the American migration. The resisters' individualized roles in their "self-recruitment" for immigration to Canada might seem to make unlikely the importance attached to social networks and mobilizing structures, both in political-process theory and as a way of understanding the consequences of the law resistance involved in the migration. Yet such mobilization structures and networks did emerge and did affect the lives of the American resisters. Similarly, the ambiguous implications of the cultural framing of the new American migrants as New Canadians, with accompanying expectations of peaceful assimilation, might also have impeded the translation of law resistance into a sustained social movement and continued social and political activism. Yet perhaps this cultural framing may alternatively have helped to meaningfully channel the directions that the migrants' social activism took as they became New Canadians.

In short, the American Vietnam war migration to Canada provides a valuable test of the scope of political-process theory for an understanding of law resistance, social movements, and the life course. In this book I explore how resistance against U.S. selective service and military laws combined with the admission of resisters to Canada through its immigration law to create turning points in the formation of a social movement, foster continuing social and political activism in individual lives, and affect relations between the United States and Canada. The Vietnam-era migration to Canada provides a unique opportunity to explore the implications of law resistance as a source of social-movement activism and its consequences in the course of human lives.

The Long View

In the 1970s several studies charted the early experiences of American war resisters who entered Canadian society.[50] Since then attention to this group has been limited, largely anecdotal and predominately autobiographical or journalistic.[51] Perhaps this is so because although Canada is a multicultural country that encourages immigrants to maintain their cultural ties, Canadian national identity is formed in counterpoint to American culture, making American immigrants, including war resisters, disinclined to identify with their American past. Jay Scott, himself an American who came to Canada with the war resisters and eventually became Canada's best-known movie critic, noted that despite Canada's multiculturalism, there are no American-Canadians and that many "dodgers simply vanished, virtually as a point of honor, into the Canadian context."[52] This ambivalence about "Americanness" in Canada dates to early and often competing cultural framings of the resisters as exiles, expatriates, and New Canadians. A worrisome result is that a unique set of life experiences is at risk of fading into obscurity as the resisters move into the later years of their lives in Canada.

In this book I draw on archival, census, and interview materials to analyze the American resister experience in Canada. The archival materials come from Canadian war resistance organization files and recently declassified Canadian Immigration Department files of the 1960s and 1970s. These files document the internal policies and practices that determined when and how American draft and military resisters were able to come to Canada. These re-

cords establish how Canadian immigration law and regulations gave the resisters a political opening for their migration to Canada.

Census materials are another important part of this study. They were used
to estimate when and how many young Americans came and stayed in Canada. This documentation of comings and goings sets the context for an analysis of the lasting effects of this migration on feelings of national identity
among war resisters who stayed. The specific social-historical context of the
time when the resisters came, including the social and legal developments
associated in Canada with the imposition of the War Measures Act in response to events in Quebec, had a major effect on the emigrants' decisions
and feelings about choosing to live in Canada.

Perhaps the most important source of information is the one hundred personal interviews I conducted with war resisters. These interviews provide
key information on the migration, settlement, and short- and longer-term
adjustment of the American war resisters to their lives in Canada. A major
problem was how to draw the sample to be interviewed, since neither official American nor Canadian records provide a meaningful sampling frame.
I decided to use a respondent-driven sampling methodology that involved
the initial subjects in guiding me to others to be interviewed. I discuss this
sampling method and its implications in Appendix A. Here it is important to
emphasize that this interview sample is not intended to represent all resisters who came to Canada, but rather those who were drawn to and who settled in metropolitan Toronto, which was a focal point of Canadian resistance
activities.

As noted earlier, slightly more U.S. women than men came to Canada
during the Vietnam war. A gender imbalance has long characterized U.S.
migration to Canada, and the numbers of men and women actually moved
closer to parity during the peak of the Vietnam period, when the growth in
male American immigration increased more quickly than that of American
women.[53] Women were still, however, a major part of the war resister migration. Although earlier samples of resisters in Canada have included only
males, Kasinsky's research demonstrated in qualitative terms that women
were an important part of this movement.[54]

The resulting dilemma is that while only the American males who came
to Canada were directly confronting the selective service and military laws
of the United States, the women who came with the men and on their own
were also prominently involved in the war resistance effort. One significant

difference was that most of the men expected that they would not be able to return to the United States without risking arrest and punishment; almost all the women knew they could return with impunity. Yet, as Glen Elder has noted, "No principle of life course study is more central than the notion of interdependent lives."[55] Consistent with this principle of what Elder calls "linked lives" is an abundance of evidence that the women who came to Canada with the men to resist the war played important parts in the resistance effort.

Doug McAdam's research on young men and women who participated in the Freedom Summer civil rights project in Mississippi provides a parallel example of the linked lives of those involved. Although both men and women were recruited, the men were generally given the more dangerous field work of voter registration, a primary purpose of Freedom Summer, while the women, against their preferences, were predominantly given more protected jobs as freedom school teachers, clerical workers, and community center staff. Nonetheless, McAdam found that the women were vital participants and were in notable ways more significantly affected by the Freedom Summer experience.[56] Such findings made it clear that women should be included in the present study. To capture differences and similarities in the male and female experience of the war resistance movement in Canada, in the following chapters I analyze responses of the men and women both separately and together.

The American Wave

The Vietnam war migration to Canada was part of a tidal wave of social and political protest that swept across the United States in the late 1960s, cresting at the close of the decade and spilling across the border into Canada. "Their presence has been felt," newly elected Prime Minister Trudeau remarked in understatement about the new arrivals during a 1969 press conference in Washington.[57]

Figure 1.1 charts the interviewees' ranking of events related to their decision to come to Canada and the timing of their arrival. The highest-ranked event in each year is presented in the figure. As might be expected, pressure began to build with the 1967 protest at the Pentagon, continued through the April and June 1968 assassinations of Martin Luther King, Jr., and Robert Kennedy, and peaked with the August 1968 riot at the Democratic Party Convention in Chicago. The growing force of the protests anticipated the peak in the movement of the sampled respondents to Canada. As shown in Figure 1.1, more than half of them came to Canada during 1968 and 1969.

Several people I interviewed came directly from the Chicago convention to Toronto, and their experiences and thoughts illustrate how this migration gained momentum. Ann Pohl and Peter Turner were inside the convention hall in August 1968 when the riot developed in the streets and parks of Chicago. Ann and Peter had been heavily involved in Eugene McCarthy's campaign for president, working at the candidate's New York office. They were put in charge of the artwork to be used on the convention floor in Chicago. Ann recalled the events of that tumultuous summer:

> We produced 2,000 posters . . . My friend Peter was the artist, I did the lettering . . . We loaded them all into the back of the station wagon . . . and then we drove to Chicago . . . The first thing that happened when we went in and started unloading the posters is somebody told us that Mayor Daly had passed this rule that nobody was allowed to take any posters into the convention—into the convention hall, on sticks or anything like that, because Humphrey already had his posters in there and they were afraid that if other people started bringing their posters in, with the tensions being

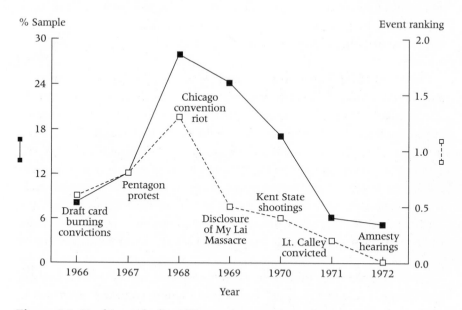

Figure 1.1 Rankings of salient Vietnam war events and proportion of sample immigrating to Canada, 1966–1972

what they were, that people might start hitting each other over the head with these posters . . . So we decided to print a poster that just said "Stop the war" on fabric . . . So we had "Stop the war"—it's like this big—I have one hanging in my office, "Stop the war" this big, in panels, huge panels, and after we finished buying all this stuff, cutting the screen, adhering it to the silk, printing the thing, dying them, cutting them up, folding them up into panels of various lengths, Peter went down to the convention hall with a package of them and gave them to all the antiwar people—all the antiwar delegates from all the candidates, as they were going in. And then there was a big demonstration in the convention hall, during the convention, and there was like—if you see clips from the convention, you often see clips of this demonstration, with the antiwar candidates holding these banners that say "Stop the war," "Stop the war."

Ann went back to New York City after the convention, taking the long route north of Lake Ontario that diverts through Toronto. Her mother, science fiction writer Judith Merrill, had also gone to the convention and was traveling with Ann. When they got to Toronto Judith decided that she would stay. Politically active and respected, she remained a resident of Toronto for the rest of her life. Ann returned to New York City with Peter. They soon sensed they were under government surveillance, perhaps resulting from their activities at the convention, and decided to join Ann's mother in Toronto.

Dee Knight also moved to Canada after working in the McCarthy campaign at the Chicago convention. Knight remembers seeing Robert Kennedy assassinated on live television as he watched from the McCarthy headquarters in Berkeley. Just two months earlier, in April, the assassination of Martin Luther King, Jr., had taken place in the hours following McCarthy's victory in the Wisconsin presidential primary. It was part of a broader rush of events that for Dee Knight culminated in the move to Canada: "Ultimately the escalation of events, from the Gulf of Tonkin Resolution through the Tet Offensive, convinced me in ever-increasing intensity of the impossibility of my participating in the war, and I would say the culminating event was Chicago."

About two-thirds of the people I interviewed reported that they had actively participated in the antiwar movement before coming to Canada. As will be seen later, the civil rights movement also played a significant role in their decision, and a parental legacy of social and political activism sometimes played an important part. However, as important as movement politics were, for most of the resisters I interviewed their migration to Canada was the result of an impassioned yet reasoned decision-making process having to do with the immediate threat of the draft and military service in Vietnam. Even if the war was or would become the ultimate focus of resistance, the selective service and military laws were the more immediate reason for the decisions that brought these young Americans to Canada. In this sense, it was law that motivated their resistance, and it was the opportunity of immigrating to Canada than gave this resistance its direction and expression.

The experience of Steven Burdick, who is today the president of a Canadian Union for Public Employees local, illustrates how the broader American political environment and the more immediate personal contingencies of the draft became intertwined. Steven heard about Robert Kennedy's assassination as he was returning from his pre-induction physical: "I was in Tallahassee at the time I was asked to take my physical for the Selected Service, and the examination was held in Jacksonville. So I was coming back on the bus from the physical, and I heard the news that Robert Kennedy had been shot. I said, 'This is unreal. This is just too much. Something is going to come apart here.' And then the Chicago convention happened." Steven realized his choices were narrowing. "The choices were to go or not to go [to Vietnam]. If you didn't go, then the choices were basically to go underground or to leave the jurisdiction. I said, 'I don't think I should suffer the consequences of somebody else's errors. So I'm not going to go underground. I'm not going to go to prison, thank you very much. I'm going to see what else I can do.'"

The contingencies of the draft were coming to a climax for many young Americans, and the dilemmas posed were intensified by political events that were shaking the foundations of American society. While classical collective-behavior and life-course theories see irrational impulses and anxieties in the reactions of individuals to such situations, contemporary perspectives look for reason and opportunity in such experiences. My interviews, first with male draft and military resisters and then with the women who joined them, help to sort out these possible motivations: Were these young people simply engaging in impulsive, ill-thought-out, individualized acts, or were they making reasoned choices, taking the opportunity of immigrating to Canada as a means of overcoming draft and military problems and in so doing becoming more engaged with social-movement politics and adding or intensifying an activist direction to their lives?

Resisting the Draft

As Steven Burdick's story illustrates, the most immediate reasons for draft resisters' coming to Canada involved the legal imperatives surrounding selective service reclassifications and the prospect of receiving pre-induction physical and induction notices. Dee Knight acknowledged this point as he explained how the Democratic convention was the culminating event in his decision to leave the United States. "I would say the culminating event was in Chicago," Knight observed, "not so much because of the riot, but because I had joined the 'McCarthy for President' campaign hoping that we could get him nominated, at which point my theory was that we could get him elected and not get drafted." Knight's earlier application for conscientious objector status had been denied. Canada beckoned as the next best option. As it turned out, Knight was able eventually to overturn his subsequent conviction for draft evasion on technical grounds. He nonetheless stayed in Canada for nearly ten years to resist the war through his position in Amex, returning to the United States in the 1970s to work for a universal and unconditional amnesty for others.

Richard Brown also played an active role in the Toronto resistance, heading the Toronto Anti-Draft Program in the early 1970s. For Richard, the initial stimulus to come to Canada involved a reclassification following an illness that required him to leave school at the University of Michigan. "Tough questions started coming up right away, and then a year later, I guess it was in the end of 1967, I had a cousin who came back after carrying a gun in the Delta and Central Highlands . . . So I sat down with him and a war buddy of his in a trailer park in a small town in Michigan over a couple of cases of beer." Richard could tell that his cousin was not yet ready to tell all of what he had seen in Vietnam. "But as edited as it was, . . . I saw that he had changed, and I realized from the stories that he was telling me there was stuff I wasn't hearing, but what I did hear I realized—no way do I want to be a part of this—absolutely no way." Richard had corresponded with his cousin while he was in Vietnam. "He wrote me a letter at one point and said, 'If there's anything you can do to stay out of this war, do it' . . . Those two events, more than anything else . . . made me realize, 'Now wait a minute, this isn't the right place for me.'" Richard Brown's story conveys a common theme in the thinking of many draft resisters in response to their reclassification and physical and induction notices: that this was an ugly war, of doubtful purpose, to be avoided if at all possible.

To some it is important to answer the question whether resisting the draft by leaving the country was an act of courage or cowardice. Interestingly, thirty years later, many draft resisters themselves still ponder this question. Philip Marchand, who is now a literary critic for the *Toronto Star* newspaper, thinks about his fear of being killed or maimed and how this compares to the feelings of young authors like Norman Mailer or Ernest Hemingway, who wrote of earlier wars from their own experience. "I might have written a meaningful Vietnam novel," Marchand reflected; "but on the other hand I might have come back without any arms or legs." He concluded, "It would have been horrible, because I would have realized I'd done it for nothing. Because I knew it was for nothing . . . I knew the war was totally wrong."

Other respondents also mentioned the fear and consequences of combat, but a more commonly expressed concern among draft resisters involved their choice to come to Canada rather than staying in United States and directly challenging the legal and political institutions by protesting militantly or violently, or by going to court and to jail.[58] Jon Caulfield, who went on to write an award-winning book about the gentrification of Toronto,[59] spoke of the unproductive choice between violent protest and coming to Canada. He noted in retrospect that "I still suspect myself . . . because it was so easy. There were people down there in jail, there were people doing horribly misguided things, like [Karl] Armstrong and other people with bombs. But they were actually trying to do something, and I wasn't. I was in a nice comfortable place . . . I wasn't part of the struggle, and I feel guilty about that." Jon's point was simply that life in Toronto was good, perhaps too good. "I still have mixed feelings about what I did in that sense . . . but on the other hand, what the hell could I have done? Go to the demonstrations?—I went to the demonstrations here—or blow something up? There didn't seem to be any middle ground . . . I don't castigate myself about it every day. I just have mixed feelings."

Others focused more specifically on the choice between prison and Canada. John Liss, a lawyer whose long career has been spent representing members of labor unions, expresses lingering reservations about not going to jail. He concedes that fear was a part of his thoughts: "I didn't know that I had it in me to withstand it . . . I was scared of jail. As the progression was developing, I wasn't going to Vietnam, I wasn't going to seek an alternative in the States that protected me . . . Well, then, living in Buffalo, it was sure easy to come up and fall in love with Toronto." Similarly, Byron Wall, who played a major office role in the Anansi publishing company and edited the sixth edition of the *Manual for Draft-Age Immigrants,* expressed admiration for those who went to jail. "I knew some guys when I was at St. John's College," Wall remembered, "who simply, you know, 'Nolo contendre,' and they went to jail . . . I admired that, but I wasn't prepared to do it."

There was, of course, the further possibility of finding a way to get a medical or some other kind of deferment. Many parents wondered why their sons did not simply do this; and, of course, many young Americans did. Charlie Diamond, who went on to a career of working in shelters for the homeless in Canada, pondered this side of the dilemma: "Either you go to jail, or you leave the country, or you lie, you fudge the facts. But the government was operating . . . in a crooked manner too . . . I can understand people doing it, but I couldn't do it personally. I think my parents wished I could have, or would have." Thirty years later such issues are still on the minds of Americans who made the decision to leave the United States.

No two thought processes were identical, but the example of Don Holman places in bold relief the kind of experiences that ultimately led to Canada. First, Don recalled what happened to a friend who went to prison. "I had heard about a friend of mine who was an Eagle Scout and a Quaker. They put him in prison. He was killed at Leavenworth. They put him right in with all these other people. Fresh meat. I wasn't anxious to go to prison. I wasn't going to kill anybody either." Second, Don became involved with SDS and did some research for an article on the Selective Service System. "I did this research around the Kansas City area, like who got drafted, who didn't— all that information is there—it wasn't hidden, they weren't trying to hide a thing, and a majority of the draftees—the largest number of people drafted—were poor blacks, the next, middle-class blacks . . . and then poor whites. . . . the upper- and middle-class whites were the last people to be drafted." These factors, combined with a physical or induction notice, convinced Don Holman and other young Americans to leave the draft and their country behind.

Although one can argue endlessly about the morality of the judgments made and still reach no certain conclusions, it is difficult to consider the kinds of thoughts recalled by the interviewees as irrational. Whatever weight these different factors had in the decisions, the factors taken into account were all very real. There is no retrospective way of sorting out the influence of these factors, much less the morality of the resulting decision. Most respondents ultimately concluded that it "just didn't make sense" for them to be drafted for the American war in Vietnam. Immigration to Canada gave them a legal opportunity to resist the draft without the consequence of imprisonment.

The resisters' conclusions paralleled the assessment that Robert McNamara articulated in a private memorandum to President Lyndon Johnson in 1967, before most draft and military resisters made their decisions. McNamara wrote, "The picture of the world's greatest superpower killing or seriously injuring 1000 noncombatants a week, while trying to pound a tiny backward nation into submission on an issue whose merits are hotly disputed, is not a pretty one . . . especially if the damage to North Vietnam is complete enough to be 'successful.'"[60] McNamara conceded in his memoirs that he should have reached this position far earlier: "I believe we could and should have withdrawn from South Vietnam either in late 1963 amid the turmoil following Diem's assassination or in late 1964 or early 1965 in the face of increasing political and military weakness in South Vietnam."[61] In November 1963, only 78 American lives had been lost in Vietnam. Against the backdrop of the loss of life that followed, the choice to migrate to Canada can be seen as a reasoned decision.

Resisting the Military

Military resisters who came to Canada often differed most significantly from draft resisters in that their decision to leave the United States evolved over a longer period that included service in the armed forces. Perhaps the best-known military resister in Canada is Andy Barrie, who is heard by over four hundred thousand Torontonians a week as the host of the Canadian Broadcasting System's radio program *Metro Morning*. Andy remembers an event while he was an undergraduate at Dartmouth College that set him on a path that led ultimately to resistance. General Louis Hershey, head of the Selective Service System, had come to Dartmouth to speak about the draft. Andy remembers the strained analogy Hershey posed in defense of the draft. "Hershey said, 'The United States is a football team, we have elected its captain, he calls the plays, the rest of us might not agree with them, but the team can't win the game unless it listens to its quarterback.' Someone stood up in the back of the room when the question period began and recalled this metaphor and said, 'I just wanted to congratulate General Hershey—Generals Goebbels, Goering, Hesse, and Hitler—for over eight million touchdowns in winning their football game.'"

Despite a two-year struggle to gain conscientious objector status, Barrie was drafted into the army. But when he received his orders to go to Vietnam, he knew he wouldn't go. The arguments for going were not compelling, and the seeds of doubt were too deeply set, even within his own family: "My brother, who was in the military, said, 'Hey, more power to you, if you don't want to go to Vietnam, don't go.' He'd gone over there very gung ho and after two years came back thinking, 'Forget it, this isn't about anything.'"

Service in the military seemed to confirm the doubts of those who were unconvinced from the outset. Allan Kazmer, who later became a successful advertising executive in Canada, did not have the financial support to sustain a student deferment, so he joined the reserves as a means of satisfying his military requirement and making financial ends meet. It didn't take long for problems to emerge: "In many of the military classes I was brazen enough to ask questions . . . I was the troublemaker, I was viewed as 'one of those' in the army that it would have been good to sort out . . . because I was counterproductive. So that had a radicalizing effect on me as well."

Jack Colhoun, who worked for many years in Canada as the editor of *Amex*, also experienced a growing sense of doubt during his exposure to the American military. In Colhoun's case, the doubts grew during ROTC training at the University of Wisconsin. Colhoun respected an exceptional ROTC instructor who candidly reported what he had seen in Vietnam. "He conceded to the ROTC cadets that it was very difficult for him, because he had to witness torture being practiced by the South Vietnamese allies against prisoners, and as a man of religious conviction, that was difficult for him. This helped to confirm my view of what I'd been hearing."

Fear of what would happen in Vietnam was also a factor. Most of the military resisters in the sample left the United States in the short periods of leave they were granted when they received their orders to go to Vietnam. John Wolfson, whose parents joined him in Canada and who went on to a career as a government civil servant, put it succinctly: "I certainly was afraid, I didn't want to go to Vietnam, I didn't want to get shot." But he was also opposed to the war and was impressed by the initiative of others who were resisting the military. He was especially struck by an article in *Life* magazine about an African American soldier he knew at Fort Bragg who refused to continue following orders and was thrown in the stockade. He said, "That was a real turning point in my own decision of 'What am I going to do about this?'"

John Wolfson was like many other young men in the military who had to make a consequential life decision in difficult circumstances. Many of these men still have difficulty recounting and clearly articulating the full range of thoughts and emotional stresses they experienced then. Half of the military resisters in the sample say that the decision to come to Canada was extremely difficult, compared to only 15 percent of the draft resisters who felt this way.

The military resisters, more than the draft resisters, tended to have continuing misgivings about their decision to come to Canada. Naomi Wall, whose counseling of resisters at the Toronto Anti-Draft Program is described in greater detail in Chapter 4, heard many expressions of such feelings. She remembers in particular that "there was a terrible guilt for a lot of deserters, because there were Americans, some of them were schoolmates, who died in Vietnam, and 'OK, I mean if I'm not gonna go I should at least be in jail.' Some draft dodgers also felt that way." Wall also recalls that folk singer Joan Baez intensified these feelings with her remarks at a widely remembered Toronto concert. "Joan Baez was up here—she's pregnant with David Harris's baby—she comes up and tells them to go home. 'How dare you be here,' she says, 'while my David is suffering in jail.' A lot of guys went home. Not in droves, but there were guys who couldn't deal with that."

Balanced against these feelings of regret or guilt about coming to Canada were experiences like the one recounted by Dennis James, who is today Clinical Director of general addictions treatment at the Centre for Addiction and Mental Health in Toronto. His background in counseling psychology makes him uniquely able to articulate the kind of tension these young men experienced. James described a chilling experience from basic training that changed his life, an experience from which he concluded there could and should be no return.

> On the personal level, I was scared—I didn't want to put myself in danger. At a psychological level, in growing up I had been an athlete. I was quite good at it, and when I went into the army, I was good at that as well. They had these awards at the end of basic training and I was awarded "soldier of the cycle" . . . It was like valedictorian, and I won that, and I shot "expert" with the M16 in advanced training. It was sort of like a sport, and I realized that at some level I really loved that. It was exciting, it was fun, it was an adrenaline high . . . That was about the time of My Lai. I could have been there. I came to the opinion that if I did go, that I—as I wanted myself to be and knew myself to be—would never come back, and part of it was, I might

get killed in the literal sense, but I was even more acutely aware that if I didn't get killed, that it would have an impact on me, and that it would change me in ways that I didn't want to be changed. Because I recognized the potential of—I would have been a mercenary, and I would have enjoyed killing people, and I would have been good at it. That was scary, and that feeling was compounded by one of the experiences I had in basic training. I came real close to killing three sergeants. We were on the range and we had cement foxholes and I had two loaded clips of ammunition. It was so horrendous the way we were being treated . . . There were two of my friends, one of them was a fraternity brother who was coincidentally there. He was a very young man who was quite obese and they just brutalized him. I was so—I vividly recall standing on that cement foxhole with my two clips. We had done enough training at that point that I knew what I was doing—and I looked around and I just targeted where the sergeants were and I did this mental calculation: "If I load my weapon, how many of them can I get before they clue in to what's going on and somebody shoots me?" And I calculated three, and I decided that it wasn't worth the trade-off. There were about six there. It was a real cold mathematical kind of assessment, and my decision to not shoot them—subjectively it felt like it was a mathematical equation. It was like I said, "I'm sure I could get three of them, and I'd trade my life for that; not good enough. If I could get five, it's good enough." It was a real calculated, subjective experience, and . . . who really knows, but I'm pretty convinced if my assessment had been closer . . . to five, I probably would have shot them . . . Tuning in to that aspect of myself was real frightening . . . I didn't want to change in a way that I knew my life would be dedicated to killing people, but the potential was there, so that was a really powerful incentive for me, in making my decision, and that was almost more scary than the prospect of getting killed, maimed, or any of that. It was absolutely clear that if I . . . went [to Vietnam] that the person that came back wouldn't be the same person who went.

As with the draft resisters, it is impossible to know retrospectively exactly what final mix of motivations led Dennis James and others to leave the military and come to Canada. Nor can we draw definitive conclusions about the morality of these decisions. But, again as with the draft resisters, the factors involved were all very real and reasonable. The resisters' decisions were rational.

The Women Who Came

The stories of the women who came to Canada during the Vietnam war are perhaps even more diverse than those of the men. Although these women were not the direct targets of the draft or military law, they were certainly affected by these laws. Naomi Wall, who met many of the women in her work at the Toronto Anti-Draft Program, recounted the diversity of their experiences. First there were the women already married to resisters: "Bonnie Klein and her husband came up.[62] They were married and he was a doctor—so there was that group—people who had family support, who were already married, or whether they were legally married or not, they already had a relationship, they knew each other. They didn't struggle as much about what to do with their relationships." Then there were the women who came with men they were only beginning to know: "Maybe they had just started the relationship and he needed to leave because he had been drafted. He'd received his notice and he needed to get out and she came with him on faith." There were also women who came later: "The women left behind, who wanted to come but for some reason, either their boyfriend said not to or their parents wouldn't let them go—women who ran away—women who eloped—women who came afterwards, who had run away from home, but who came on their own and then had to find the guy they came to be with." There were also women who came on their own: "The women who came because they didn't like the war—the American government—they made their own antiwar statement by leaving the States." And there were women who came for nonwar but other law-related reasons: "The women having legal difficulties, maybe they were busted for dope; they heard of Toronto, how lenient things might be, and they just wanted to get away and hoped they wouldn't get extradited." Finally, there were a few women who were resisting the United States in a very long-term way: "The older women, like Judith Merrill, who came up because they were opposed to U.S. foreign policy." Overall, the numbers were large, and the variety was great.

About half of both the draft and military resisters in the sample came with a partner or spouse. The motivations of the women who came are especially interesting, because their decision was not forced in the same way as many of the men, so in this sense it was more freely made. All of the women in the sample reported that they played a role in the decision of the men they joined in coming to Canada. Most indicated that their involvement in the decision was major. Some said they were more convinced about coming than the men.

Kristine King today is president and owner of an international record promotion company and is married to Bill King, a jazz musician, publisher of the international magazine *The Jazz Report,* and the artistic director of the Beaches International Jazz Festival. Kristine began our interview by saying simply, "It was my idea to come to Canada." At the time Bill was drafted, he was Music Director of Janis Joplin's new band, Full Tilt Boogie. Four days after they were married Bill received his orders for Vietnam. They didn't realize that Bill was scheduled to report for duty on the day of the biggest national Moratorium against the War, October 16, 1969, and that the largest demonstrations were planned for Fort Dix, New Jersey, putting everyone on the base in a high state of alert.

Kristine went to Fort Dix with Bill in hopes of spending their last night together. Her account of their ordeal is intense, but nonetheless clearly reflective of two people making a joint, rational decision to take the opportunity that Canada provided.

We hitchhiked to New Jersey from Manhattan and got into a cab when we got near the base. As soon as we passed through the gates we were pulled over by an MP. He reached in and grabbed Bill by the collar and threatened that if he saw him on base again with that hair on his face there would be serious consequences. Soon after another MP pulled us over. He repeated the same threats before we were allowed to continue to the processing center.

After bill processed in, he asked the commanding officer if he could spend the night with his wife. After much wrangling they finally gave him permission but said that if the guest house was full, she would have to leave and he would have to go back to his barracks and await the 5 A.M. flight to Saigon.

The guest house was full when we arrived. As we walked back across the field, Bill turned to me and said, "Well, what do you think? Do you want to go to Canada?" For three months I had been pushing for Canada, so he knew my answer. I told him this had to be his decision; we knew we may never step foot in the U.S. again. We would not be able to visit friends or relatives. I didn't want him to resent me for the rest of my life because he couldn't go home. As we stood looking into each other's eyes, Bill made the decision to go to Canada.

We walked back to his barracks, where he picked up a change of clothes and a few personal items, then tried to hitchhike off the base. With the demonstration going on, the Military Police were nervous and agitated. They seemed to be everywhere. We hid in the ditch until we could see if it was an MP's car. It wasn't long before a sympathetic officer's son picked us up. He hid us under coats or blankets and delivered us to a local gas station not far from the base. Bill changed his clothes and threw everything in the garbage. We hitchhiked back to Manhattan and spent the night with friends before heading out to Long Island to pick up some belongings. We said our good-byes and hit the highway, stuck out our thumbs, and began our trip to Canada.

Allan and Karen Kazmer, who later did voluntary work for the Toronto Anti-Draft Program, came to their decision only slightly more easily than the Kings. As noted earlier, Allan was serving in the army reserves when he received his orders to go to Vietnam. Karen played a more indirect role in the decision to go instead to Canada than Kristine King, but nonetheless her involvement was crucial. Karen was working at a U.S. Steel plant as an assistant to the public relations director, who knew of her coming marriage to Allan and his antiwar feelings. Karen reports that "at one point he said to me, 'Did you ever think of going to Canada?' and I said, 'No, what do you mean?' He said that a lot of people had done that—something to think about. So that thought was put in my mind." Allan picked up the story: "Two days before I had to report, Friday night about midnight, Karen said, 'There's still one option you haven't considered—Canada.' It was an American realization of the notion that we don't think about Canada even though it's a skip and a throw away." Allan continued to debate how he could resist the war from within the military. The answers weren't satisfying: "Then Karen said at one in the morning, Friday night, 'Canada.'" From this point on their decision was made. They left without telling their families, for fear of someone's revealing their destination to the FBI.

Most women in the sample felt that the decision to come to Canada was jointly and equally made. Carolyn Egan, now a counselor and educator in a health clinic in Toronto, remembers that the decision seemed clear: "The only other thing to do was to go underground, and that didn't make a lot of sense, or to become a symbol and go to prison, which also, although we knew people through the Catholic Workers' Movement who did do that, that didn't seem reasonable . . . I don't think it was one of us. We both came to the conclusion." Although Carolyn and her husband later separated, they both have stayed in Canada.

One of the most politically active of the people I interviewed is Sandra Foster, who has been involved in urban political issues, working extensively on housing problems at the mayoral, municipal, regional, and provincial levels and serving both in elected and appointed positions. She too remembers participating equally in the decision to come Canada. "The decision was very equal," she says. Both felt that Sandra's husband was at risk of being arrested for his antidraft work. "What was the point of having him arrested? We weren't interested in that statement. So it was equal." Sandra also recalls details of actually crossing the border that many other women must also have experienced. "They spent considerable time questioning my husband, but had very few questions for me. The assumption was that I had done absolutely nothing but was somehow a young person being swept up by this man who was resisting the draft." The immigration officers could not have known how active a Canadian politician this young American woman would become.

Turning Points

American selective service and military laws and Canadian immigration law and regulations acted as institutional gates and channeling mechanisms that strongly influenced the direction of the lives of American resisters who came to Canada. The intersecting influence of American and Canadian laws was directly felt by the many young American men who came north, and less directly but probably no less significantly by the young women who were linked to these men. Early life-course and social-movement theories anticipated contemporary novels in offering a pessimistic view of the motives and meanings of youthful American dissenters from the demands of the Vietnam-era laws of conscription and military service. In contrast, contemporary life-course theory and the political-process theory of social movements converge in making the point that dissent and disorder often are rational and responsible reflections of human agency, representing sensible responses to opportunities that can introduce purposeful turning points into human lives. Although the political-process theory of social movements is hesitant to treat marginalized, individually initiated, or "spin-off" movements like the Vietnam war migration to Canada in the same way as more established social movements, I contend that the possibility of immigration to Canada was an opportunity that made draft and military resistance a rational route for many young Americans to follow.

For many, the American migration began as an individualized form of draft and military law resistance that often involved a process of self-recruitment for immigration to Canada, and this might seem to make this movement an unlikely subject for social or collective explanation. However, the ways in which social processes initiate, mediate, and transform human experiences should not be underestimated. For example, the mobilizing structures of the resistance movement in Toronto supplied information and support that assisted many resisters in coming to Toronto and channeled choices about what to do once they arrived. The story of this migration is therefore important not only because it involves a large and neglected exile movement in American social history, but also because it can better inform us about the breadth and scope of the political-process account of social movements and of the role of law and legal resistance in social activism and the life course. My goal in this book is to broaden and thereby enhance our understanding of social processes that have the potential to change our lives and the societies in which we live.

In the chapters that follow I explore the war resister migration to Canada as a rationally motivated and legally channeled turning point that emerged in response to the alternative opportunities that Canada provided. These opportunities had important consequences on multiple levels beyond these individuals' simple relocation across a national border. At the macro level, Canada embraced the prospect of a long-term trend toward increased Canadian autonomy and the chance to separate itself from U.S. foreign policy domination. At the meso level, a social movement resulted in changes that affected its members' lifelong commitment to and involvement in political activism. At the micro level, individuals made permanent changes in their perceived national identity. The American war resister experience offers a unique context in which to explore the roles of law and legal resistance in the formation of social movements and social activism, and their function as sources of important turning points in human lives.

CHAPTER 2

Opening the Gates

In 1969 the American embassy in Ottawa stood directly opposite Parliament Hill, the Peace Tower, and Center Block, which housed the Prime Minister's Office, the Cabinet Room, the Senate, and the House of Commons. The lore of the Hill was that during important meetings the curtains of the Cabinet Room were closed to prevent surveillance from the embassy. If this story was ever true, it would have been so in the spring of 1969, when the cabinet of Prime Minister Pierre Elliott Trudeau met to decide the fate of American servicemen who were seeking refuge in Canada.

On May 22, 1969, the Canadian Minister of Immigration, Allan Mac-Eachen, rose in the House of Commons to announce the cabinet's decision: that henceforth American Vietnam draft and military resisters—that is, both "dodgers" and "deserters"—would be admitted to Canada without regard to their military status. MacEachen explained that this decision was the extension of a policy of "liberalization" in the treatment of "military applicants" that had been evolving for more than a year and that followed from a policy already in place allowing draft resisters the legal status of "landed immigrants" in Canada. "Our basic position," Minister MacEachen proclaimed, "is that the question of an individual's membership or potential membership in the armed services of his own country is a matter to be settled between the individual and his government, and is not a matter in which we should become involved." This position fit well with Prime Minister Trudeau's frequently quoted observation, "You can't look into a man's heart." Toronto's *Globe and Mail* cautiously surmised in a headline that now "Deserters Will Be Eligible for Status as Immigrants," while the *New York Times* more dramatically heralded an invitation in its headline, "Canada to Admit Any U.S. Deserter."[1]

MacEachen's statement opened the legal gates to Canada, providing the opportunity for immigration that many American resisters had been looking for. The number of draft-age males entering Canada as landed immigrants each month tripled between April and August of 1969, as word of the open immigration policy spread through the mainstream media and the underground Vietnam war resistance movement.[2] Young Americans who were subject to prosecution and imprisonment under selective service and military law in the United States now could take refuge under Canadian immigration law. This was a turning point that resulted in the migration of more than 50,000 draft-age Americans to Canada—the largest northward exodus since the American revolution.[3]

Immigration Minister MacEachen's public framing of his announcement as the extension of a policy of liberalization claimed the operation of what sociologists and political scientists often call policy feedback[4] or perhaps more aptly, given the prospective influence and momentum involved, a policy process that "feeds forward."[5] This concept refers to the process by which "policies, once enacted, restructure subsequent political processes." Attention to this policy dynamic encourages researchers interested in processes of law formation and enforcement to "make social policies the starting points as well as the end points of analysis."[6] Recently, Nicholas Pedriana and Robin Stryker have demonstrated how cultural resource strategies, built around central societal values and expressed through symbolic framing processes, can be combined with forward-feeding policies, such as the immigration minister's presumed liberalization of immigration procedures, to explain changes in social and legal policies.[7] In this chapter I elaborate on Pedriana and Stryker's approach by considering how a second dimension of political power, identified by Steven Lukes, influenced the evolution of cultural images and symbolic framing processes that at first reflected the American characterization of U.S. military resisters as irresponsible.[8]

Lukes distinguishes a dimension of political power beyond the more easily observed behavior of interest groups and their representatives.[9] Lukes's added dimension broadens analysis of political power by focusing on non–decision-making as well as decision-making, potential as well as current issues, covert as well as overt conflict, and grievances that can prefigure political participation. His point is that this second dimension of political power operates in less public ways than is suggested by a simpler model. Lukes's perspective helps to explain how the covert and surreptitious use of political power by the immigration minister initially interfered with the framing of Canadian immigration policy on American Vietnam war resisters as an issue of Canadian autonomy from the United States. American Vietnam war resisters ultimately emerged as unexpected symbols of Canadian sovereignty, but this was only after the immigration minister initially characterized military resisters as irresponsible and therefore as unsuitable immigrants to Canada.

It is easy to understand the eagerness of governments to engage in myth-making as a means of legitimation and prospective influence. Even the members of the opposition party in the Canadian House of Commons rejoiced in the policy potential of Minister MacEachen's May 22, 1969, opening of the Canadian border to the American resisters. Edward Broadbent spoke for the New Democratic Party in reminding House colleagues that Canada had an important tradition of welcoming political refugees that reached back to the Empire Loyalists, who fled the American Revolution and led to the mid-twentieth century, when Hungarians and Czechoslovakians escaped repressive regimes by coming to Canada. This tradition made MacEachen's claim that his ministry was simply extending a policy of liberalization plausible and is the foundation of current belief that "his arguments carried the day."[10]

However, MacEachen's claim is also the stuff of which myths are made, for a deeper probing of the path to his announcement reveals that his policy was anything but the completion of a linear trajectory of liberalization. To the contrary, MacEachen and the department of immigration exercised their political power to divert public attention from policies and practices that were regressive, rather than progressive, with regard to the liberalization of American war resister immigration. The story of the development of Canada's immigration policies and practices illustrates Lukes's idea that "the question of the control over the agenda of politics and of the ways in which potential issues are kept out of the political process" must be considered in an analysis of political power relations.[11] This factor was crucial in the framing of the debate over American Vietnam war resisters in Canada.

MacEachen's immigration ministry had been wracked by rumor and retrenchment through much of the year leading up to the spring statement. The turmoil in the ministry and the resulting controversy that spread through the media to the public were the ultimate reflection of divisions between powerful political, religious, and bureaucratic forces that were in conflict over the issue of allowing American Vietnam draft, and especially military, resisters into Canada. In the end, MacEachen's speech proved to be a turning point in the lives of many American war resisters and marked a shift in Canadian feelings and expressions of independence from the United States.

To get beyond the public discourse that surrounded the American war resister issue in Canada, this chapter examines recently declassified historical records in the National Archives of Canada, as well as recent interviews with former government ministers on the events of this period. The collection of historical records can be traced to an October 26, 1966, meeting between representatives of the Immigration Department and the Royal Canadian Mounted Police (RCMP), which led the department to set up an official file of reports, related materials, and communications with its four field units, the RCMP, and other departments of government.[12] This file grew to contain fourteen heavily stuffed folders, which provide a detailed background to a rancorous public discourse that lasted for more than five years. The documents reveal how the Canadian immigration department and its minister misled the public about its policy and practices regarding American military resisters in ways that diverted and distorted public discussion of the issues. Only after this deception was exposed by the news media could countervailing cultural resources be brought into play to support a policy of liberalization, and these cultural resources prevailed only after the Nixon administration revealed its own indecisiveness about the war resister migration. The result was, in Lukesian terms, a form of American nondecision involving that country's failing to object to the opening of the Canadian border. However, the Canadian immigration files further reveal that this was neither the beginning nor the end of the intricately choreographed power politics that shaped this highly symbolic episode in Canadian-American relations.

The Shifting Sands of Policy

Canadian policy on American Vietnam war resisters had its roots in the work of Tom Kent, an English immigrant who came to Canada as a newspaper editor and became a prominent policy adviser to Prime Minister Lester Pearson, eventually serving as Deputy Minister of Immigration.[13] It was Kent, under Minister of Immigration Jean Marchand, who first moved the department of immigration from unwritten to written policies regarding draft and military resisters. It is important to note that Canada's Immigration Act makes no mention of draft or military service, and by the time of the Vietnam war Canada had taken in many previous draft and military resisters as immigrants—for example, from Hungary and Czechoslovakia. The presence of these and earlier groups makes it extremely unlikely that Canada would ever include references to draft or military status in its immigration legislation.

Nonetheless, on January 14, 1966, the immigration department implemented Operational Memorandum (OM) number 117, which drew a written distinction between draft and military resisters and articulated what had until then been an unwritten policy excluding American servicemen. Although this policy was now in a written form that circulated among ministers and immigration officers, it was not publicly published, and thus its terms and the issues it raised remained covert and beyond public discussion.

The memorandum first laid out an ambivalent position on draft resisters: "Officers will not refuse an immigrant solely on the grounds that he is known to be, or suspected of being, a draft evader. Nonetheless, they will take this factor into consideration in determining whether he is a bona fide immigrant and in assessing the likelihood of his successful permanent establishment." It then committed to print a previously unwritten policy, saying that a military resister "will not be issued a visa or granted admission until he has submitted proof of his discharge."[14] The problem that would haunt the department of immigration for years following was, again, that the Immigration Act itself did not exclude draft or military resisters, while it did explicitly exclude certain "prohibited groups," such as convicted criminals.[15] This point did not attract attention until Tom Kent began to explore its implications nearly two years later—largely because so few American servicemen were then seeking entry to Canada.

Initially, it was American draft resisters who attracted attention as they began to migrate to Canada. In the early fall of 1966 Kent began to articulate publicly the point that the Immigration Act was silent on the issue of draft status. In a letter to *Ramparts* magazine, Kent observed, "There is not any prohibition in the Immigration Act or Regulations against the admission of persons who may be seeking to avoid induction into the Armed Services and, therefore, provided they meet immigration requirements we have no bases in law for barring them entry."[16] "I just decided," Kent recalled some thirty years later, "that persons shouldn't be questioned about their draft status . . . It was made known that draft status had nothing to do with it."[17]

The Powers Without and Within

Although Tom Kent was neither a lawyer nor a legislator, he foresaw the potential gap that would become apparent between the provisions and prohibitions of the Immigration Act and its interpretation through the day-to-day regulations, memorandums, and activities of the department. Kent began to address this problem by developing an official point system that was put into use by immigration officers on October 1, 1967. According to Kent, "Not the least important aspect of the reform was that the details of the immigration process were for the first time set out in law, as regulations under the statute, instead of being mere administrative directions within the department."[18] The goal was to make the legal gatekeeping role played by officers in extending the opportunity of immigration more objective.

Under the new system, applicants were evaluated on nine factors using a hundred-point scale, with a score of fifty required for admission. All but one of the factors involved relatively objective considerations of age, education, employment, occupation, knowledge of English and French, financial resources, and relatives in Canada. A ninth factor, worth a maximum of fifteen points, involved the officer's "judgment of the personal suitability of the applicant and his family to become successfully established in Canada." In addition, the officer could refuse an applicant who earned more than fifty points "if in his opinion there are good reasons why those norms do not reflect the particular applicant's chances of establishing himself in Canada and those reasons have been submitted in writing to, and approved by, an officer of the Department designated by the Minister." These discretionary aspects of the point system later became the basis of internal department directives[19] and of a symbolic package that framed military resisters as unsuitable for immigration to Canada, even though these provisions were a carefully circumscribed part of Kent's efforts to make selection standards for immigration overt and objective, and even though military resisters were not identified in the Immigration Act as a prohibited class.

Kent reasoned that in the longer term U.S. military resisters could only be legally barred from Canada if they were identified as a "prohibited class" in the Immigration Act. Since this was unlikely to happen, Kent was concerned with what the routine exclusion of this group by immigration officers would mean in the future. Kent signaled his concern in a letter written in the late fall of 1967 to the Canadian Under-Secretary of State for External Affairs. His letter anticipated changing public opinion about American war resisters, as well as the significance of the absence of an explicit prohibition of military resisters in the Immigration Act.

"There seems to be little doubt," Kent wrote to his counterpart in External Affairs, "that public opinion is developing in a way that would make any deportation of a deserter highly controversial." He noted that potential problems involving draft resisters were being sorted out, as immigration officers were being discouraged from asking about draft status. "With deserters, however, we run into a much different problem." The problem was not that the act required different treatment of military resisters for, Kent pointed out, "legally this is not so. There is nothing in our law that makes the deserter as such a prohibited person." Rather, the problems were practical and political—more specifically, problems of American power and influence and Canadian immigration department bias and recalcitrance.

The United States had not at this stage given any indication of how it might react to Canada admitting its fleeing servicemen. In Lukesian terms, the Americans were in a state of inaction that amounted to nondecision. Kent argued "that the problem is not that we should be concerned to exclude deserters but that the United States, if it is really concerned, should provide means to prevent such persons leaving the country." Kent's mission was both to inform and to enlist assistance, and thus he hopefully noted that "the time may approach when you might wish to explore the views of the United States government through channels open to your department." He closed by accurately predicting that although the number of deserters wanting to come to Canada was now small, it would grow.[20]

Three decades later, when I asked Tom Kent what was in his mind with regard to the American resisters during his time as Deputy Minister, he said that his inclination was to initiate, though not complete, a policy of liberalization. He made a decision on draft resisters and a nondecision on military resisters.

> I never thought there was an issue as far as the draft evader was concerned . . . Nine times out of ten he was going to be a very good Canadian. If he didn't stay forever, well so what? He was going to contribute something. There was no moral policy or legal basis for rejecting people on the basis that they were liable to the draft . . . Desertion is another matter. Many of us would tend to be sympathetic to the deserter too, but it was a very different issue from the draft evader. I mean I'm quite sure that if I had still had responsibility for immigration over that period, . . . I would have wanted to bring it to a head and make sure that the deserter was treated like the draft evader, but that had to evolve.[21]

When I interviewed the former Minister of External Affairs, Mitchell Sharp, he recalled the same initial inclination: "The general feeling in the circles in which I moved in the civil service and in the public service was that the Americans had made a mistake . . . We didn't say these things publicly, but when we thought about deserters: from what? . . . Maybe they should never have gone, that was the sort of underlying thinking."[22] Again, Minister Sharp's public silence was an expression of nondecision; the liberal impulses that lay behind this thinking did not therefore feed forward into policy. From Lukes's perspective, nondecision at the ministerial level left the fate of military resisters to be dealt with covertly at the administrative level in a manner that challenged the overt, explicit provisions of the Immigration Act.

Tom Kent believed that probably the biggest reason the liberalization policy did not feed forward to the military resisters was the fear of offending Canada's powerful American neighbor. Anticipation of *potential* American opposition likely stalled the liberalization policy before it could be extended to military resisters.

> There is no question there was a strong conviction on the part of the RCMP and also External Affairs that—we're talking about my day, 1966, 1967, and the beginning of 1968—there was a very firm view that the Americans would protest, would be angry; exactly how far it would go, et cetera, no idea, but we couldn't, openly at least, accept deserters, treat deserters like draft evaders. There was no question that there was a sense of an American presence . . . how far it was expressed formally, informally, diplomatically, I have no idea, but I think there was no question there was, as there always is, on the part of many officials, and some politicians, a great reluctance to offend Americans.[23]

At this same time, many immigration officers within Kent's own department were covertly resisting implementation of the liberalization policy even with regard to draft resisters. As the front-line administrators of immigration policy, these officers possessed covert, discretionary power to subvert legal departmental policy. Their reasons for subverting a liberalization policy were not difficult to understand. In 1969, 234 of the 353 immigration officers in Canada were military veterans.[24] As such, they often had more in common culturally with the paramilitary RCMP, the FBI, and American immigration officers than they did with their own ministerial superiors. The immigration officers were less compelled culturally by notions of national sovereignty than by their earlier experience as veterans and by their current occupational identity as paramilitary officials in frequent contact with their American counterparts, who had similar experiences and identities.

Kent further explained that immigration officers "tended to be ex-non-commissioned officer-type veterans . . . So there was a natural tendency, I think, to regard anybody of military age coming from the United States as probably a bad guy, . . . who was dodging his civic responsibilities."[25] This culturally embedded notion of "dodging responsibility" would soon emerge as the immigration department's justification for using officer discretion to deny military resisters admission to Canada. In the fall of 1967, the Vancouver Committee to Aid American War Objectors wrote to Ottawa to complain about immigration officer behavior. Kent responded, "I do not in any way resist the immediate conclusion that some of our officers at least have not been fully following instructions . . . Our instructions not to inquire into draft status could not be in plainer English (and French) . . . We have more recently emphasized to our senior field staff that any departures from these instructions must be treated as a serious disciplinary matter."[26]

As 1967 came to a close Kent found himself hamstrung by Canadian fears of displeasing its powerful American neighbor and the covert recalcitrance of immigration officers in following his instructions at border crossing points. Kent did not feel he could do much more than insist on an open admission policy for draft resisters, while leaving military resisters at the mercy of the unsympathetic border officers. As Kent had earlier anticipated, American servicemen were beginning to arrive at border stations seeking admission to Canada in growing numbers. At the same time, official Ottawa was gearing up for the federal election that would soon make Pierre Elliott Trudeau the new Prime Minister of Canada. The attention of Kent and other political appointees in government was diverted, and the issue of the military resisters was left in the hands of others. Kent knew that he would seek a new posting after the election. A career departmental administrator, Director of Immigration J. C. Morrison, was left to instruct the immigration staff. This was a definite reversal of fortune for a policy of liberalization.

A Secret Smoking Gun

Director Morrison filled the policy vacuum with a January 9, 1967, "personal and confidential" letter to the regional directors of immigration, which quoted OM 117's statement that "permanent admission to Canada is not to be granted to military deserters." He then added, "The Department's view is, as firmly as ever, that we do not want deserters as immigrants. But a recent review has revealed that we may have no legal basis on which to order the deportation of an applicant in Canada for the sole reason that he is a deserter." Even more to the point, he noted, "there is real reason to doubt that the present Act contains the authority necessary to exclude military deserters by regulation." Given the approaching federal election, it is perhaps not surprising that Morrison reported that there was no plan to try to change the act or even the regulations, "because anything so dramatic might rouse talk." Morrison took the opportunity presented by Kent's nondecision to confirm a covert exclusion of military resisters; and by doing this in an "undramatic" way that would not "rouse talk," he further used his covert administrative power to eliminate potential widespread debate. Morrison simply wrote, "There has been no change of attitude so far as the Department is concerned."

Morrison's letter went on to spell out an early version of a symbolic package and cultural strategy that expanded on the circumscribed discretionary references to "suitability" for immigration incorporated in the October 1967 point system. This strategy extended the concept of suitability by calling on cultural norms of moral obligation and social responsibility to justify the rejection of military applicants as "unsuitable" for admission to Canada. But Morrison's clear purpose was to exclude military servicemen per se; he stated that if the examining immigration officer at the border could not find other reasons to exclude a deserter, "This type of case, instead of being finally decided locally, is in the future to be referred to headquarters." This instruction was effective immediately and over the following months resulted in officials' denying admission to military resisters.[27]

Allan MacEachen was sworn in on July 5, 1968, as Minister of Immigration in Prime Minister Trudeau's newly elected Liberal party government. Kent left as Deputy Minister the next day. Thirty years later, he was quick to say of his inaction with regard to the military resister issue, "I just didn't take on that battle at that time."[28] MacEachen was ill-disposed and ill-prepared to do so in Kent's place. Like many ministers with new portfolios, he knew little about his new responsibilities. As well, MacEachen could not have failed to see potential American storm clouds on the Canadian political horizon and to have noted the hostility to war resisters within his new department.

Richard Nixon was preparing to run for President of the United States on a law-and-order platform. Within a month of MacEachen's becoming Minister, Lewis Hershey, Director of the U.S. Selective Service System, announced that he wanted "to stem the flow of American youths who are fleeing across the border to avoid the draft," adding that he was going to Calgary to address the Army, Navy, and Air Force Veterans of Canada and "to talk with officials."[29] Although Hershey canceled his trip the next day, saying his wife was ill, and further noted that the State Department was the source of policy on such matters, he did send the Assistant Director to Calgary in his place. This U.S. official instructed his Canadian audience a few days later that "Parliament should pass legislation to make it illegal for persons eligible for the U.S. draft to enter Canada."[30] Other than through the above newspaper reports, there is no certainty about when, how, to whom, or with what authority these sentiments were communicated directly to Canadian officials. Yet, as Kent's interview comments suggest, it is difficult to believe that the effect on Canadian officials was insignificant, and it is therefore probably not coincidental that MacEachen followed his administrators' lead in authorizing revisions to the department's operational regulations on July 29, 1968.

Perhaps the most significant revision was the addition of a paragraph officially rejecting deserters to the department's operations manual, which was never made public. Paragraph 12(g) explicitly cited the example of a "military deserter" as a person to be excluded from the country on the grounds of that person's failing to keep "moral and legal contractual obligations." This was a more explicit elaboration of the symbolic package and cultural strategy justifying exclusion on the basis of normative "unsuitability." At the same time a confidential memorandum was sent to all border station officials, instructing them that military resisters could be rejected on the basis of the officer's discretion, however great an applicant's qualifications might otherwise be. This discretion was linked to section 32(4) of the regulations and the earlier provision of the point system, which authorized rejection of the applicant "if in [the officer's] opinion there are good reasons why those norms do not reflect the particular applicant's chances of establishing himself successfully in Canada." The memo went on to designate three reasons for such rejection, citing as examples of "contractual obligations" excessive debts, marital disruption, and military desertion.[31]

Within a month of the July 29 memo Ron Haggart, a nationally syndicated newspaper columnist, caught wind of the newly formalized covert policy and began a series of columns (the first entitled "Lawbreakers Who Work for the Government") documenting how immigration officers were refusing U.S. military resisters entry into Canada. The effect of this publicity was to take what had been a potential issue, one that to this point had been suppressed through the department's covert policies and practices, into the public domain, where interests could begin to coalesce in support of the military resisters. Some of Haggart's columns were written with the help of Bill Spira, a middle-aged businessman who was helping military resisters enter and settle in Canada through the Toronto Anti-Draft Program. Early in 1969 a Haggart column estimated that there were probably 2,000 deserters in Canada. The problem, Spira noted through Haggart, was how to help these military resisters get immigrant status so that they could get on with their lives in Canada.

The military resisters had a legitimate grievance about their treatment as applicants for immigration who had been forced underground. Spira was helping to hide them, often in his own home and in the homes of friends and neighbors, and sought with Haggart's help to bring the military resisters' grievance to the public. Haggart wrote: "In recent weeks there has been a sharp change of attitude among Immigration officials. Deserters are still arriving at the rate of five a day, says Spira, but almost none are being accepted as landed immigrants. The reason is a departmental memo of July 29, 1968, which instructed examining officers to take into account whether prospective immigrants are currently serving in the armed forces. This flies in the face of the Immigration Act." Haggart went on to say that these were "new bureaucratic policies which are, all at the same time, secret, illegal, and stupid."[32] Haggart's columns raised the public's suspicions about the politics of the immigration department's administration.

A Timely Test

Notwithstanding the existence of the policy and the protests, immigration officials steadfastly denied in public that military resisters were covertly being refused admission to Canada. For example, early in 1969 a ministry official said that although the absolute number of deserters recently denied entry may have increased, this was only because the total number applying for entry had grown, while the proportion admitted presumably was stable.[33] This assertion was necessary to sustain the fiction that military resisters per se were not being excluded, given the absence of any prohibition by the Immigration Act. The goal was to silence public debate on the issue.

To test the department's claim, five York University undergraduates associated with the student newspaper *Pro Tem* conducted a field test of border practices. The results of their experiment were publicized as the following lead story on the February 9, 1969, evening edition of the television *CBC National News:*

On Canada's border this weekend, five York University students put this country's immigration laws to the test. They did it by posing as American deserters, using a real deserter's name [John Heintzelman] and carrying photocopies of his identity papers. Then, from the American side they tried to enter this country as Landed Immigrants at five different border posts in southern Ontario. Four were turned back—the fifth was asked to fill in an application form but didn't go through with it. One of the Canadians who posed as a deserter was Graham Muir, Editor of a student newspaper at York University in Toronto.

Muir was then asked what had happened. He said, "In my case I went back to the Canadian border and I was told, even before making out an application for landed immigrant status, that it wasn't much good because I was a deserter and the people at the border are under instructions not to let deserters in. That is what the immigration official told me." Thus, Muir and the others demonstrated that the covert policy of the immigration department was to exclude military resisters.

Minister MacEachen's initial response was to condemn the "impersonation tactics" employed by the students and to deny the existence of a covert policy, saying that "at no time since he had become minister had border officials been instructed to weed out deserters."[34] However, within two days of the border revelations MacEachen received a memo from his departmental administrators reminding him that during the ministerial transition the preceding July he had authorized changes in internal departmental regulations:

> You will recall from our discussions last week and earlier advice to you that guidelines were issued last July to all of our officers abroad and at ports of entry suggesting that they should take into account such obligations in their assessment of an individual's application. In addition to membership in the armed forces, other examples of such obligations were, as you will recall, pending disposition of criminal charges, suspected desertion of families, or debtors who would be leaving behind them large debts for which no settlements had been made.[35]

As will be seen, Minister MacEachen probably did not fully understand, either earlier in July 1968, or early in 1969, the import of this and other aspects of his department's covert regulations, or indeed the Immigration Act from which they presumably gained their authority.

A New Power Within

When MacEachen appeared in the House of Commons following the student border experiment, and when he met with reporters afterward, he defended his department by using arguments of suitability and responsibility. These abstractions now became his primary cultural resource in defending the recasting of internal departmental regulations (or "guidelines," as he preferred to call them) and interpreting the purposes of the Immigration Act. News reports noted that he "refused to be pinned down on whether military desertion alone is a grounds for denial of landed immigrant status to persons applying at the border."[36] Instead, he emphasized that officers had wide discretionary power at the border. In making this assertion, Mac Eachen was elaborating on the circumscribed discretion allowed by the point system that had been passed in Parliament, borrowing language from the unpublicized internal departmental regulations and cultural norms of responsibility that likened military desertion to "heavy financial obligations and desertion of a man from his wife," which he emphasized were "substantial moral or contractual obligations."[37] MacEachen was now fully joined with his department in using an elaborate cultural strategy framed around notions of suitability, responsibility, and obligation to justify the covert exclusion of military resisters. This view recalled the American characterization of its draft and military resisters as wrong-minded and irresponsible, and the assumptions of 1950s normative life-course theory, which portrayed military resisters as "castoffs," "misfits," and "irresponsible troublemakers."

The admission of military resisters had by 1969 thus progressed from being a potential to an actual issue of public discussion, with MacEachen and the department framing the issue in terms of suitability and responsibility, but refusing to admit the covert policy of excluding military resisters per se. MacEachen probably felt that he was on the right track with this strategy when he accepted an invitation to speak and answer questions about immigration before the Board of Evangelism and Social Service of the United Church in Toronto.

In issuing its invitation to the minister, this board of the largest and most powerful Protestant denomination in Canada was fulfilling its evolving commitment to a position that "the Church is to be the conscience of the state."[38] Such a relationship between church and state obviously distinguished Canada from strict notions of separation held in the United States,[39] and in this instance, unknown to MacEachen, the United Church was positioning itself to be the conscience of Canada in prodding the government to reassert its sovereign power in relation the United States with regard to the immigration of American military resisters. In short, the church leadership was a cultural elite preparing to exercise strongly felt moral and political responsibilities.[40]

Before MacEachen arrived at the Toronto meeting, the church board had already passed a detailed resolution, based on the York students' findings, expressing concern that border officials were rejecting military resisters "on the grounds of desertion alone" and noting "the apparent change in the policy earlier set forth by Tom Kent, as the former Deputy Minister, in which he stated that there is no specific reference in assessment for immigration purposes, 'to someone's military status in his home country.'" The board had also passed a sweeping motion before MacEachen's arrival reviewing other problematic aspects of the situation—"involving unpublicized bureaucratic processes, unwarranted allocation of discretion to officers, influences from outside Canada, and misleading renderings of Canadian laws."[41] This motion stridently advanced the argument that MacEachen's department was covertly flouting an explicit law, the Immigration Act, by illegally excluding a group that was not prohibited entry by law. At the same time, the motion introduced an alternative symbolic package built around concerns for the sovereignty of Canada. This would become a competing framing of the issue in opposition to the focus on the Americans' suitability. The strategies and elements of the opposing suitability and sovereignty packages are summarized in Table 2.1.

It is an understatement to say that Minister MacEachen confronted a hostile audience in his meeting with the United Church Board. The *Globe and Mail* summarized the event in a scathing editorial entitled "Who's in Charge Here?" The editorial was from the outset dismissive of MacEachen's strategy of assessing suitability for immigration on the basis of contractual obligations including military service. A questioner at the meeting asked, "How can you say that a minor of 18 or a man of 21 who is a conscientious objector but has been drafted against his will has a contract, which is a meeting of minds?" The *Globe* suggested that although MacEachen seemed beyond his depth on this preliminary issue, at this point "he was only entering the shallows." The editorial went on to detail MacEachen's display of his limited knowledge of the Immigration Act. It stated, "If the Government wants to exclude deserters it can do so legally only by changing the Immigration Act

Table 2.1 The recasting of American military resisters as symbols of sovereignty in the Canadian immigration debate, January 1968–May 1969

Symbolic package	Frame	Signature elements	Cultural strategies
Personal unsuitability	Contractual responsibilities and obligations	Castoffs/misfits/ irresponsible persons	Emphasize officer discretion in enforcement regulations of Immigration Act intended to select suitable New Canadians who are free of unfulfilled obligations—marital, financial, or military.
Canadian sovereignty	Independence from United States	Refugees/rational persons of conscience	Emphasize similarities to United Empire Loyalists, Hungarians, Czechs who received refugee status in Canada—unprohibited by the Immigration Act.

or by altering its extradition treaties so that desertion becomes an extraditable offense." The *Globe* noted that this would mean turning away not only American servicemen, but servicemen from other countries as well. It then asked, "Are we going to rewrite our laws or treaties for the benefit of one country?" The sovereignty issue was now framed in a way many Canadians could support.[42]

It was the United Church leadership that began to give the sovereignty strategy its full moral power. Rev. Ernest E. Long brought the meeting to its climax by insisting that "one of the fundamental rights in a human society is the right of political refuge. Our problem is that we can't imagine political refugees coming from the U.S. But the U.S. is a sufficiently troubled society that in the next decade we shall see an increased flow of refugees. Unless we clarify this matter now we are liable to be a very unjust society."[43] Reverend Long was insisting that if the Canadian state was to act in good conscience, it must exercise its sovereignty and act independently of American law and foreign policy. Long used the moral authority of the United Church to re-cast the American military resisters from being symbols of unsuitability into symbols of Canadian sovereignty. The moral power of this action was some-thing that the leadership of the United Church as a cultural elite alone could provide.[44]

To Be Sovereign or Servile?

The United Church was more in touch with the quickly changing opinions of the Canadian public than MacEachen's department of immigration. In the fall of 1968, just under a third of sampled Canadians reported they sym-pathized with "young Americans who dodge the draft."[45] By the spring of 1969, more than half of Canadians reported feeling sympathetic, while those reporting qualified support increased from 2 to 19 percent.[46] Addi-tional public opinion data indicate that between 1966 and 1970 the propor-tion of Canadians who felt Canada and the United States were growing fur-ther apart increased from 8 to 28 percent.[47]

A reading of the minister's mail during this period provides a further sense of the public mind. Some Canadians wrote the minister expressing their op-position to the admission of military resisters to Canada, with comments like the following:

> "Why should we as Canadians keep these 'bums' in our country when they have no loyalty to their own?"
> "I have never in my life ever seen such trash as these American Draft Dodgers . . . whom we as Canadians have to support and cater to, after they haven't got the guts to fight for their own country."
> "I say our whole existence is threatened if we continue to allow this type of rabble into our country."
> "We trust that a sterner line will be taken by our government to halt this influx of undesirables to our country."
> "I can only term them as cowards and feel that we in Canada are aiding and abetting them in a traitorous act."
> "I have met several of these American deserters, and to a man, they were scruffy rascals, types we can well do without in Canada."
> "You allow Yellow Bellies to come from the U.S.A. We go to war for Can-ada. Do not do this."
> "Keep Canada a proud land, not a country that allows garbage in."

Such statements were consistent with the earlier reported finding that in the fall of 1968 only a minority of sampled Canadians reported that they sympathized with American war resisters.[48]

Nonetheless, a far greater number of letters to the minister supported the admission of the resisters, most often on grounds that placed concerns about sovereignty ahead of sympathy:

"We are not merely the administrators of domestic American law north of the longest unprotected boundary in the world."

"It is the realistic fear that our fates are in the clumsy hands of people more disturbed by actions distasteful to their American masters than they are excited by the promise of this nation."

"As a Canadian citizen I favour an independent decision regarding exiles; one that is not subject to the dictates of the American government."

"It would appear that Canada is once again bending to pressure from Washington. I am exasperated with Canadians who are more American than the Americans themselves."

"If the government is really so cowed by the U.S. government as to want to bar these men, it should at least have the courage to shoulder the blame itself."

"Since when is it a function of the Canadian government to enforce U.S. laws respecting the draft?"

"When Canada . . . acts as the military policeman for the U.S.A., she becomes party to American policy as such and this cannot be assumed to coincide with our own any more than the policy of any other foreign power."

"Why should Canada change its traditional open door policy merely to help the United States carry out a purpose which is odious to many thoughtful and altruistic people on both sides of the border?"

"I suggest that you, as Minister, have an obligation to stress to all border installations that military laws of a foreign power are of no concern to Canada."[49]

Between 1968 and 1969, the balance of letters shifted toward opening the border and offering the opportunity of immigration and refuge to American military resisters as an expression of Canadian sovereignty.

Clearly the United Church was not acting alone or apart from many, perhaps most, Canadians in seeing the war resister issue in national terms. Canadians in 1969 were still basking in the afterglow of a nationwide 1967 centennial celebration of the country's confederation. Canada's most popular historian, Pierre Berton, was so taken with the "turning point" qualities of this year-long celebration that he later wrote a book entitled *1967: The Last Good Year.* In it, he contrasted the new national mood that emerged in 1967 with a stereotype that plagued Canadians in relation to the United States: "We tended to see ourselves (as, indeed, others saw us) as stick-in-the-muds, while the Americans looked like gamblers and risk-takers. No more. Nineteen-sixty-seven was a watershed year in more ways than one, a revolutionary year . . . But the greatest revolution was the revelation that we had created a world-class, forward-looking nation."[50] It was in this context that the United Church leadership saw the application of Canada's immigration law as an issue of sovereignty.

The greatest threat to Canadian sovereignty, of course, had long been the United States. This made the issue of the admission of American draft and military resisters all the more important as a symbol of a newfound sense of national sovereignty. The United Church had identified a timely symbol to give new and aptly directed expression to a growing national mood. Recognizing the power of this issue, the opposition New Democratic Party in the House of Commons also railed against the newly apparent policies and practices of the department of immigration. David Lewis demanded that the "secret" and "illegal" directives dating from the previous July that banned U.S. military resisters be tabled in the House. The immigration department responded by citing an obscure 1946 precedent for treating intradepartmental communications as confidential. It insisted, "They are extracts from our *Manual of Instructions for the Guidance of Immigration and Visa Officers.* All such instructions are issued under a 'restricted' classification."[51]

Lewis also asserted the sovereignty issue, saying, "I see no reason whatsoever, except a servile attitude on the part of Canada, for treating American young men who object to fighting an immoral war in Viet Nam differently from the way we treated literally tens of thousands of immigrants all through the years who refused to accept military service in their countries for similar reasons."[52] He concluded that "Canada was acting in a servile way if it turned down U.S. deserters." With this Lewis challenged the cultural framing of servicemen who had left the American military as unsuitable castoffs, misfits, and troublemakers, portraying them instead as refugees and rational persons of conscience who deserved the opportunity to immigrate in opposition to the Vietnam war and as appropriate symbols of Canadian sovereignty. Lewis and the New Democrats were happy to provide the American resisters the opportunity to open a new front in the antiwar movement while solving their draft and military problems by immigrating to Canada.

Nonetheless, an apparently unswayed Minister MacEachen began in early March 1969 to prepare a confidential memorandum for the Cabinet whose purpose was to produce parliamentary approval for a new overt, specific regulation to exclude American military resisters from Canada. These efforts suggest that MacEachen was still responding to perceived concerns of his departmental administrators and the United States. From MacEachen's perspective, the memorandum was a compromise extracted from those in the department who wanted to reopen the draft resister issue while excluding military resisters. The memorandum declared, "There is a need for a re-affirmation of Canada's policy of disregarding draft status in determining a person's admissibility to Canada, and for the passage of a regulation to exclude military deserters." The key argument at this stage was now more candidly stated as involving Canada's relationship to its powerful neighbor: MacEachen asserted, "To grant asylum to deserters as refugees would constitute a blanket condemnation of the United States and its political and judicial system . . . Many critics of the present policy are less interested in the welfare of the deserters than in using them as a focal point for a continuing campaign against the United States."[53] MacEachen clearly saw the opportunity that open immigration would provide not only for draft and military resistance but also for antiwar mobilization.

To be sure, some members of MacEachen's own party in Parliament were lobbying for a policy of liberalization. One minister reminded MacEachen, "Many immigrants to Canada in the past have been deserters, and we have seen no reason not to admit them. I submit that we should maintain our traditional policy, and that is the only course for a liberal Government to follow."[54] As suggested later, MacEachen resisted growing support for this view not only because of the position adopted by his administrators, but also because as the Cabinet memo was being prepared, newly elected Prime Minister Trudeau was planning to meet newly elected President Nixon later in the month in Washington.

Trudeau's views on war resisters at this stage are uncertain. In the memo MacEachen wrote to his deputy after returning from the difficult meeting with the United Church Board in Toronto, he described a telephone conversation with the Prime Minister. MacEachen reported of Trudeau, "He made reference to the contractual business and stated as follows: 'surely a person who deserts from the armed forces of the U.S. is guilty of a criminal offense and accordingly would be inadmissible to Canada on that ground alone.'"[55] This was perhaps an unexpected position for Trudeau to take, since he had begun his life in politics as a student in Montreal campaigning during World War II for a candidate who opposed conscription. In any case, Trudeau was assuming that desertion was an extraditable offense; but the U.S. State Department had discarded this position in May 1968 Senate hearings, where its representative testified that "[t]he exception from extradition for military crimes is one of long standing and great tradition."[56] This is why MacEachen's deputy soon replied, "Our legal advisers in the department find themselves unable to agree that a person by the act of desertion commits a crime in the ordinary sense. True he commits an offence against U.S. military law but there is a real question whether that is in itself a criminal offence."[57] It was becoming increasingly clear that neither the Canadian Immigration Act nor the extradition treaty with the United States provided legal authority for excluding American servicemen from immigration to Canada.

The Elephant Didn't Twitch

In the days leading up to Trudeau's departure for Washington, MacEachen struggled to write both a follow-up letter to the leadership of the United Church about the ill-fated meeting in Toronto and a final draft of the memo to the Cabinet about American war resisters. An early draft of his letter to the United Church rearticulated the argument of suitability as justification for circumventing the explicit provisions of the Immigration Act. This draft is a striking example of the process Pedriana and Stryker describe in which a central symbolic value is mobilized in a cultural strategy designed to recast the interpretation of an explicit legal rule. MacEachen wrote:

> It has been drawn to my attention on a number of occasions that these sections [of the Immigration Act] do not refer specifically to an applicant's military status. Notwithstanding this, it is my considered opinion that obligations such as exist between a serving member of the armed services of the United States and his government are such that we must seriously question whether an individual who seeks to come to Canada to escape such obligations would not also forsake equally serious obligations in Canada. In my

opinion an individual's attitude on such matters has a definite bearing on his ability to establish himself successfully in Canada.

MacEachen's own handwriting reveals that he rewrote this paragraph several times before striking it completely from his letter, explaining in a dated note alongside the draft, "We should not anticipate outcome of Cabinet review."[58] In the end, MacEachen sent the church an innocuous note, which its recipient found insulting in its lack of substance. Though not revealed in his writing of this letter, MacEachen was beginning to have second thoughts and was coming to realize that cultural norms of responsibility and obligation would not provide sufficient leverage for him to widen the definition of suitability as circumscribed in the immigration point system. This he needed to do in order to overcome the absence of a prohibition against military resisters in the Immigration Act. The problem was that the real goal—to exclude U.S. military resisters per se—had become too obvious.

In effect, MacEachen's opponents, the advocates of liberalization, were mobilizing the legal realists' classic critique of the gap between the "law in the books" and the "law in action" for their assault on the "lawless discretion" covertly being exercised by the immigration department and its officers. In practical as well as theoretical terms, the issue was how far the relative autonomy of law could be stretched. The treatment of the military resisters in Canada shows how alternative interpretations of the constraints imposed by an existing law can shape and reshape the way operational policy is made and interpreted. Minister MacEachen and his administrator Morrison both came to realize that they were vulnerable in their elaboration of the discretion the existing law provided. This did not keep them from covertly using their political power to suppress the issue posed by the exclusion of military resisters from Canada for nearly a year. When this abuse of power was revealed it became possible for the opposition to reframe the issue of immigration as one of sovereignty rather than suitability.

Several days after MacEachen penned his second thoughts in the margin of the United Church letter, and as Trudeau left for Washington, MacEachen signed off on his confidential "Statement on Draft Dodgers and Military Deserters" for the Cabinet Committee on Social Policy. This statement acknowledged that "instructions were issued to immigration officers in July 1968 setting out as guidelines examples of obligations, including the obligations assumed by members of the armed forces of foreign countries, which officers should take into account in exercising their discretionary power. They were advised to consider using their discretionary power to refuse such persons."

This last sentence finally acknowledged, but in the secrecy of the Cabinet, that the purpose of the July directive was to have officers covertly refuse servicemen at the border. The statement built to this conclusion: "The Government believes it is not, on balance, in Canada's interest to accept military deserters from foreign countries. It has therefore been decided to provide a regulation under the authority of section 61 of the Immigration Act . . . This will have the effect of prohibiting military deserters from coming to Canada wherever they may apply."[59] The effect of this change in the Immigration Act would have been to make public and legal what the department was already doing by covert instruction of its border officers—that is, it would have brought the explicit rule of law embodied in the Immigration Act into conformity with existing covert practice and the cultural strategy based on suitability. The content and timing of MacEachen's Cabinet memo was tied to the Prime Minister's visit to Washington.

The tie between the Cabinet document and Trudeau's Washington trip is revealed in a section of the confidential briefing papers prepared for the Prime Minister's state visit. A part of this document, entitled "Draft Dodgers and Deserters," summarized the Cabinet statement and offered an assessment for the Prime Minister of attitudes he was likely to encounter on this issue in the United States, noting that while Canada's acceptance of resisters was a source of irritation to the United States, "it has not so far resulted in any formal U.S.A. representations." The document concluded, "It is not expected that President Nixon will raise the question. Should he do so, however, it would probably be sufficient to indicate that Cabinet is now awaiting the conclusions and recommendations of the departmental review . . . If it were desirable to be more forthcoming it could be said that preliminary indications are that the review will lead to all deserters, but not draft dodgers, being refused admission to Canada."[60] This advice was presumably in Trudeau's mind when he met with Nixon, and it seems clearly to have been in his thinking during remarks he delivered at the National Press Club toward the end of his visit.

As predicted in the briefing materials, Nixon did not raise the resister issue during their talks. It is easy to find reasons why. Nixon was more immediately preoccupied with domestic protests and resistance activities, and the resisters in Canada probably would have seemed to him far removed. There were also other military issues that Nixon considered more important, including Trudeau's public speculation about reducing or eliminating Canadian participation in NATO and Canadian opposition to Nixon's plans to develop an antiballistic missile system with sites near the Canadian border. Trudeau was accommodating in his discussions with Nixon on both of these issues.[61]

The topic of the resisters finally came up on the second day of Trudeau's visit, during his appearance at the National Press Club. Trudeau began by offering his classic description, still famous in Canada, of the view from the north of the Canadian–U.S. relationship. Trudeau likened this relationship to "sleeping with an elephant . . . no matter how friendly and even-tempered the beast, . . . one is affected by every twitch and grunt." This comment likely hinted at Trudeau's watchfulness of America in its attitudes about the war resister issue.

It was in this context that Trudeau later moved beyond a reporter's question about Canada's admission of U.S. "draft dodgers" as immigrants to speak about "deserters." Drawing on his briefing materials' references to the issue of suitability, Trudeau said Canada banned some servicemen because they had moral and legal obligations "at home." Then he opened the door to a more liberal policy by noting that nonetheless some deserters had been accepted. A following *Globe and Mail* editorial implied that Trudeau was trying to test American reactions to this topic that Nixon had not broached.[62] The *Globe* already supported the admission of military resisters and would have preferred Trudeau either to have taken a stronger stand or to have ignored the issue. The *Globe* nonetheless implicitly conceded the wisdom of Trudeau's approach when it acknowledged that "we do have to live with the elephant."[63]

The Cabinet Considers, the Church Responds

When MacEachen met with Cabinet members about the war resister issue in the beginning of April 1969, the political equation was far different from what it had been ten months earlier. Then the head of the American Selective Service had signaled the apparent wish of the United States that Canada slow the exodus of war resisters. Then Canadians had been unsympathetic to American Vietnam war resisters and felt closer to the United States. These factors had made the cultural strategy of suitability seem a plausible justification for first covertly and then more overtly excluding American servicemen as inappropriate immigrants, even though the Immigration Act did not prohibit them. In this context, MacEachen had been rushed into approving changes in the internal departmental regulations that excluded military resisters. This in turn had made it seem prudent to plan for a change in the Immigration Act that would legalize the overt exclusion of American servicemen. But by the spring of 1969 the Canadian public had developed sympathy for the American war resisters and their grievances, against both the United States and Canadian immigration officials. Although these grievances earlier had been forced underground by the immigration department's covert tactics, which excluded admission on the basis of unsuitability, the military resisters were now, with the support of a growing number of Canadians, gaining a public voice.

Canadians had also started to see their country as being more separate from the United States; and newly elected President Nixon, through his inaction during and after Trudeau's visit, had sidestepped the issue of Canadian admission of military resisters. The American President had chosen to focus his power and influence on the issues of NATO and his planned new missile system. His inaction with regard to the military resisters was a Lukesian nondecision with consequences. It was in these new circumstances that an emboldened symbolism of sovereignty could emerge as the master frame for interpreting the immigration to Canada of American military resisters.

Nonetheless, MacEachen took his departmental proposal to change the Immigration Act to the members of the Cabinet at the beginning of April. Thirty years later he explained, "Here was my department . . . It was a difficult situation. I decided to bring forward the Cabinet document, so the departmental view would be fully expressed. It had cogency . . . Well, not to abandon these people, you know, . . . in the political process, I certainly was content with that policy."[64] Yet he did not seem convinced about the policy, and his earlier handwritten remarks on the draft of the letter to the United Church reflected these doubts. Cabinet members were even more doubtful. Notes from two aides who attended the meeting confirm that the former Minister of Immigration, Jean Marchand, spoke strongly along with others against what was seen as a clear break with a more liberal policy and the Immigration Act itself. One aide reported that "Mr. Marchand pointed out that desertion is not mentioned in the immigration law. As a result, he really questions whether we should have restrictions against deserters entering Canada. He expressed his view fairly forcefully that he didn't feel we should

. . . that the law should not authorize the government to make any prohibited classes by regulation."[65]

MacEachen and Marchand were clearly at odds in this meeting. At a minimum this reveals that the later characterization by MacEachen of the background to his May 22, 1969, opening of the border to military resisters as a simple extension of a policy of "liberalization" was not shared by Marchand and others who were previously involved. Marchand and Kent had sought to place the immigration policy on resisters on a path that was subsequently systematically subverted by MacEachen's departmental administrators. The Cabinet was divided in this meeting and decided to postpone taking any definite action.

Meanwhile, the United Church of Canada leadership had received MacEachen's revised, vacuous response to the Toronto board meeting and decided to go over the minister's head by sending a public telegram to the Prime Minister. The telegram emphasized the illegality of the government's covert exclusion of American servicemen under the Immigration Act and brought forward the symbolic package of sovereignty as a fully formed master framing of the issue.

"The basic problem," the General Council of the Church now charged in its telegram, "is . . . the existence of two sets of criteria for Immigration purposes . . . The bending of the law through secret 'guidelines' is not the manner in which any issue should be faced." The telegram then went to the symbolic heart of the issue by raising the issue of sovereignty, charging that Canada was acting as a "military policeman" for the United States. The Church Council asserted, "The exclusion of deserters from foreign armed forces from Canada, simply by reason of that fact, we would challenge on its own grounds. Canada is not bound by law or obligation to be military policemen for any foreign power and has a long tradition of receiving persons from many lands who have sought escape from forced service in foreign wars."[66] MacEachen responded angrily to the Church by return telegram, and the Church shot another telegram back over his head to the Prime Minister. The newspapers had a field day.

The significance of the leadership of the United Church taking this strong position on an important social issue was not accidental and did not go unnoticed. The *Globe and Mail* ran an editorial applauding "The New Church" and noting that until recently the social policy of the United Church consisted of little more than a call for more evangelistic campaigns and stricter laws against liquor and gambling. In this context, the cultural package based on suitability would have seemed a more persuasive framing of the issue to the Church than the new concern with sovereignty. MacEachen had assumed that the suitability strategy would prevail, but Canada was changing and the Church was too. The *Globe* noted that the three main resolutions passed by the board at its recent annual meeting had dealt not with bingo or lotteries or the regulation of beer parlors, but with major social and political issues—medicare, housing, and the admission of U.S. deserters to Canada as immigrants. The Church had stepped in to fill a power vacuum left by the nondecision of the United States on the war resister issue. "This is a far cry," The *Globe* emphasized, "from the narrow self-centered puritanism which used to be characteristic of the United Church."[67] The American resisters both provoked and benefited from some of this change.

The Newly Suitable Symbols of Sovereignty

The *Toronto Telegram* struck once more on behalf of the cultural strategy of suitability, even chastising Minister MacEachen for "pussy footing" around the issue that "deserters from the United States aren't welcome in Canada as immigrants." The *Telegram* editorial reasoned that *draft* resisters were suitable because they had made no commitment to their government to serve in the military forces. But "deserters are entirely different. They have made a commitment to the government of their country. This isn't the kind of citizen Canada wants."[68]

Nonetheless, the tide had turned. The day after the *Telegram* editorial, the *Toronto Star* became the last major Toronto paper to give its opinion by siding with sovereignty. "A man's status, or lack of it, in the military of another country has little bearing on his value to this one." The *Star* reasoned that "it is in principle and in practice, irrelevant, and should be treated that way— whether the military in question is American, Czechoslovakian, Cuban, Hungarian, or British. To act otherwise is to relinquish a part of the selection of our population to another sovereignty." The *Star* then warned that "clusters of pressure groups are forming . . . for the express purpose of forcing the government into a reasonable stand on this issue. Mr MacEachen need have no illusions; the public is not going to shut up, and the question is not going to go away."[69]

The *Star's* editorial was accompanied by an op-ed piece written by Professor Stephen Clarkson of the University of Toronto. Clarkson's piece[70] cut to the American linguistic core of the Canadian sovereignty issue and the characterization of American military resisters as unsuitable immigrants. He noted, "By talking of 'draft dodgers' and 'deserters' we are accepting the official American view of these applicants for Canadian residence. In 1956 we called the Hungarian immigrants 'freedom fighters,' not disloyal, contract-breaking citizens (which of course they were from Budapest's point of view). If we would call these young Americans what they are—political refugees—we would be part way toward removing the mote from our own eye." Clarkson then traced the opposition to the American military resisters to fears of the neighboring power of the United States: "What seems to be Ottawa's major hang-up is the Pavlovian apprehension that, should Canada take a clear stance, there would be some immediate American government retaliation."

It was now several weeks since Trudeau's visit to Washington, and there was still no indication that the American government would challenge the admission of draft or military resisters to Canada. Clarkson acknowledged, "We should, of course, measure the implications of our actions . . . but it is hard to imagine how this would be a major concern for the Nixon administration." At the same time, Clarkson argued that Canada had an important opportunity to make a difference in American public thought. Nixon's Lukesian nondecision gave Canada the freedom to act: "We should be interested in influencing U.S. opinion," Clarkson insisted, "and if this simple act would bolster public resistance to the continued U.S. fighting in Viet Nam, this is a further argument in its favor." Clarkson concluded that "this is a concrete challenge for the Trudeau government's American policy: Is it going to adopt a coherently liberal policy or is it, like the well-trained concubine, going to pander to its master without even being asked?"

The pressure continued to mount over the following weeks. A Committee for Fair Immigration Policy formed, with a membership that was a Who's Who of Canadian writers, scholars, and civil libertarians.[71] This committee was then cloned in Ottawa, Vancouver, and Montreal. Yet another eloquent plea addressed the competing narratives of suitability and sovereignty, this time by Jack Ludwig in the *Globe,* under the title "Why We Should Not Desert Our Sovereignty."[72]

Like Clarkson, Ludwig was conscious of the power of the national origins of words (such as "deserter"), in this case used to define the resistance issue. He based his argument on the covert directives that MacEachen had refused to make public and that undermined Canadian sovereignty on the presumed ground of suitability for immigration, noting that "the officers have somehow interpreted the directive to mean they must consider a man's military status; more, that his failure to honor U.S. obligations establishes him as someone clearly incapable of establishing himself successfully in Canada. Thus, in what seems a tiny way, Canadian determination of fitness or unfitness yields to U.S. definitions. Hardly the way for the smaller country to guard its precious sovereignty."

Ludwig's ultimate concern was about the threat to Canadian independence posed by the country's direct or indirect submission to American influence. He wrote, "Pressures from the United States, real or imagined, must be resisted with cool. The United States, in that way, develops the habit of consultation, consideration, and respect for sovereignty and even neutrality. The metaphor we search for is so simple: a man must be master even in his own small house."

The cultural strategy of suitability was now clearly overwhelmed by the more central value of Canadian sovereignty as a symbolic package; and this idea, with the assistance of the American government's nondecision, was rapidly gaining strength. Few would have questioned, and indeed the most articulate advocates such as Clarkson and Ludwig made this part of their argument, that American inaction was helpful to this groundswell of national sentiment.

In the end, both the Liberal Caucus and the Cabinet came to the conclusion that American military as well as draft resisters should be treated like other applicants and be given the opportunity to immigrate to Canada. The then Minister of External Affairs, Mitchell Sharp, later mused, "I think in Cabinet that the feeling was very strong, even stronger as the thing went on, that somehow these were not deserters in the sense of deserters from people who were defending the United States, you know, they were just deserters for a cause, and it wasn't that they were opposed to military action, it was just that they thought they were involved in an unjust war, a useless war."[73]

It was in this context that on May 22, 1969, Allan MacEachen stood in the House of Commons and reversed his nearly year-long stand on the admission of military resisters to Canada, opening the border and claiming that doing so was the extension of an ongoing policy of liberalization. The day after this speech the Assistant Deputy Minister was back at his desk, revising the Immigration Manual to remove provisions of the never disclosed, covert directives that contradicted the liberalization claim. The deputy discussed the changes in a memo that confirmed what had been widely suspected.

While 24.03 12(g) was designed to exclude deserters, the public posture has been that its purpose was to give examples of various "substantial legal, contractual, or moral obligations" to our officers which they should take into account in the exercise of their discretion. To repeal the entire section at this time would indicate the true purpose of the July 29 1968 amendment should it become known. For that reason I suggest we delete the example of membership in the armed forces and rewrite the final paragraph to make clear that such membership is not to be taken into account.[74]

Minister MacEachen took this advice, and the explicit reference to military desertion was excised from the department's manual as quietly as it was covertly inserted nearly a year before.

Cultural Symbols, Political Power, and Legal Gatekeeping

In the end, Canada's immigration policy on the admission of American Vietnam war resisters was the result of interconnections between competing cultural and symbolic claims about American military resisters as immigrants and the exercise of political power within Canada concerning its relationship with the United States. Canadians were increasingly opposed to the war in Vietnam, and eventually they were pleased to have its country's immigration policy reflect their opposition by opening the legal gates and allowing American war resisters the opportunity to immigrate. Yet the country's position did not evolve consistently; it developed in regressive as well as progressive ways.

The analysis in this chapter of the evolution of Canadian immigration policy toward American war resisters focused on what Steven Lukes calls a second dimension of political power that often precedes the more visible clashes of first-dimension power and interest-group conflict emphasized in pluralist political theory. The exercise of second-dimension political power often interacts with and influences the symbolic packaging and cultural framing of policies through nondecisions as well as decisions, and it involves covert as well as overt conflict around potential as well as fully realized issues, often expressed by an airing of subjective grievances before they result in actual political participation. Lukes goes on to identify a third dimension of power politics, in which actors are kept unaware of real grievances, which they therefore do not subjectively perceive or express.[75] The American Vietnam servicemen who were initially denied admission to Canada on the basis of unwritten rules experienced this kind of third-dimension political power in that they initially were unaware that they had rights as unprohibited applicants for immigration to Canada.

Lukes's point is that at each level of remove from the first dimension of overt interest-group behavior, the exercise of political power is no less important but more difficult to discern. Still, it is often the covert and surreptitious exercise of political power of Lukes's second dimension that stimulates political discourse framed in cultural and symbolic terms, which can change the public's understanding of the issues involved.

The policy of liberalization with regard to Vietnam war resisters was publicly proclaimed by Canadian Immigration Minister Allan MacEachen in the spring of 1969. Yet Canada's immigration policy actually had been conducted outside of public view and in ways that were purposefully obscured for much of the preceding year by MacEachen's own ministry. What had been a retrenchment in immigration policy went back at least to the summer of 1968 and coincided with comments of the Director General of the U.S. Selective Service System, Louis Hershey, who criticized Canadian immigration policy. First with unwritten rules, and then with written but unpublicized internal departmental rules and directives, Canadian immigration administrators covertly closed the gates to legal admission of American servicemen to Canada.

The immigration department's exclusion of military resisters visibly entered Lukes's second dimension of the political process when a nationally published newspaper columnist became aware of the covert policies and practices and began writing about them. The immigration department and its minister denied allegations of the existence of the exclusionary policies and practices; even after changing them, they never publicly admitted that they were followed. For more than half a year the department and its minister instead defended a position built on what were intended to be circumscribed discretionary provisions in the immigration point system, opposing admission of American servicemen by emphasizing cultural norms that defined them as unsuitable for immigration because they had irresponsibly failed to keep moral and legal obligations to complete their military service. The Immigration Act of Canada did not prohibit admission of military resisters, and in the past servicemen from other countries had been accepted. Nonetheless, until Canadian student news reporters demonstrated that immigration officers were summarily excluding military resisters on the basis of their military status per se, the debate surrounding this issue was defensively framed as an issue of personal suitability for immigration.

An alternative to the symbolic package of suitability only emerged when the covert policy of exclusion was fully revealed and when Canadians began to understand that their Immigration Act did not prohibit admission of military resisters. To this point, those practicing the covert tactics of exclusion had managed to suppress this issue of potential national interest. The issue came to the fore as the cultural elite of Canada, through the leadership of the United Church of Canada, supported by the New Democratic Party and an array of civil libertarian groups, advanced the argument that the Immigration Act was being subverted by observing distinctions of American military and selective service law that were legally irrelevant in Canada. Building on a wave of national feeling that was already growing in Canada, the grievances of American military resisters now were framed as symbolic of Canadian sovereignty. This assertion of sovereignty became a cultural resource that its proponents used to take the offensive in the battle to open the legal gates of admission for American military resisters to Canada. Yet the emergence of this symbolic package as a master framing of the issue also was contingent on the inaction, or nondecision, of the Nixon Administration that left unopposed the immigration of American military resisters to Canada.

In this new context, a spring 1969 policy of liberalization on the admission of draft and military resisters assumed center stage. The failure of President Nixon in 1969 to oppose the admission of American draft or military resisters to Canada encouraged a call by the large and powerful United Church for Canadian sovereignty in the application of its Immigration Act. The symbolic appeal of sovereignty, and its support by the United Church and other cultural elite groups, was a powerful resource that helped Canadians to reject Americans' distinguishing between draft and military resisters and their attaching particular stigma to the latter. This change, along with the rejection of the notion of resisters as unsuitable for immigration, probably would not have occurred without the cultural resource that the symbolism of sovereignty provided.

The evolution of Canadian immigration policy on war resisters was an intricately choreographed dance with regressive and progressive steps linked to covert policies and practices of the immigration department and its minister and to perceived shifts in American demands and expectations. This improvised dance eventually led to the American draft "dodgers" and military "deserters" becoming Canadian symbols of sovereignty. In the end, Canada used its immigration policy to practically as well as symbolically open the legal gates of political opportunity in Canada for a new and peaceful defiance of the American Vietnam war. This was a turning point for Canada, as well as for the American war resisters now streaming into the country.

CHAPTER 3

Toronto's
American Ghetto

By the early 1970s there were more than 20,000 American war resisters in Toronto. The opportunity offered by Canadian immigration law to resist U.S. selective service and military laws set in motion the formation of a new immigrant community. Robert Fulford captured the pace of change when he told the story of a young Texan draft dodger he knew who moved into a boarding house on Admiral Road, a gracefully winding, shady street in the Annex section of Toronto. Within two hours of arriving in the house the transplanted Texan discovered another draft dodger staying just down the hall. They went out for a walk and, a couple of houses away, discovered three young men working on a motorcycle. They stopped to talk and discovered that these three were also draft dodgers. "Five of us on the street!" the startled friend exclaimed. "Wait a minute," said one of the motorcyclists. "Next door there's two more, and a couple of houses down the street there's another one." This made eight draft dodgers on Admiral Road. Probably more, remarked Fulford, but who could know for sure?[1]

These new immigrants stood out, not only because of their youth but probably also because of their American exuberance. They had a tendency toward outspokenness. This, combined with their uprootedness and displacement, created an impression that was often boisterous and sometimes disturbing, especially because of their ignorance of things Canadian. Douglas Fetherling, one of the newcomers, later remarked in understatement, "We were a noisy community of strangers."[2]

This chapter focuses on the city of Toronto, specifically the neighborhoods in which the largest concentrations of American war resisters settled and caught their collective breath. I then sketch the backgrounds of some of the more entrepreneurial new arrivals and describe how they established a countercultural American ghetto in the heart of the city, giving particular attention to the neighborhoods in and around the University of Toronto, where American immigrants clustered on their arrival. Most of the new arrivals spent their first nights and days in this downtown area, and many settled in for periods that lasted from weeks to years. The organizations that were the indigenous mobilizing structures of the war resistance movement in Toronto were also clustered around the university campus. In this way, the neighborhoods and the campus became a residential base of overlapping organizational and social ties. Using the classic example of the Paris Commune of 1871, Roger Gould has demonstrated how powerful a source of solidarity and commitment the combination of organizational and residential ties can be for social-movement activity.[3] A similar network could be seen at work in Toronto during the late 1960s. This setting was, of course, further energized by the migration experience itself, especially through the formation of the American ghetto.

Toronto and Its Newest Minority

The University of Toronto is located in the heart of Canada's largest city, a metropolis whose population is today nearly half composed of persons born outside this nation's borders, making Toronto one of the most diverse urban settings in the world. This diversity is relatively recent, having taken place over the last third of the twentieth century; and the American migration was part of the city's transformation.

In the 1920s Hemingway lamented his return from Paris to a newspaper job in "Toronto, the city of churches."[4] This was much the same city that a few decades later world-renowned but still very Anglo-Canadian classicist and literary critic Northrop Frye appreciatively described as "a good place for minding your own business."[5] These perceptions of Toronto by two very different personalities expressed their separate national backgrounds as much as their personal tastes or times. For if American cities sought to provide opportunities for life, liberty, and the pursuit of happiness, Toronto was a more somber expression of a historic Canadian concern for peace, order, and good government. This difference of attitude dated at least to the eighteenth century and the immigration of the United Empire Loyalists, American counter-revolutionaries who chose to leave the rebellious colonies and live in the more British part of North America.[6] It is estimated that as many as 100,000 loyalists came to Canada.[7]

Modern Americans sometimes see virtues in a Canadian distinctiveness that is traced to Loyalist times. A New York magazine article lauded a contemporary "return of New York" and speculated that in its renewal "New York could become something like Toronto, happy and edgeless and Canadian."[8] But the "edgeless" part of this image was a thing of the past by the middle 1960s. In October 1965 the University of Toronto hosted an International Teach-In, with President Claude Bissell as Honorary Chair and professors and students providing organizational leadership. An explicit purpose of this event was to bring the emerging peace movement and the university together. The teach-in was called "Revolution and Response" and focused on the growing American military involvement in the Vietnam war. One participant recalled, "People came with banners, they came with literature and slogans, classes were cancelled. I mean it was *huge*. Sure, the organizers brought in some big Yanks but they also brought George Grant, the Red Tory, who talked about nationalism and technological empires and multiversities and dehumanization and manipulation by the social sciences."[9] The event was certainly a success, lasting three days, with seventeen speakers, one hundred twenty journalists, more than four thousand students, and an estimated radio audience of more than a million listeners. One consequence of the success of the teach-in was renewed efforts by the Student Union for Peace Action (SUPA) to press the question of Canadian response to the Vietnam war.

SUPA was initially linked to the American Students for a Democratic Society, and members of SUPA went on to found the Toronto Anti-Draft Program (TADP), which played a leading role in bringing American war resisters to Canada. To this extent, Canadian Vietnam war resistance can be regarded as a spin-off of its American counterpart, but the story rapidly becomes more complicated. As the previous chapter and the quote about the Toronto teach-in suggest, movement activity in Canada also was strongly indigenous.

In any case, by the late 1960s Toronto was no longer as staid as it once was, and it was rapidly sharpening its newfound edges. The most noticeable change was the increasingly diverse but still hierarchically stratified ethnic makeup of the country, which John Porter incisively called Canada's "vertical mosaic."[10] Power and privilege were still governing parts of the civic equation, even in the face of the growing ethnic diversity. City planners joined with government officials in attempting to eradicate some of Toronto's most distinctive ethnic neighborhoods, only some of which were poor and most of which had a richness of life and architecture that begged to be preserved. Urban sociologist and transplanted American war resister Jon Caulfield writes that from the 1940s through the 1960s, Toronto city planning was dominated by schemes for demolition and reconstruction; if the planners had their say, it seemed that little would stand in their way.[11]

For example, city government supported plans to route an expressway from north of the city through the established midtown districts that formed the white- and blue-collar residential heart of Toronto, south through the historic neighborhoods of Spadina Avenue, feeding finally into the railway and freeway lands located along the waterfront. A "Stop the Spadina Expressway" movement halted this project literally in its tracks, replacing the planned expressway with the new Spadina subway line. A subsequent citizen revolt stopped a similarly destructive plan to construct high-rise buildings in the Southeast Spadina neighborhood that housed many recent American arrivals as well as other immigrant groups. Jane Jacobs, an urban scholar and activist who moved with her husband and draft-age sons from New York City to participate in the Toronto Vietnam war resistance in the 1960s, helped theorize and organize resistance to these plans, a process that was essential in ensuring that Toronto would retain the vitality of its core streets and neighborhoods.[12] In short, the mid- to late 1960s was a time of urban protest and uncertainty, with the recent American immigrants very much a part of the mix.

It is surely more than mere coincidence that as Toronto began to throw off some of the stodginess of an inward-looking British enclave, it included Marshall McLuhan among its new luminaries. While McLuhan may have been British trained and tweedy in manner, he was anything but conventional in his thoughts about the emerging "global village." While a member of the faculty at the University of Toronto, McLuhan wrote of the influence of television, which he early recognized was making "Vietnam our first TV war, just as World War II was a radio war." McLuhan's thinking was doubtless influenced by the explicitly expansionist immigration policy Canada was adopting. Television was bringing the news of the world to a city whose gates were simultaneously swinging open to increasing numbers of the globe's people. Toronto would soon take pride in being home to over one hundred immigrant groups, and this fact, as much or more than television and general population growth, was making the city a global entity.

McLuhan argued that Canada was more than an ordinary part of the new global village by virtue of its position apart from but nonetheless alongside its dominant southern neighbor. For McLuhan, "Canada is a kind of . . .

cultural counter-environment. The Canadian is an outsider to the United States." This is important, he asserted, because "you must live outside an environment to understand it; to participate in it is to blind yourself to all the hidden effects it may have on you."[13] The American war resisters gathering in Toronto were more than ready to accept and act on McLuhan's assertion, but they were only beginning to attain the global perspective on the United States that Canada now provided. Most were still wondering what exactly this perspective was.

Robert Fulford captured the irony of this situation for the new arrivals. "They come into my office," Fulford reported in 1969, "a steady stream of refugees, looking for work—but not for work only, for something else. A confirmation that they exist; no, that *Canada* exists; that there's something here you can grasp." The American immigrants also wondered where they might fit into this uncertain cultural terrain. In fact, they were more than just cultural curiosities, more than a novel source of national interest and even amazement; they were also cultural objects, new elements in Anglo-Canadians' perennial search for cultural bearings and meaning. At first, however, the new American arrivals could only see themselves as blurred images in a shifting Toronto cityscape, with no clear directions home. Compounding their uncertainty was their discovery that the locals weren't sure of their bearings either.

Robert Fulford voiced the bewilderment and consternation of the Americans: "The Canadians they meet aren't quite sure that their own country exists, and the newcomers are profoundly confused. It's hard enough growing up with the Great Canadian Identity Crisis; think how much harder it is to be forced to adopt it."[14] Where, if anywhere, were these American immigrants to fit? It was not even clear what to call them. Were they draft dodgers and deserters? Draft and military resisters? War resisters? Expatriates and exiles? Pacifists and radicals? New Canadians? All that initially was clear was that by the summer of 1969 they were becoming Canada's fastest-growing and newest minority. Out of these cultural conundrums emerged a provisional set of social solutions that in various ways involved the new American immigrants as well as their Canadian hosts.

The American Ghetto

One setting that would provide both a formative context and the mobilizing structures for war resistance and related social activism was the American ghetto. This ghetto was both real and imagined, although the term itself was only occasionally used. The outer boundaries of this ghetto were the borders of the world's largest national land mass, Canada itself, which the U.S. Exclusion Act along with that country's selective service and military laws formalized when the newly exiled war resisters wished to return for visits to parents and families in the United States. If they attempted to cross the border, they risked rejection, if not imprisonment. This legal reality led the resisters back to their newly adopted homes and the self-selected boundaries of the American ghettos to be found in the central parts of Canadian cites, most notably in Toronto.

The emotional heart of the American ghetto in Toronto consisted of the shops and businesses begun by American war resisters on Baldwin Street, in a mixed Chinese and Jewish neighborhood just south of the University of Toronto. In the early days of the migration it seemed that in every direction one went in and around the university campus, one bumped into arriving Americans. Ordinarily welcoming Canadians at times began to worry about American domination of their educational system, especially in such places as the University of Toronto.[15] The newly landed and struggling American resisters, who were unfamiliar with Canadians' ambivalent feelings about the United States, were taken aback by the reception they received. In an attempt to get their bearings and fit into their new surroundings, the resisters created housing cooperatives, community newspapers, voluntary organizations (including war resistance organizations), and small businesses. More than a few became university professors.

Amex, a newspaper that was founded in 1968 by the Union of American Exiles and that was the longest-lasting and probably most widely read expression of American Vietnam war resistance in Canada, used its own mailing list to map what it called the "American Refugee Ghetto" in Toronto.[16] This map included locations as distant in the city as the Beaches neighborhood in the east ("scores of American exiles live here"), York University to the north (a sometimes more radical campus outpost than the University of Toronto), the High Park residential neighborhood to the west (a site of weekly expatriate softball games), and the Toronto Islands to the south (a "groovy ferry is the only way to get there"). The heart of the American ghetto, however, was the University of Toronto's downtown St. George campus. Its focal points included the Rochdale College residence on the northern border of the campus, the Toronto Anti-Draft Program office housed in shifting sites on the east side of campus (for a time moving north to a midtown location), the *Amex* office in the middle of the campus, and several collectives to the south, initially including The Yellow Ford Truck ("a trading post") and Ragnarokr ("leathercraft") on Baldwin Street itself.

Most American war resisters who came to Toronto did not live in this ghetto, and the territory that included the American ghetto was probably identified by most of Toronto's citizens as many things other than American. Still, the lives of literally thousands of American war resisters were touched and given new direction by the institutions that made up this community. Many began their lives in their new country with a night or two of housing found through the referral service of the Toronto Anti-Draft Program. More than a thousand new arrivals took advantage of this housing service in 1969 alone, and they often reciprocated later by taking subsequent arrivals into their own homes.[17] For newcomers, the American ghetto was real and important, and this community retained its identity, at least in its early years, through several groups of individuals located in and around the university campus. These groups provided a supportive base with overlapping and intersecting residential and organizational ties that formed the foundation for much of the war resistance activity that subsequently developed in Toronto.

An Ambient Annex and the Raucousness of Rochdale

The first of these groups is in some ways the best known, although also probably the most loosely connected, and perhaps even apocryphal in its significance. Its residential location was in the Annex neighborhood, which stretched north and west from the university. It included a number of literary figures and social activists who were all in some way connected to the Vietnam war resistance. An at least symbolic figure near the center of this loose social network was Margaret Atwood, who was, and probably still is, Canada's best-known literary icon.

Then recently returned from graduate work at Harvard University and married to James Polk, a draft resister and descendant of the eleventh President of the United States, Atwood took a supportive and protective interest in the resistance community. She was involved in various ways with Anansi Press, which published some of her earliest work as well as the *Manual for Draft-Age Immigrants*, the guide that gave many resisters their first real introduction to Canada. Atwood's first book of literary criticism, *Survival*, featured a comparative theme that played off Canada and the United States. Her critique was greatly influenced by Jim Polk's understanding of the literary underpinnings of these two societies, which derived partly from his own experiences in the United States. Polk eventually occupied a managerial role in Anansi, became an accomplished writer in his own right, and acted as a consultant assisting Canadian publishing ventures for the Ontario Ministry of Culture and Recreation.

Atwood was in these early years already attracting international attention as a writer, and she generously used her growing reputation and influence to assist friends in the American ghetto. These included Jennifer Glossop, Atwood's editor and the partner of an American war resister. Among Atwood's American admirers was Douglas Fetherling, an ardent and often angry resister who later wrote of his own journey to Toronto in *Travels by Night: A Memoir of the Sixties*.[18] Given the recognition that Atwood was already receiving, it is especially telling that Fetherling later would write of Atwood that while "she had many impressive qualities, . . . I think loyalty was the most attractive of her many attributes." She nurtured an extensive network: "Sometimes it seemed she had been at the University of Toronto with about half of the individuals I was coming into contact with in my professional dealings: the magazine editors, publishing people and other writers who were all starting to get their first really important jobs." Fetherling recalls that "Peggy was loyal to all of them and they to her."[19]

However, this Annex-centered circle could be as piercingly political as it was loftily literary, and both in a combatively anti-American way. For example, Atwood's characterization of an American draft dodger, in her novel *The Robber Bride*, was far from sympathetic. Fetherling identified strongly with the critical thrust of Atwood's fiction and with others who followed this lead, noting that

> Margaret Atwood, for her part, was characteristically the most forthright and unambiguous in locating the villain somewhere between patriarchy as a social system and maleness considered as a pathological condition. In fact, it seemed to me with certainty then, and still seems to me even now, that they were all, at some fundamental level, against more or less the same thing: Americanism, with its republican brutality and hatred of culture. I wasn't an important writer but I found a great sense of discovery in locating a group of people who hated the same enemy I did (even if, because I had been born there, they sometimes found it necessary to hate me in the bargain).[20]

Jack Granatstein would later dub the onset of this mind-set in the resistance community as "the arrival of the anti-American Americans."[21] Fetherling spoke fiercely for himself when he wrote, "My only ambition now was to be a last-generation American and a first-generation Canadian."[22] Such sentiments suggest that it is too simple to regard the American resisters in Canada as a mere spin-off of the American antiwar movement.

The most controversial part of the Annex was Rochdale College, which stood on the neighborhood's southern flank, adjacent to the University of Toronto. Rochdale's intent was to be an open university for experiments in education, but it soon became more like Haight-Ashbury, one year too late. It opened its doors on Bloor Street in September of 1968. In short order it became a haven for drugs and the violence that too often follows. Fetherling writes that Rochdale became "a closed dystopian society of the most rigid kind, an authoritarian nightmare of a place where biker gangs, hired as security forces, set up checkpoints in the lobby and patrolled the corridors with vicious dogs." Few were happy with the results. From the viewpoint of the resistance community, it was especially regrettable that Rochdale was so clearly a part of the new American Ghetto in Toronto. Fetherling put it starkly: "It became the most Americanized place in Toronto, not excluding the U.S. Consulate on University Avenue: a kind of tower of urban decay and social chaos, reaching to the sky above the Annex."[23] If the Annex was home to some of the very best and most creative of the Americans in Canada, Rochdale became a symbol of some of the worst elements of American culture brought along by the new arrivals.

Getting Organized at TADP

Meanwhile, only blocks away, the Toronto Anti-Draft Program (TADP) and Amex were frequently allied in the work of getting the new American arrivals settled and providing a forum for their evolving thoughts and interests. Prominent figures in this group were Mark Satin and Bill Spira, who helped many draft and military resisters come to Canada through TADP; and Stan Pietlock, Dee Knight, and Jack Colhoun, who started and then guided Amex as it became more actively politicized over the nearly ten years of its existence.

Oliver Clausen, a *New York Times Magazine* reporter, encountered Mark Satin just a month after he had arrived in Toronto and had taken a $25-a-week job from the Student Union for Peace Action as a counselor for American war resisters. Clausen adopted a patronizing attitude toward Satin that was common at the beginning of the resistance movement, concluding that "Satin . . . is, in his way, a very good American. His trouble may be in a sophomoric Muirhead kind of way, he is too good."[24] The facts suggest that Satin was probably more savvy than sophomoric.

Mark Satin was the son of a Texas university professor and had developed an interest in urban planning at the University of Illinois. Later he joined SDS at the State University of New York in Binghampton. After he left school and lost his deferment, he encountered a SUPA pamphlet entitled "Escape from Freedom," which was circulating in the United States. The publication explained how to become a landed immigrant in Canada. Satin was so affected by his experience of reading this pamphlet that after arriving in Canada he helped create the first edition of the *Manual for Draft-Age Immigrants,* which was published under his name by Anansi Press in conjunction with SUPA and later by TADP. Fetherling observed that Satin was highly publicity conscious and reports once having heard him say, "Anonymity would kill me."[25] Perhaps Satin's interests ran in the family, for his mother was interviewed about her son in the *Ladies' Home Journal* and his father started a publishing house.[26]

Satin became a key figure in the transition of the draft counseling program from SUPA to TADP. A reporter who interviewed Satin in the fall of 1967 described him as "unremarkable looking. Not tall, not terribly tidy, with brown hair and eyes and a bit of length to his nose. A bit of length to his hair, too, though not enough to startle."[27] SUPA helped Satin open an Anti-Draft Program on Spadina Avenue.

Since SUPA was at this stage heavily influenced by the United States' SDS, it could be thought the Canadian draft and military resistance effort was just a spin-off of the American movement. Actually, the connection between SUPA and TADP became a source of conflict with SDS. According to Renée Kasinsky,

> In the United States, the Students for a Democratic Society were not happy that SUPA was involved in counseling and creating propaganda designed to encourage more men to come to Canada. The leaders of SDS, like Tom Hayden and Rennie Davis, expressed the fear that their revolutionary forces in America might "split" to Canada instead of working for the "Revolution" at home. They put enormous pressure on SUPA to disassociate itself from the counseling of draft dodgers.[28]

SUPA soon did disassociate from TADP, and the latter became a self-sustaining organization. Although there was a connection between TADP and the American war resistance movement, there also was conflict, and the connection remained strained until the later stages of the Canadian resistance movement, when attention shifted to the issue of amnesty (described in detail in Chapter 5).

The Spadina Avenue office of TADP looked like a cross between a social club and a committee room, or a small insurance or real estate office, except for its sunny yellow door with a peace dove in the center. Satin was a well-known and popular figure in this area of the city, where draft dodgers often spent their first days or months. A reporter joined Satin for a walk up the street to the Company of Young Canadians' office and noted, "We kept passing studious-looking young men . . . Satin knows over a hundred by their first names—probably a hundred more by sight. It really excites him to think there are so many people from America that close together."[29]

TADP soon moved on to an office in a once-grand but by then somewhat decrepit Victorian home on Spadina Road adjoining the Annex.[30] This run-down gingerbread house, a stone's throw from the more solid, stately, and faintly forbidding brick and stone mansions of the Annex, became an essential institution for resisters who were seeking initial lodging or assistance with draft-related problems. Satin himself eventually returned to Texas and published an autobiographical novel as well as a highly successful pamphlet that at least popularized, if it did not originate, the briefly ubiquitous neologism "new age."[31] Before he moved on, however, Satin was a colorful and innovative force in the emergence of the American ghetto in Toronto.

TADP's main activities were getting its clients situated, finding them shelter and sustenance, and addressing their draft and immigration-related problems by offering legal advice, lending money, providing room and board, and assisting in finding work. Staffed mainly by resisters who received meager compensation from local peace and religious groups, the Program routinely lent hundreds of dollars and found jobs for resisters who had been admitted to the country as visitors and who needed to return to the border with proof of employment and financial resources to reapply for landed immigrant status. While these matters were being arranged, TADP provided lodging in the homes of participating families and settled resisters and in hostels run by the organization. TADP's contact with resisters ranged from brief to long lasting; a high proportion of the resisters offered return involvement and support. The unconditional attention of TADP to the most basic subsistence and settlement needs of the resisters helped form strong ties of mutual support and solidarity among the new arrivals.

By 1968 young American draft and military resisters were arriving in Toronto in significant numbers. The resisters were coming sooner and faster to Toronto than elsewhere, but the numbers were increasing throughout Canada. The summer of 1969 was especially important for the increasing numbers of military resisters who were now being allowed into the country. At one point the numbers became so large that TADP began to feel a need to deal more with the specific problems of the military resisters, whose difficulties with immigration and personal adjustment were often more severe. Still, both kinds of resisters continued to arrive, and TADP remained the major point of entry and settlement into the city.

By 1969 a loose network, which some called an underground railroad, began helping resisters come to Canada. For example, Kevin Vrieze, who later with his wife made great contributions to the development of education for deaf children in Toronto, began his journey from Texas.

> I knew of the existence of the Toronto Anti-Draft Program . . . I had written to the Anti-Draft Program and they'd basically said, "Let us know when you get here." That's it. The people in Houston were supportive, but they didn't have a whole lot to offer, except that Canada was a possibility. However, they knew some people and they basically got the underground railroad thing working for me . . . They made a phone call. I knew this former English teacher who was living in St. Louis. And so they got me to St. Louis. They said, "Let's get you some connections in Indiana too." This guy they knew in Indiana, they got me to his town where this next connection was. He met me at this corner. My bags were out, he met me with a car and took me to Ann Arbor . . . Then someone got me across through Windsor as a visitor, and at that point I was hitchhiking the rest of the way to Toronto. I got a ride right to Yonge and Eglinton, where TADP was. They said, "Get yourself settled and come back." I had a friend at Rochdale College on Bloor Street. So I took the subway to Yonge/Bloor . . . walked from there to Rochdale. I stayed there until the middle 1970s, but at that point it got too crazy even for me. Anyway, they [TADP] had it all down. I was quite surprised how organized it was.

The interviewees introduced in Chapter 1 further suggest how large a part the Toronto Anti-Draft Program played in bringing and settling resisters into Toronto. Like Kevin Vrieze, about a third of the sample corresponded with TADP before they came to Canada. More than a third of the sample had read the Program's *Manual for Draft-Age Immigrants* while still in the United States. This small book played an enormous role in shaping resisters' early thoughts about Canada and in helping them find their way to Toronto and other major cities. Nearly another quarter of the sample acquired the *Manual* once they arrived. Many still have battered copies of the book in their homes. Some have joked that this must be one of the all-time best-selling books in Canadian publishing history, with over 65,000 copies printed. This compact manual was a manifesto for the mobilization of the resistance movement.[32]

Many resisters needed the support of the *Manual* and TADP to counterbalance the lack of support they received from parents and family. About half of the sample found the decision to come to Canada either difficult or extremely difficult, with deserters finding the decision most difficult. Only about one-third of the sampled resisters' parents approved of them coming to Canada. Another one-third neither approved nor disapproved, while fully one-third of the sample members' parents clearly disapproved. However, once the resisters were in Canada, more than two-thirds of the parents of sampled resisters became supportive. For others, the reconciliation took many years. During the early part of this period, TADP played an essential role. About half of the sample received help from TADP after they arrived in Toronto. Recognizing the extent of TADP's role, the National Council of Churches in the United States and the Canadian Council of Churches both eventually provided the Program with financial assistance.

Although Mark Satin played the leading role in getting the Toronto Anti-Draft Program up and operating, and men such as Richard Brown, Danny Zimmerman, Bernie Jaffee, and Richard Burroughs played major roles in keeping it operating, women such as Naomi Wall, Mona Stevens, and Katie McGovern also played important roles. Naomi Wall took over from Mark Satin in leading the TADP through its early and middle years, with major support from Mona Stevens. Katie McGovern sustained the Program through its last years, ultimately winding it down from her own home when financial support finally gave out.

Phil Mullins arrived in Toronto in March 1968 and stayed at a hostel operated by TADP at 27 John Street.[33] Ten years later, he still vividly remembered the John Street hostel.

There were four guys in the front room. There were a couple of bunks in the second room, there must have been four or five guys there. Upstairs there were three bedrooms, they were smaller. The younger single guys stayed downstairs and the married couples stayed upstairs. I think there was another room way up in the attic. So that would be four couples and maybe eight or ten single guys. Then we cleaned out the basement and there were another three or four single guys there. There was always a good quantity of people and it changed all the time.

Mullins described a sequence of entry and "landing" that TADP often helped to orchestrate for the new American arrivals: "The TADP had this whole system worked out where you would go to their office . . . They would basically set you up and find what kind of documents you had, . . . what kind of documents you ought to get, and if you didn't have a place to live, they would tell you where to live . . . And then you went back later when you had all your documents."

This assistance extended to planning and initiating a recrossing of the border to obtain "landed immigrant" status.

> So you would go back to TADP on your second or third visit and they would tell you where to go to get immigrated, like they had all the up-to-date data. You were supposed to report to them what happened when you immigrated and they would remember it, and they would say OK, this is a good place to go to, or this is bad place to go to. And they knew what time of the day and they would arrange it so that not a whole bunch of people would go there at once. They would have a guy go on the morning shift and a guy go on the afternoon shift . . . They knew who was there and they knew who was sympathetic and who wasn't. They had it down, that was their main job, to get people immigrated. And it was all based on feedback from people who had gone there and talked to these guys. They had maps with all the places on it and information about each guy that worked there.

TADP even staged encounters with the immigration officers. They would match up better- and worse-looking prospects to be driven down and to cross the border and re-enter Canada together. For example, a well-dressed, well-spoken resister would be paired with another whose accent and appearance might be more likely to cause problems. Usually, both would cross successfully—for example, with the better-spoken of a pair helping to make a successful case for both. The counselors at TADP were often self-educated experts on draft, military, and immigration law, and they had help from some of the best young legal minds in the city, including Clay Ruby, John Liss, and Paul Copeland.

Bill Spira was also a major figure in this early period. His work began in late 1966 when SUPA asked him to assist in housing and often hiding the then occasional military resisters who were contacting their Anti-Draft Program. Spira was a successful middle-aged businessman, but with an unusual background. More than a decade earlier, during the McCarthy-era witch-hunts, he had migrated to Canada from the United States after losing his job as a draftsman in an aircraft plant when he refused to identify radical friends. By the mid-1960s he was a stocky, well-jowled partner in a structural steel business with twenty employees, a million dollars a year in sales, and his company's name on prominent signs at school and post office construction sites across the city.

In the beginning only a few deserters needed Spira's help, and he often provided them food and housing in his own home. By the fall of 1967, Spira was relying increasingly on friends and neighbors and eventually found himself with seventeen deserters staying in his own basement and in nearby homes. At that point he knew he had to expand his organization. By January 1969, Spira reported that he personally had helped more than 600 of the more than 2,000 deserters who had come to Canada.[34]

The Politics of Amex

The more ideologically and politically engaged counterpart to TADP was the organization and news magazine for resisters, *Amex.* Started by Stan Pietlock, who would later become a Catholic priest assigned to a southern Ontario parish, Amex was an outgrowth of the Union of New Canadians. The Union's name suggested that its main concern would be helping new arrivals settle in Canada. But for many resisters, this concern was soon superseded by an abiding desire to persist in opposing the war in Vietnam, which involved focusing on the political scene in the United States.

The interest in American Vietnam war politics foreshadowed a growing split in the leadership of Amex. An early reflection of the division and direction of a coming shift in priorities was the renaming of the Union of New Canadians as the Union of American Exiles (UAE). Another indication that the organization was changing was that it began to become less a place to discuss individuals' adjustment problems and more an organization oriented toward political action. This change resulted in the UAE's sponsoring protests at the American Consulate on University Avenue, located just blocks away from Baldwin Street and the American ghetto. The renaming of UAE and its targeting of the U.S. Consulate symbolized the Union's new focus on American and international issues. This shift became more pronounced later, when serious discussions of amnesty began in the United States; but by the end of the 1960s the control of Amex was becoming contentious; and by the early 1970s Jack Colhoun and then Dee Knight became much more interested than Pietlock in focusing Amex on the amnesty issue.

For most of its history, Amex was housed in a donated room in a building shared with the student newspaper of the University of Toronto in the middle of the campus on St. George Street. Jack Colhoun, who was to give Amex its most determined and strident direction traced his American routes to the *Mayflower* and to his namesake, John C. Colhoun, who was an early colonial governor of Rhode Island. The twentieth-century Colhoun left the University of Wisconsin at Madison after declining a post-ROTC commission as a second lieutenant in the military police and came to Toronto in 1970, where he earned a doctoral degree in history from York University while working at Amex. Strains of indignant patriotism regularly spilled out in Colhoun's conversations. "If I didn't feel so strongly about America," he commented in the early 1970s, "I wouldn't be here in Toronto. I would have sold out like everyone else."[35]

Dee Knight, who shared editorial duties with Colhoun, was a campaign worker for Senator Eugene McCarthy and, as noted in Chapter 1, came to Toronto directly from the 1968 Chicago Convention. Knight, with his conventionally cropped hair and carefully framed opinions, seemed cautious and considered in comparison with Colhoun, who with his shoulder-length locks and colorful headbands was the more provocative and incendiary of the two. They joked that this was why Knight was always chosen to appear on television, McLuhan's "cool" medium, while Colhoun did the "hotter" radio talk shows. They made a good team.

Together, Colhoun and Knight expanded *Amex*'s role, transforming it from news magazine to lobbying group and eventually joining with the National Coalition for Universal and Unconditional Amnesty to campaign for a Vietnam war amnesty in the United States (as recounted in Chapter 5). For more than half a decade, they were recognized fixtures of the American ghetto scene in Toronto, giving expression to a wide range of resister concerns.[36] TADP often worried that Amex's more political positions would arouse public suspicions about American war resisters and in this way interfere with the Canadian government's typically benign attitudes toward the immigration and settlement of this group. Nonetheless, the two organizations were generally supportive of each other and more often than not joined together in working on behalf of the interests of the resister community. The overlapping interests of these two groups reflected their roles as mobilizing structures of the Canadian resistance movement. Meanwhile, the symbolic heart of the day-to-day life of this growing political movement was found in the residential and commercial redevelopment of the neighborhood to the south of the University of Toronto campus.

Baldwin Street and Beyond

The area around Baldwin Street was the most conspicuous everyday embodiment of the American ghetto. The people, collectives, apartments and houses, stores, and street life along Baldwin and neighboring McCaul and Dundas Streets provided a focal point for the relationships, politics, and daily life of the growing exile community and its organized resistance activities, including fund-raising rock concerts, street demonstrations, festivals, and celebrations. Phil Mullins, Dave Woodward, Mary Rauton, Jim and Pat Wilson, Kent and Karen Lawrence, John Phillips, Laura Jones, Janice Spellerberg, Steven Burdick and Lisa Steele formed a core set of actors around whom a much larger, looser social network formed. Again, while most American war resisters did not live or spend extended periods of time in this community, the simple presence of this neighborhood attracted young Americans to the city and helped to draw them into war resistance efforts. The fact that the Baldwin Street scene was exciting and entertaining did not detract from the war resistance efforts that developed there. To the contrary, Baldwin Street and its countercultural entrepreneurs provided an energetic seedbed in which the resistance efforts grew in purpose and intensity.

The Americanness of the Baldwin countercultural experience was in some ways best reflected by the contrast it presented to the Yorkville area north of Bloor and west of Yonge Streets. Yorkville was already well known by the late 1960s for its clubs where rock and folk musicians played. Many of Canada's best new musicians regularly appeared there, including Bruce Coburn, Gordon Lightfoot, Joni Mitchell, Neil Young, and Ian and Sylvia. Tom Kane remembered that "it was pricier. The club, the Riverboat, was there. So were the suburban hippies who came on Saturdays. Lots of people on the street, sitting on the street. A trailer served coffee and offered counseling to the kids." Most remember Yorkville as a much more Toronto-based, Canadian scene than Baldwin Street, with its older, more politicized, and American residents.

The summer and fall of 1968 were identifiable starting points of American ghetto community life. By then enough Americans were in the city that their gatherings were becoming regular events. In August, the Union of American Exiles held a demonstration at the American Consulate on University Avenue. By September, the UAE was holding meetings every other Sunday at 89 St. George Street, and in October the UAE sponsored another demonstration, the International Days of Protest, at the Consulate. Baldwin Street became a kind of staging area for such efforts, with flyers and posters blanketing the neighborhood in the days leading up to sponsored events and demonstrations. An annual Baldwin Street Festival began in June 1969; an alternative newspaper, *Harbinger,* became a symbol of the collective identity of the Baldwin Street scene.

The new arrivals to Baldwin Street saw irony in the fact that the area had been largely a Jewish business community made up of many first-generation immigrants from Europe who had begun their life in the New World as rag and scrap merchants. Several of the earlier residents were now in their later years and contemplating closing their small surplus and wholesale clothing businesses. Cross-generational friendships developed between some of the older merchants and shopkeepers of the area and the new American arrivals. The newcomers were respectful, but also obviously much different in their behavior and attitudes. For their part, the older merchants were relatively tolerant of the drugs and the general sense of freeness and experimentation with regard to sexuality and lifestyles that began to permeate the area.

The daily life of this community was organized around fledgling efforts at collectivized commerce. By the late 1970s most of these experiments in alternative entrepreneurship had ended. Nonetheless, many of the members of the Baldwin Street scene, now spread more broadly across the city and in some cases beyond, still maintained contact with one another. As one means of marking the significance of the neighborhood, in the late 1970s several original community members joined a citywide effort to record oral histories of ethnic, religious, and national communities for preservation in the Ontario Archives and at the Multicultural History Society of Ontario.[37] These tapes provide a sense of the individuals and the setting that formed the symbolic core of the Baldwin Street experience during the Vietnam war resistance period in Toronto.

I have supplemented these oral histories with excerpts from my own recent interviews. The accounts that follow concentrate on the men who started the Baldwin Street businesses. In most cases, the women's contributions were as great or greater than the men's, particularly when measured by the length of time they were involved. The stories of these women are told in Chapter 4. The following accounts are not intended to be representative of American war resisters in Toronto generally during this period. Rather, they represent what was happening on Baldwin Street as a focal point of the American migration to Toronto.

Baldwin Street was the first Toronto setting in which many American immigrants recognized that they could be a collective force for continued war resistance and social activism in Canada. This neighborhood was one of the first places where the mobilization of the Canadian resistance took hold, and it became the most concentrated expression of this movement. The Baldwin Street experience was also symbolic: through the media and the cultural underground the image of the community drew thousands of American war resisters to Toronto. The organized war resistance efforts of TADP and Amex interacted with the counterculturalism of Baldwin Street to create a transformative context for social-movement activism. Some descriptions of the focal institutions of Baldwin Street convey a sense of some of the interconnections between the countercultural commerce and politics of the American ghetto.

The Yellow Ford Truck

The first collective effort that most remember as the beginning of the American ghetto was a store established by Jim and Pat Wilson, Phil Mullins, and Dave Woodward.[38] The store initially was more grandly to be called "The Yellow Ford Truck, a Liberation Tribal Store, Another Socioeconomic Alternative." The Wilsons, Mullins, and Woodward each took credit for a part of the name. It was an ambitious title for what began as an abandoned storefront with boarded-up windows. The group tracked down the owner through a records search at city hall. Jim Wilson and his colleagues were convinced that they should shorten the name when they signed the lease for the store and contemplated the task of painting the sign to hang out front.

Jim Wilson came from a large midwestern family with Republican, Roman Catholic, and military roots. He could recall reading about Canada from the age of ten, including adventure stories by Jack London and Robert Service that depicted early contacts of northern native groups with the Hudson's Bay Company. Wilson's lifelong interest in aboriginal society would later be reflected in products sold at the store.

From 1962 to 1968 Wilson was an undergraduate sociology and anthropology major at the University of North Carolina at Chapel Hill, where he first became involved in civil rights activities through the Congress of Racial Equality, the Student Nonviolent Coordinating Committee, and later as a Volunteer in Service to America (VISTA). He was exposed through this work to civil rights leaders such as James Farmer, Stokley Carmichael, and Floyd McKissic. Later he joined the Student Peace Union and SDS, where he became involved in antiwar efforts. He met his wife, Pat, at the University of North Carolina. They lived in communes in the Chapel Hill area and were both involved in sit-ins and other forms of civil disobedience that led to extended court cases.

Jim and Pat Wilson spent their first nights in Toronto in August 1968 at the hostel on John Street run by the Toronto Anti-Draft Program. There they met Phil Mullins; Dave Woodward, who went on to form the Downchild Blues Band; soon after, a group of resisters from Kansas City; and later, several individuals who were involved in acting and the theater. This evolving collective soon began to discuss opening a communal craft shop. They lived in a communal flat and then a house before renting 11 Baldwin Street for the craft store in September of 1968.

When they first came to Baldwin Street, Wilson described it as a "backstreet, rag trade, secondhand, run-down set of stores that seemed either to be never open or open just to wholesale business." His reaction to the area was "to what it *wasn't* rather than to what it was." He recalled that the group was "really not interested in a completed image, we were more interested in developing an image on a blank sheet." The boarded storefront that became the The Yellow Ford Truck "sure left a lot of room for that." Wilson traced his image for the store to his desire to create an alternative kind of business that could support people who for political and other reasons would otherwise have trouble finding employment.

The plan for the store involved the group's living at a basic subsistence level and reinvesting their profits in supporting the stock and the other people involved, which quickly grew to ten. The Wilsons' politics also were reflected in the merchandise sold in their store, which included not only the usual countercultural paraphernalia of the day, such as hash pipes and smoking accessories, but also First Nation's arts and handicraft work, including clothing with beadwork done by First Nations Canadians.

The shop also served as a meeting place for the First Nation's Society and as a location where aboriginal people from Ontario reserves could come to create and sell their craftwork. A unique feature of The Yellow Ford Truck was that it offered an opportunity for native peoples to be more directly involved in retailing their crafts instead of relying on wholesaling to less scrupulous retailers or bartering or selling their wares on the street. The life of The Yellow Ford Truck followed the Wilsons' marriage, which came apart in the late 1970s when Jim Wilson moved to rural Ontario to pursue his interests in aboriginal peoples. Pat Wilson continued to live for some time in Toronto, but eventually returned to North Carolina.

Ragnarokr

A shop called Ragnarokr evolved out of the leather work done at The Yellow Ford Truck, taking over the 11 Baldwin Street location when the The Yellow Ford Truck moved on to 25 Baldwin in April 1969. Jim Wilson noted that during this period he and others were much impressed with the idea of expanding the Baldwin Street commercial scene so that it could support increasing numbers of members of the evolving American ghetto community. However, he also observed that while "we saw this as an expansion of the commune, in reality it was just the growth of the community."

Wilson began to realize that at this point the movement they were involved in was much bigger than he had anticipated and was growing in new and unexpected directions. Dave Woodward was becoming much more involved with the Downchild Blues Band, which was gaining a following. This added to the variety and reputation of the Baldwin Street scene and the larger American ghetto. Wilson likened the commune at this stage to a cell that was not only growing but also beginning to separate.

So it seemed natural that a second business venture would soon emerge out of The Yellow Ford Truck, and that initiative was the leather shop. The name of the new shop, Ragnarokr, had its origin in The Fantastic Four, an alternative comic book series of the day; the name originally involved a reference to the end of the world in Germanic mythology, out of which "things began anew," an idea later popularized in Wagner's Ring cycle. Phil Mullins was central to the development of the new store.[39]

Mullins was an "army brat" whose father's military career took his family to a number of towns in the south and overseas before settling in northern Florida during Phil's high school years. During a summer break from college in 1966 Mullins worked in New York City and became involved in the War Resisters League and the Lower East Side Mobilization for Peace Action. He took what he learned in New York back to Florida State University, where he increased his involvement in antiwar organizational efforts. In October of the following fall Mullins participated in a national antiwar demonstration that involved sending his draft card back to his draft board. This resulted in his being declared delinquent; and by the middle of the year, when the university hastened his graduation, Mullins was classified lA delinquent; this made it impossible for him to find employment.

About this time Mullins became involved in disrupting a Dow recruiting program at the University at Florida and wound up serving a brief jail sentence. During the court case leading up to the time in jail Phil accumulated reading material that included an early version of Mark Satin's *Manual for Draft-Age Immigrants*. It was while reading this document in jail that Mullins made the decision to come to Canada. The options, once he was released from jail, seemed clear: go to war, go back to jail, or go to Canada. Not wanting to go to war, having already gone to jail, and feeling the futility of returning, probably for a long term given judicial attitudes in Florida, he decided that "Canada looked like a reasonable place to live."

Mullins arrived in a snowstorm in the middle of March 1968 and went directly to the TADP hostel on John Street. He lived at the John Street hostel for several months and then moved into an apartment with another resister. He continued to be involved with TADP through his work on an employment program, and he helped form the Union of American Exiles. In August 1968 he met Jim and Pat Wilson, Dave Woodward, and others who were renting a co-op house on McCaul Street; together they opened The Yellow Ford Truck at 11 Baldwin Street. Mullins was involved in The Yellow Ford Truck and later spent a considerable amount of time out of the city in a rural "back to the land" setting in northern Ontario. Gradually he helped form a group that moved back and forth from the country to the city and operated the leather shop that became Ragnarokr.

Jim Wilson paid the first month's rent for Ragnarokr, in April 1969, when The Yellow Ford Truck moved to 25 Baldwin Street and Ragnarokr opened at 11 Baldwin. Around that time Mullins met Mary Rauton, who had left an abusive marriage in Georgia. She brought her draft-age son with her to Toronto. Rauton worked with Mullins and several others in developing Ragnarokr as a craft shop specializing in leather goods. Mary and many others put their own leather work on sale in the store. From about 1972 to 1978 the cooperative moved members back and forth in three-month spells from the settlement in northern Ontario to their work in the store. This arrangement combined a modest income stream from the store with the group's desire to have a "back to the land" kind of lifestyle, at least until the group began to have children who needed to attend school.

Rauton, who had a business degree, ultimately wound up being a partner in Ragnarokr, working in a cooperative arrangement with Mullins. However, the store was always as much or more a social and political force as a place to work. Each year the store would sponsor a street festival on Baldwin Street; it also offered prospective jobs to help resisters satisfy immigration requirements to get into the country. Mullins and Rauton also helped bail out members of the community who were arrested in demonstrations at the U.S. Consulate.

Steve Spring became a partner, bringing an element of Buddhist spirituality into the co-op. In the early 1970s, members of the collective organized by Wilson and others eventually also bought land and lived in a ninety-seven-acre location called Frost Pocket in northern Ontario. Mary Rauton and Steve Spring continued operating Ragnarokr into the late 1990s, relocating the store in the growing alternative commercial area of Queen Street West before finally closing.

The Cosmic Egg

Kent and Karen Lawrence began a surplus and wholesale clothing store called the Cosmic Egg on Baldwin Street.[40] An only child, Kent was brought up in a bucolic valley nestled in the mountains of Vermont. There were several family break-ups and changes of households, including a move to Connecticut. Although he had always been considered college material and went to university with high expectations, he flunked out after his first year and got a job in a record shop. Things were going reasonably well until Kent received his induction notice in the mail.

Kent got in touch with an antidraft group and received counseling, but under the influence of his family made a fateful decision to enlist in the army. Within three days he walked away from a New Jersey pre-induction center and began a battle with the U.S. army that included alternate periods in the stockade and living underground in New York City. He eventually escaped to Canada with his partner, Karen.

They arrived at Toronto's International Airport at ten o'clock at night, and after being given visitor status by immigration were housed for several days by a friendly family arranged by TADP. The Program also helped Kent get a job at a food store and work out the details of his exit and reentry into the country with a job offer, which was required for his obtaining official landed immigrant status. At first Kent and Karen felt isolated and lonely in Toronto, even though they loved the city from the outset. Gradually their sense of foreignness began to lessen, and Kent especially appreciated his declining sense of paranoia about the police and military issues. He felt that "Toronto was a blessing, it was a real blessing."

Kent had a distinct sense of wanting "to set up shop and start fresh," and Toronto would soon allow him to do this. He had a job driving a delivery truck for a surplus dealer on Spadina Avenue. He liked the idea of recycling surplus goods, and the job also enabled him to learn about the surplus-goods business and about his new city and province, across which he was making deliveries. In time he learned how one bought surplus goods and materials from the government and eventually put in a bid for a batch of clothing himself.

Kent's first purchase involved his picking up a ton of clothing—jackets, pants, shirts—in London, Ontario. It was in boxes and he hadn't seen it. He paid for the shipment and took it back to Toronto. He told his employer he had done this by mistake and asked if the employer would want to purchase the goods at a lower price. Instead, he was fired for poking his nose into the business. At that point, Kent realized he would have to find and open his own store.

He began combing the city for possibilities and was drawn to Baldwin Street: "Especially in those days, Baldwin Street had a very strong feeling to it, very magnetic." There were only about eight storefronts and none was for rent. Instead he had to rent a store on Avenue Road. Later he received a phone call from Pat Wilson, who offered Kent a store to rent. He rented the location, named his store the Cosmic Egg, and began selling secondhand clothing; the store later came to specialize in antique clothing. He recalls that the first couple of years were tough; he didn't begin to draw a wage out of the business until the third year. But Kent enjoyed being self-employed and especially grew to love the neighborhood, where he and Karen also lived during this period.

Kent described the new American ghetto on Baldwin Street in idealistic terms, as a beautiful, attractive community with a meaningful economic base, where people were self-sufficient, supporting themselves in an alternative kind of way, outside "the bread and butter, nine to five" kind of system. His description of Baldwin Street comes about as close as one could imagine in downtown Toronto to the "Beloved Community" of Freedom

Summer in Mississippi studied by Doug McAdam. Kent recalled that Baldwin Street had

> a kind of small town feeling to it, almost a sense of isolation, whereby after you had been there for a while and you know your neighbors . . . it's like being in a small town anywhere. A feeling of acceptance, a feeling of relaxation, a feeling of familiarity to everything around you. But with it also comes the tremendous blessing of being in the middle of a huge city, whereby you could walk literally to any store downtown in about five or ten minutes, and you can choose to have access to any of the facilities that a big city offers you. But you can also choose to be in a very isolated position away from it, and that is one of the unique things about Baldwin Street, among many others. My coming to Baldwin was like a grand fulfillment, as I really liked the place a lot, and I dreamed about being here. Coming here was quite an amazing experience for me.

Kent felt that life on Baldwin Street helped him grow stronger as a person and, in the words of the day, "get in touch with his own thoughts and feelings."

The business ultimately lasted as long for Kent as his marriage to Karen, which came apart in the middle 1970s. Kent went on to take part in an amnesty program and returned to the United States. Helen and Dave Zimmerman became involved in the store after Kent and Karen split up, and in this form the Cosmic Egg lasted into the late 1970s.

The Whole Earth Natural Foods Store

Karen and Kent Lawrence also lived for a period in a communal arrangement in a house at Kennedy and Steeles Avenues in the northern part of the city. The big, old mansion had once belonged to a wealthy Toronto business family. Kent and Karen lived in this house with a group of Americans and Canadians who ran the Whole Earth Natural Foods Store on McCaul Street.

The Whole Earth Store was developed by Michael Ormsby, who had come to Toronto from Berkeley, California, where he had been involved in the attempt to create People's Park. He recalled, "The university owned this piece of property and wasn't doing much with it. We took it over and made it into a park. The university or police then fenced the area off. We demonstrated and got into several battles with the police." Ormsby's problem was that he believed there was a warrant out for his arrest because he had not shown up for his pre-induction physical. There was a warrant out for his brother, who had already moved to Canada; Michael assumed there was a warrant out for him as well. "I began to get very paranoid. I was thinking that this warrant was out for me, and if the police arrested me I figured I was in deep trouble." Michael talked to his brother in Toronto, who said things were good and to come up; but Michael found it difficult to leave California. His wife's family was there, and they had many close friends. "But," he recalls, "we got our stuff together, said our goodbyes, and headed off in our van."[41]

Ormsby worked with his brother and others in developing the food store. The Whole Earth concept was a novelty for Toronto. At this time health food stores in the city were still selling packaged foods in an antiseptic, sterile way following a European tradition, with Swiss herbal remedies, lots of vitamins, and powders for muscle building. Ormsby's commune had something more Californian in mind. The members of the commune would package the food in their house, then take turns bringing the food they would sell into the city. The food was sold in bulk, with customers serving themselves from bins. Many of the members of this group later became interested in carpentry and cabinetmaking and moved on to this type of work, although the Whole Earth Store continued for many years in various incarnations and locations.

The Baldwin Street Gallery

John Phillips founded the Baldwin Street Gallery with Laura Jones in June 1969.[42] Phillips was born in the small town of Cherokee, Iowa, in 1945 and grew up in Algona, a wealthy farming community of about five thousand people in northern Iowa. He attended Grinnell College, which he remembers as being very liberal and quite expensive for its time and place in Iowa. Phillips helped edit the college newspaper and yearbook. The latter became so controversial for its provocative and explicit content that the school decided to ban its publication. The episode got extensive national press coverage as "the college yearbook that was censored."[43]

As a member of the newspaper staff, Phillips decided to cover the civil rights struggle that was then focused on voter registration in Selma, Alabama. He spent ten days there photographing the events, hearing Martin Luther King, Jr., give speeches in small churches, being chased by the state troopers, seeing people get beat up: "It changed my life, it was so powerful, words can't describe it." He came back to Grinnell a different person. He felt that his social conscience had gained a focus.

Phillips left Grinnell before graduating and returned to Selma with a summer job as a photographer for an African-American newspaper. At this time he also became involved with a radical Quaker international education program called Friends World Institute. He traveled with this institute to Harlem, Mexico City, and elsewhere, and in the process met his wife-to-be, Laura Jones. When he finished the Friends program the following year, he received his induction notice.

Phillips returned to Iowa and applied for conscientious objector status on the basis of his Quaker beliefs. The bewildered farmers on his rural draft board responded that they had never given C.O. status to anybody and that he wasn't going to be the first. He was dismayed, feeling that his Quaker training made his case clear and certain. "I felt like I had a right to it because at that point my philosophical and religious beliefs were pretty clear on the subject of the war, and there was no way I was going to be involved in that, or in killing anybody in any situation, or in being part of killing anybody. My feelings were very sincere . . . , but there was no way they were going to give it to me."

Phillips found this experience traumatic because he believed that he would ultimately be able to find a way through the system to get his beliefs recognized. Instead, members of his draft board wound up calling him "a coward, a hippie, a nigger-loving radical." Emotionally devastated, he recalls having to drive home from the draft board office but stopping along the way, broken down and in tears. He realized that he was either going to have to go to jail or leave the country. He resigned himself to going to jail but decided first to go with Laura to Expo 67 in Montreal. Canada was a revelation: "I had no knowledge of it whatsoever, Canada was a meaningless word to me, I knew nothing about it. So once I was in Canada and traveled around in it for a few weeks, I decided that going to jail for a few years was not the right thing to do."

John and Laura went back to the States for a final visit. Laura was only eighteen at the time; her parents, especially her father, objected to the move. Nonetheless, they married and took off for Canada. Immigration proved to be no problem. John's friend Henry Wilhelm photographed the departure and the crossing at the border to encourage others to follow; the picture appeared as part of a January 1968 story in the *Saturday Evening Post*.[44] Once in Toronto the couple quickly connected with Rochdale College, which at that point reminded John of his experience with the Quakers. They felt at home, with more draft dodgers joining them by the day. Phillips describes the day he drove away from Canadian Immigration and into Canada as being ecstatic, among the happiest of his life.

John and Laura got jobs almost immediately with the Company of Young Canadians (CYC), a Canadian government organization that in their still-American minds seemed to mix elements of the Peace Corps and SDS. They stayed with CYC for more than two years, working in the Baldwin Street area, where they operated a drop-in center for young people that among other things taught photography to children. They began to live in what Phillips fondly remembers as "a very beautiful old Victorian house" at 23 Baldwin Street. When they left CYC in April 1969 they turned the house into the Baldwin Street Gallery of Photography.

John and Laura proudly promoted the Baldwin Gallery as the first privately operated gallery in Canada devoted entirely to the pursuit of photography as a documentary and fine art. The gallery presented monthly exhibitions of original photographic prints and served as an informal meeting place and clearing house for information about the art of photography in Toronto and in Canada generally. The gallery also stocked over 15,000 different book titles for sale and maintained a reference library of illustrated twentieth-century photography books.

Phillips and Jones had a clear sense of what their gallery was about, and correspondingly about what it did and did not do:

> There is *no* admission charge to visit the Baldwin Street Gallery of Photography. The Baldwin Gallery is *not* a commercial photography studio. It is *not* a school for photography nor is it affiliated with any school. It functions independently. It *is* a place where, without charge, anyone can see original prints of some of the most important documentary and fine art photographers working today. It *is* a place that allows free access for unlimited browsing (sorry, no loaning) through one of North America's largest collections of photography books. It *is* a place where you may purchase if you wish, an untouched copy of most of the books in the open shelf collection. It *is* a place to meet other people who take photography seriously. There *is* no membership. Everyone is welcome.[45]

The gallery was run on a nonprofit basis, with all funds from book sales as well as much of John and Laura's income from other work reinvested in the facilities and services of the gallery. Some grants were received from the Ontario Arts Council and there was much volunteer help, but the overwhelming investment was of the time, talent, and energy of John Phillips and Laura Jones.

Phillips and Jones always had tenants living in the home that housed the gallery; they estimated that over the first five years they had over one hun-

dred different draft and military resisters who lived there at one point or another. The resisters usually would not stay longer than a couple of months,
but the gallery was one of the first places resisters would look to stay, and
there was a constant flow of these new immigrants through the house. John
described the result as an environment that was both chaotic and fulfilling,
and this ultimately burned him out.

By 1974 a sense of fatigue set in, compounded by the arrival of an eviction
notice that resulted from the owner's sale of the house. The new owner
wanted to tear down the existing structure and build something new. Attempts were made to litigate the eviction, but they failed. Meanwhile, a
number of fires occurred on Baldwin Street in a short space of time, which
led to suspicions that an arsonist was at work, and the gallery itself received
threats. The result was that the gallery closed for about a year. John became
a filmmaker, and the gallery reopened later with a focus on photographs by
and about women.

Snowflake

In 1971 and 1972, after a year or two of settling in, many of the resistance
couples began having babies. Members of the community then created a
day-care center called Snowflake, which soon became a central institution
in the Baldwin Street neighborhood. Snowflake began as a Local Initiatives
Project (LIP) funded by the Canadian government. Karen Lawrence, who
still was involved with the Cosmic Egg and later went on to become a
teacher, and Laura Jones, from the Baldwin Gallery, played leading roles in
designing what was explicitly a "parent-child center" in which parents were
expected to contribute their time as well as their money for the care that was
provided. The similar ages of many of the parents and their children, the
ease of movement of children among homes in the neighborhood, and even
the predominance of vegetarianism offered a near-seamless foundation on
which to build a community-based child-care program.

Canadian residents of the community joined with their new American
neighbors to write the LIP grant application. A guiding principle was that
participating parents rather than hired workers should be prominent in the
care the center provided. This attitude reflected the participants' general dis-
trust of bureaucracy. Snowflake remained in operation for about fifteen
years, first on McCaul Street and then on Queen Street, and continued beyond this in various reconfigurations formed to address perennial funding

problems. A whole generation of American children began their lives in Canada in what might be described as the ultimate alternative childhood experience that the parent-workers of Snowflake provided.

Something Happening Here

By 1969 the American resisters' businesses on Baldwin Street were an established presence, and the street itself had undergone a remarkable transformation. Nondescript and previously neglected storefronts were full of new life and color. Beyond this, Baldwin Street was also a "construction site" in the metaphorical sense suggested by Stephen Cornell and Douglas Hartmann:[46] a concentrated social and geographical setting in which a new group of immigrants began to cope with their new national surroundings, make sense of the world around them, identify themselves and others, and pursue social and political objectives, most notably involving Vietnam war resistance. The American immigrants were simultaneously banding together and exploring new and diverse social and political environments that they themselves were helping to create, giving new direction and purpose to their lives in Toronto.

The sidewalks and back lanes of Baldwin Street were alive with a mixture of people, Americans and Canadians, young and old, in all manner of accent and attire. The stores and businesses provided many of the American war resisters who worked in them a needed sense of security and belonging. The residents of this neighborhood developed a new pride of place, a unique identity that was neither fully American nor entirely Canadian. Baldwin Street was both an alternative place and a way to live, a dramatic focal point for the larger migration of young Americans that was capturing widespread attention in Toronto and beyond. Resistance and exile were the unifying themes, binding together the people and purposes of this rapidly evolving community setting.

The life span of the American ghetto was by many measures brief. It probably peaked in the early and middle 1970s, and its Americanness began to fade with the decline and disappearance of most of the resisters by the end of that decade. In some ways the resisters were like many other immigrant groups who, after a period of clustering in residential and commercial enclaves, move up and out into the larger society. In the case of the commercial collectives located on Baldwin Street, however, the process was not so much a matter of moving up socioeconomically as choosing to experiment with other ways of "doing their own thing," including moving on to collectives in rural Ontario and deciding to pursue other kinds of work and new forms of social and political cooperation. In any case, Baldwin Street as an American ghetto seemed at most to have about a ten-year life span. In this short period it captured the attention of not only its American inhabitants, but also the surrounding community and country, with its colorful, flamboyant, and boisterously creative ways of working and living.

And, of course, this new and sometimes strident group wanted to be noticed, especially when it expressed its views about the Vietnam war. Baldwin Street was neither the Paris Commune nor the Beloved Community of Freedom Summer, but it did collectively encourage a growing Vietnam war resistance movement in Toronto. Just blocks from Baldwin Street, resistance organizations came to life by staging demonstrations in front of the U.S. Consulate on University Avenue with increasing frequency. These confrontational events shocked this eminently civilized Canadian boulevard, consisting as it did of statues and monuments flanked by banks, museums, courthouses, insurance companies, and hospitals, all leading solemnly forward to the majestic Provincial Legislature, which headed Queen's Park to the north. Young American resisters, many of whom lived and gathered in the Baldwin Street area, marched up and down University Avenue, carrying signs and symbols of the times and increasingly confronting Toronto's mounted and helmeted riot police, who were charged with protecting the solemnity and propriety of University Avenue, as well as the foreign property of the U.S. Consulate.

Michael Ormsby recalled one of these demonstrations:

Yeah, we went to a major demonstration at the Consulate on University Avenue. It was a major event and I was there with my wife who was pregnant—really quite large, you know, with child. The police were there on horses and there was a lot of pushing and shoving. I remember getting pushed more and more toward the horses, which were huge. At one point I remember getting shoved from behind and really out of fear more than anything else, I remember slamming back with my elbow as hard as I could . . . When I looked back I realized it was a cop. I was arrested and charged and eventually convicted and sentenced to 30 days in the Don Jail. After I got out the Department of Immigration wanted to deport me, but my lawyer was eventually able to help me out.[47]

Predictably, these demonstrations attracted more attention from the local Toronto press than in the United States. From the American perspective, the

Americans in Canada were a marginal, spin-off group whose activities paled in perceived importance to parallel events occurring in the United States. From the Canadian side of the border, things looked much different. This was a sizable, growing group of resisters whose voices were increasingly heard in opposition to the Vietnam war.

One of the popular songs of the late sixties, "For What It's Worth," evoked the ominous urgency of the escalating American demonstrations and riots. Something similar was happening in Toronto, and where it would lead was also unclear. The American war resisters were sometimes unintentionally, but also often willingly, becoming symbols of change and confrontation in Canada, and not all Canadians were comfortable with the challenges these young Americans represented in the midst of their country's perennial uncertainties. It was a situation that only a few years earlier probably few Americans or Canadians would ever have predicted, much less understood. University of Toronto sociologist Lewis Feurer, who recently had moved from Berkeley, offered a classically Freudian-based explanation in his *Conflict of Generations*. Scott Young, a newspaper columnist and father of Neil Young, the rising rock star and member of Buffalo Springfield, which recorded "For What It's Worth," penned a vicious attack that questioned the purposes of the resisters. The title of Young's angry column said it all: "Draft Dodgers: A Passive Breed Doing Nothing and Going Nowhere."[48] It was the familiar and frequently repeated charge of misguided irresponsibility.

Yet it was hardly the new immigrants' passiveness that attracted the attention of the Canadian public and its government. It was more their exuberance and activism that provoked response. A rock concert that got out of hand can serve as an example of what was happening.

On a hot late-summer evening in Toronto in 1969 a group of about twenty students attacked a police cruiser after a Rochdale College student was arrested for causing a disturbance by leaping onto the car while it moved through a crowd of about five hundred young people who were dancing to rock music. The crowd protested by pounding and kicking the police cruiser; dancing on its hood, roof, and trunk; burning an American flag; and forming a barrier across the street.

After the arrest the response of the authorities became more accommodating. Inspector William Bolton arrived on the scene. He told a *Toronto Daily Star* reporter, "These kids haven't really done any harm. Strictly speaking they're breaking the law by blocking the sidewalk and the street, and I suppose they are disturbing some people in the neighborhood." But Inspector Bolton took no action until 5:30 A.M., when he told the organizers that there had been several complaints and that they should stop the music. They did so without argument and set about cleaning up the street. Bolton concluded, "You see, they do cooperate if you approach them the right way. It's all a question of tact."[49]

Of course, not all Canadians thought that acceptance and accommodation were the right responses as the 1960s came to a close. Some felt that the Americans should not be on the Canadian side of the border at all, and that civil disturbances should be strictly controlled and repressed. However, the die had been cast when the Minister of Immigration, Allan MacEachen, opened the border. A period of uncertainty followed, with the resisters cast as lightning rods in a continuing conflict of cultural symbols that struck to the very core of what these Americans represented, to themselves and to Canada. Nineteen sixty-nine was an important year of change—a turning point both for the young Americans entering Canada and for the Canadian government that opened its gates. The opportunity of immigration had been granted and the mobilization of a movement was under way. Something was happening here: battle lines were being drawn.

CHAPTER 4

Activism by Exile

Young Americans who chose to oppose the selective service and military laws of the United States by becoming exiles in Canada exercised a fundamental American freedom. "America," Steven Decatur offered: "love it or leave it." They left. Their decision to leave was a form of activism, an act of resistance that brought them further choices about whether and how to extend active opposition to the war and to become involved in related social and political causes in their new Canadian setting.

This chapter explores whether the new immigrants' involvement in war resistance activity in Toronto was for them a turning point in the development of long-term commitments to social and political activism, with related implications for their vocational and occupational life outcomes. As indicated in earlier chapters, the American migration to Canada became more than the sum of the individual acts of draft and military defiance with which it began. This was so in spite of the marginal status of the Canadian exiles in the minds of many Americans, including members of the American antiwar movement. What began as individual migratory acts of resistance against the requirements of American selective service and military laws became a collectively organized experience with long-lasting political and socioeconomic consequences.

These consequences are explored in several ways in this chapter. Particular attention is given to the resisters' own descriptions of their lives in Canada, and to an analysis of the resisters' involvement in social and political activism in relation to their marital and occupational histories. Comparisons are made between the resisters who came to Canada and their siblings who stayed in the United States, as well as with participants in earlier civil rights efforts in the United States. These comparisons offer benchmarks that can be used in assessing to what degree the decision to leave the United States and come to Canada was a turning point. The lives of both the men and the women are considered, because these experiences in some ways were gender specific and in other ways closely linked. Narrative accounts involving some of the leading figures in this movement are introduced first to develop a further sense of how the early settlement process was structurally intertwined with the mobilization of war resistance efforts in Toronto.

Naomi Wall's Resistance

Naomi Wall was older than most Americans who came to Canada to resist the Vietnam war, and she did not come to Canada for this purpose. She arrived in 1963 with her husband, who had accepted an assistant professorship in the Department of Psychology at the University of Toronto. Yet by 1967 Naomi was heavily involved in the war resistance movement, and nobody should have been surprised. Activism and resistance were a family tradition. Wall remarked that "my mother was from a very young age really critical of the U.S. government. She just thought it was a crock right from the word go; she never bought into that sort of patriotism." Naomi, like her sister, was already strongly committed to social justice by the mid-1950s. She grew up in Washington, D.C., and remarked, "I made political speeches in high school, for example, when the decision was made to desegregate the schools . . . I was politically aware because my mother was politically aware." Wall's sister was also actively involved as a political artist in the 1960s. In the vernacular of movement politics, Naomi and her sister were "red diaper babies," and they were not the only ones in the Toronto resistance movement.

Within six months of Wall's arrival in Toronto she became involved in an ongoing civil rights protest in front of the U.S. Consulate on University Avenue. A Canadian activist had heard about the events unfolding in Selma, Alabama, and decided to make a placard and begin a vigil. Soon the Student Union for Peace Action (SUPA), which also initially supported Mark Satin's counseling of American draft dodgers, was encouraging its members to join the protest. It was the dead of winter, and conditions were harsh. Wall spent a full week camped out in front of the U.S. Consulate and getting to know members of SUPA and Mark Satin. A result was that "the emerging antidraft program and Mark Satin became aware that I was this middle-class American with a house who would probably be willing to put up American draft dodgers and help in the Program." She was more than willing: "We started housing young men and the women who came with them, sometimes the dogs and babies, and from that point on we usually had one or two draft dodgers living with us." This was just the beginning. Wall worked at TADP for a few years without pay, and beginning in 1968 received a token salary for her full-time efforts.

Her early work was with draft resisters. Mark Satin had already drawn up a list of people who would house newly arriving resisters and was helping to publish and distribute the *Manual for Draft-Age Immigrants*. Naomi helped in both tasks and particularly recalls "sending the manuals off everywhere . . . We had this communal house on Lenox. We ran them off on photocopiers, gestetners, and collated them in our bedroom." She also introduced a program that arranged job offers to be used by resisters when they applied for landed immigrant status. A great deal of time was spent developing the leads and contacts for these job offers, collecting information about which offices and border crossings were treating resisters best, and preparing resisters for their interviews with immigration officers. The network of contacts was remarkable. "We had contacts with Friends Committees and other church people on the other side of the border—Buffalo, Niagara Falls, Queenston, Lewiston Bridge, we had contacts both sides of that bridge—we had contacts in the Sioux, Thousand Islands, Gananoque." These contacts became increasingly important as the composition of the resister population began to change.

Especially after the massive Washington antiwar demonstrations and the revelation of the My Lai massacre in 1969, the number of military resisters began to increase, and their problems proved to be greater than those of the draft resisters. The disadvantaged class backgrounds and circumstances of the growing number of military resisters presented unique problems. The military resisters were less likely to have the education or work experience that would ease their immigration under the point system. Even those who had such credentials often had not thought to bring their records when they bolted from their units: "They came to Toronto empty-handed; they had nothing. They had trouble getting job offers and immigration points." Wall found that meeting the military resisters transformed her political perspective: "Particularly as a result of my work with deserters, I began to see that this was a classist and racist war, not only in terms of the Vietnamese, who were southeast Asian and being bombed into oblivion, but also in terms of who the deserters were."

Wall described how different the problems of many of the military deserters could be:

> There were so many deserters and they had such pressing needs. They didn't come with proper identification or money. Often they had only the clothes on their backs. We had to set up an operation that would allow us to get all that stuff. We had to find housing for them. We had deserters who'd deserted from 'Nam and made their way to places like Amsterdam and places in Europe, and then they'd come here. We had deserters who claimed, and we had no reason not to believe them, that they were running from the CIA, that they were CIA operatives . . . We had guys who threatened to jump out of windows at Rochdale . . . Their needs were very pressing, very serious. They didn't often have support from family members at home . . . The welfare class and working-class guys, often it wasn't that their families didn't want to support them—they had no way to support them. They weren't able to support them. The FBI was much harder on their families than on the middle-class families. The class politics that we learned during that period have stayed with all of us ever since. That's where I really began to understand, on the ground, what class means to a person who has to move from one country to another.

At this point TADP had to establish its priorities, which often meant giving precedence to the more pressing problems of the military resisters over the less immediate needs of the draft resisters, who were often better equipped to solve their own problems.

New problems required new solutions. Some of these solutions required trust and generosity, and some involved the participants putting themselves at considerable risk. In the category of trust and generosity is the frequently recalled story of the "float," a sum of cash that was held at TADP and circulated from one resister to the next as they went for their interviews with immigration. The rules instructed immigration officers to assign points to those arriving in the country with some money to support themselves. Wall recalled, "We had a floating fund where the guys could come across with money in their pocket, and then the money would be returned to us. We only lost the money once . . . sometimes it was up to $1,000. We'd give out $1,000 and get $1,000 back."

At one point during my research an elderly American couple, who were retiring and leaving Canada, came to my office to tell me about a more dangerous undertaking during the resistance period. This involved providing contraband and forged discharge forms and other kinds of identification papers for resisters to use when they needed to return to the United States, either to obtain copies of diplomas and other credentials or simply to cross over into the United States in order to come back and apply for immigration status at the border. The couple, in their seventies when they visited me, had been involved in radical politics since coming to Canada from the United States during the McCarthy era. They left me with copies of the kinds of documents used by military resisters. They wanted to make sure that the documents found their way into the proper archives, and they still worried about the consequences of being associated with the events of this period.

Some resisters came into conflict with Canadian legal authorities, and TADP was concerned that these young people were completely without support and assistance. A further concern was that these young people were at risk of being returned to American immigration authorities, who would turn them over to military courts and prisons. Wall at one point developed a plan that involved getting herself put in jail to investigate this problem: "I had hundreds of dollars of parking tickets, and in those days you could go to jail to serve time instead of paying. I went in specifically to find . . . how many American guys were being held . . . We found out there were several. We had a hard time getting their names, but it resulted in a useful newspaper article." TADP made skillful use of the media, frequently placing stories that would help in pressuring the government to reassess its policies.

Wall worked with Bill Spira, the expatriate American businessman and early leader in helping military resisters, to pressure the federal government in Ottawa during the winter of 1968 and spring of 1969 to open the border to American servicemen. This was a source of pressure that led to the May 1969 decision to open the border to military and draft resisters alike. "We wanted the government to say it clearly," Naomi recalled, "because we realized that it would be very good politically, as an antiwar strategy, to have the government come out and say, 'We do not have an extradition treaty with the U.S. regarding draft evasion and desertion, period, and that includes all [military as well as draft resisters].'" She remembers that getting Minister MacEachen to make such a policy statement in the House of Commons was particularly important in increasing the flow of military resisters to Canada. According to Wall, television journalist Barbara Frum and the organization Canadians for a Fair Immigration Policy were especially strong spokespersons in this cause.

The effect was to bring into the open the underground military resistance movement Naomi Wall had been building with Bill Spira through TADP. This meant that the humanitarian efforts of this mobilizing structure could now become more overtly political: "Once we had MacEachen's statement, this underground network went above ground, and we were then able to bring deserters up." The significance of this extended beyond the resisters themselves: "We were now political activists, not just humanitarian types who wanted to help these guys and their wives or girlfriends get settled. We wanted to do more, to do our bit to end the war." This was also the period when Jane Fonda was involved with the coffeehouse movement around American military bases. A combination of forces was now working to bring military as well as draft resisters to Canada.

A sense of the impact of the support services provided by Naomi Wall and other counselors at TADP is provided in the account of Dennis James, whose departure from the American military was described in Chapter 1. Like many resisters, James came into Canada as a visitor, without the papers he needed to win landed immigrant status. After getting his parents to cooperate in collecting and sending the necessary papers, such as birth certificates and diplomas, James needed to return across the U.S. border and reenter Canada to apply for landed immigrant status. At this time resisters of all kinds believed they were subjects of government surveillance and subject to prosecution, if not persecution. James did not have the draft or discharge papers he would need to get back into the United States. He called TADP and was told to "watch the mail": "A few days later I received this package, which was a whole bunch of newspapers, and tucked in the middle was a blank discharge—a general discharge."

James was now ready to cross back into the United States and return to apply for landed immigrant status. The timing was memorable: "It was Christmas Eve that we actually went down. They had a network, and when I called and said I'm ready to go, and he said, 'So, you'll be going tomorrow,' and I said, 'Yeah,' so he consulted with somebody, he said, 'OK, go to Windsor, and use the tunnel and not the bridge.'" James was then given a telephone number to use when he arrived in Windsor, with the instruction to "call this number and say you're a friend of mine." He did exactly as instructed.

James stopped at this point in the interview to regain his composure, remarking that it was an emotional experience remembering the help he had received from people he didn't even know and to whom he would always be grateful.

So I get down there and I say, "I'm a friend of ———," and this woman gave me instructions on how to get to her house, and then she gave us very explicit instructions, told my wife to drive, she gave me $500 in cash, to help round out my points when I came back over. So off we went to the American side. We went through the tunnel, and it was one of those things you could write for a movie. As we were coming up out of the tunnel, there were three or four entering points. So we pull into the shortest line. The others kept going through and ours was delayed. So I'm sitting there and they had given instructions that I should be in the passenger seat, because they always ask more questions of the driver as a routine, so my wife is driving and our St. Bernard is in the back seat and the car that was right ahead was a Volkswagen Beetle. All I could see was the guy in the car had a huge Afro. There was this mass of hair, and as he pulled in I saw the American immigration officer kind of lean down, and they talked back and forth for a bit, and then the driver handed this guy a card, no idea what the card was. The inspector looked at it and pointed over to this building that was off to the side. So the car pulled over and I said, "Oh, shit" . . . Then we pulled up and this guy asked my wife, "Where were you born?" "How long are you planning on staying?" pretty routine kinds of stuff, and he leaned down and he said to me, "And where were you born?" and I told him, "I was born in Kansas City." Just at that moment, our dog, who had been sleeping in the back seat, sat up—so this guy looked and here's this huge St. Bernard's head, and he said, "Wow, how much does it cost to feed that animal?" I made up some figure and he just said, "He's really beautiful, go on." And so off we went back into the United States.

At this point, all James and his wife wanted was to get back safely into Canada, as landed immigrants, as soon as possible. Nonetheless, they followed instructions to spend a few hours in Detroit before crossing back to Canadian immigration. With the float money in hand and an arranged job offer at the Clarke Institute of Psychiatry in Toronto, the reentry to Canada and application for landed immigration status went smoothly. Dennis actually wound up getting the job at the Clarke Institute. "So I was enormously grateful—by the end of January I had landed immigrant status and a job, having come up in December." After the minimum waiting period of five years, Dennis James became a Canadian citizen. He has never since crossed back into the United States.

Resistance in Black and White

Relatively few African American resisters made it to Canada, and those who did found the adjustment difficult. Rob Winslow's story is a good example. Rob graduated with an English major and a physical education minor from North Carolina State University in 1969. He was the first college graduate of a proud black family. His father died when he was young, and his mother worked as a receptionist in a doctor's office in northwest Washington, D.C., to put Rob and his siblings through school. When Winslow graduated, he had good reasons to be optimistic about his future. A large paper company was one of several firms interested in employing him: "They flew me in. I toured the plant. They said they liked me . . . 'There's only one thing about the application here—one thing, your draft status.'" When he went to his draft board and consulted the woman in charge, he realized he had a real problem: "She threw this book open and she goes—right to the page—and she goes, 'Winslow, Winslow, Winslow, oh yes, November, you go in November.'"

Rob now realized he needed a different plan. He got a job offer that could qualify him for an occupational deferment as a teacher in Washington. This seemed promising, but "I came back from the Board of Education office . . . I opened the door and walked in, and . . . the mail was scattered on the floor underneath the mail slot, and I could tell by the envelope that it was my draft notice." Winslow knew he would have to go back with the new job offer to the draft board. He took the employment letter from the Washington Board of Education, and his draft notice, with him to the draft board. "I presented them to the lady and she put them on her desk, and she looked at the one and she looked at the other, and then she said—'Uh, this draft notice was mailed to you, you received it on Monday, and it was mailed on Friday, it takes precedence over the contract you signed.'" By November of 1969, Winslow was in the army.

The physical and academic requirements of basic training posed little challenge for Rob. From the beginning, however, he had serious doubts about life in the army. He recalled, "One night we're there eating and this guy says, 'You know, this is the first time I've ever had three meals a day. You know what else, this is the first time I've ever had shoes that didn't leak.' And I looked at him and I was thinking, so that's why, that's how the army works."

Winslow's leadership potential was recognized early in basic training, but this only led to his becoming aware of other inequities. He soon realized "we were all the same age, same background, same demographics, you know, but they were the reserves and I was drafted. That was when it became real odd, because I thought, 'Wait a minute, we're from the same space and time, but they're gonna be here for two months, and I'm gonna be here for two years.'" It didn't take much longer for him to assess the probabilities that followed from this situation: "They were probably going to live and I was more likely on another track. You know, always on my mind was the inequity of it, and that it was like a plot, all these wars to eliminate specific groups of people—whether it's the people you're fighting against, the Vietnamese, or the people going over there." Winslow went AWOL after four months in the service. After being arrested back in Washington and spending a short period in the stockade, he made his way to Canada with the help of his mother and brother. "My brother drove up with me, when I first came. It was a big drag is what it was—with $174. My mother gave me $174, to come to live in Canada. $174."

The transition was difficult. He was a black American without contacts or networks of support, other than TADP. Perhaps as a result of these factors, he married too quickly and then worried about having to depend on support from his new wife. His mother also sent money, which didn't improve his self-esteem. He could only find menial jobs, and one of his first jobs, in an auto repair shop, led to an early layoff. This was probably the low point in Winslow's young life. Fortunately, on this and other occasions, Naomi Wall was there to offer support.

> I came in the fourth day—there's nothing. The painting's finished. The body guy, he's finished—everybody is standing around. I'm pushing my broom, back and forth, up and back, all day long, there's no dirt in front of my broom, but I'm still sweeping—'cause I know the cardinal rule, I'm looking busy—I'm gonna look like I'm working—so he calls me in and says, "I gotta lay you off" . . . I'll never forget it. I went home that day and I went to the liquor store, and I bought a bottle of wine and a bottle of something deadly. And I drank it up, just drank it up. Straight. At the time I was living on Bedford Road, had a room. I got married by this time. I was so depressed. It was depressing enough to not have a job and I was depending on my wife . . . all really humiliating. My mother was sending me a check for $30 a week, and every time I cashed that check at the bank I felt horrible—terrible—and then I get fired from this new job. So I get drunk. So I took the bus up to

Davisville and I transferred—I was OK but I felt horrible by the time I got to Eglinton Avenue. The TADP was just north of Eglinton. By the time I got off that bus at Eglinton Station I couldn't hold my head up—all I could do was see my feet . . . Looking at my feet, walking, 'cause I couldn't hold my head up. So I got there, I went right to the bathroom, and I stayed in that bathroom about eight hours. Eight hours! I was sick. Naomi came in every now and then and checked me out—"OK, Rob, want something?" "No . . ."— Then she came in and said, "We're gonna close up now—I'm gonna take you home with me." So, OK, she dragged me out, she had one of those old Volkswagen vans. She said, "I gotta go pick up David," that was her son. So I got in the back of the van, and she drove me . . . I didn't want to go home. She took me to her place . . . I go in, go upstairs. By midnight I kind of woke up and I kind of felt better. She gave me some tea or something, and she took me home. My wife thought I had run away. 'Cause I had left this cryptic message—something about losing my job. She thought I had gone back to the States. So she was mad. She had ripped up all my stuff—I came in and a pile of pictures and stuff were torn up—and I thought, "If I'd gone, why would I have left these things?" And she said, "Oh, yeah."

Naomi and I go way back. Naomi saved my life on more than one occasion.

The difficulties that Rob Winslow faced in making a life in Canada speak to the question that often emerges in accounts of the era—namely, why more black resisters did not emigrate from the United States. One answer is that they had less of the knowledge, networks, experience, and familiarity with the prospect of moving to another country. Winslow notes the cruel irony of this situation: "Lack of knowledge. The unknown. Fear of the unknown. More fear of the unknown here than of the 'going to the war' scenario. 'Cause they knew what was happening in the war."

Pam Oxendine, a white woman who married and helped a black military resister, Julius, come to Canada, described the barriers to this migration even more starkly than Rob Winslow. She observed that it was her involvement that made the prospect of her husband's migration appear plausible when it otherwise might have seemed impossible. The story of Pam and Julius is an exception that helps nonetheless to explain why so few African American men who resisted the draft and military came to Canada and instead went underground. Pam explained, "Canada was not an option, and that was a well-known fact in the black community, because they're black and they're not going to get in. It was just as clear as if you close the door, it closes." Pam concluded that "the only reason that Julius got up here was because I was white and I had two years of university and we hid his blackness and then I sponsored him." Julius was atypical in having Pam Oxendine to help him. Even with her help, however, he still found the transition to Canada difficult and after several years returned to live in the United States.

The support that Rob Winslow received from his family, Naomi Wall, TADP, and his own initiative eventually resulted in his making a successful transition to a new life in Canada. He ultimately obtained his teaching credentials and began a career as an educator. In addition to becoming a gifted teacher, over the years he has been one of the most articulate voices of American war resisters, featured in numerous newspaper articles, television shows, and documentaries. His experience of being helped, and later giving help in return, was common in the Canadian war resistance community. His eventual success in turning his life around in Canada was repeated by many other military resisters who also began their immigrant experience in difficult circumstances.

Activism in Exile

In many ways the most interesting questions about the American exodus to Canada during the Vietnam war involve the decades following the arrival and settlement. To what extent were those who came political activists, and did they retain their activism once in Canada? As noted earlier, to refer to all those who came as "resisters" is a presumption built on the assumption that leaving America and coming to Canada in response to the demands of the draft or the military was in itself an act of resistance. This was a frequently defended view in the Canadian Vietnam war resistance movement, often articulated by people with unquestioned activist credentials that justified their taking this position on behalf of others who also came, but who after arriving were less involved in actively opposing the war.

Katie McGovern felt strongly that all Americans who came to Canada rather than support the war in Vietnam deserved to be called resisters. McGovern's own life is a statement about political activism. She came to Canada in 1970 from the University of Illinois, where she worked in the antiwar movement and with the United Farm Workers. She originally came to Toronto to help move a girlfriend whose boyfriend was escaping the draft. Katie soon hooked up with the nascent farm labor movement in Ontario and then began to work with TADP. She remains active in a wide array of causes to this day, often in her role as a community liaison worker with the Toronto School Board. Her years of political involvement have given her a perspective on the activism of Americans who came to Canada because of the Vietnam war. According to McGovern, "There has been controversy over the terms *dodger* and *deserter*," but "the more correct term . . . would be *resister* . . . People resisted in a whole lot of ways . . . You couldn't expect everyone to be out there burning flags and marching in the street . . . Anybody who removes their body from the war machine is by definition a resister, and had to be respected as such."

When McGovern looked back, she realized how deep her own involvement in the antiwar movement had been and how it influenced her later choices. At the time, she did not think much about the impact the work she was doing at TADP with military resisters would have on her own life. "What we were doing," she noted in retrospect, "was listening to people who were involved in the most hideous offenses against human rights and human nature." It was one thing to know about such atrocities in the abstract, but it was another to hear the raw emotion of the stories firsthand. "We knew about what was going on overseas through the deserters that were coming in, and we talked to people who were involved in the torture and murder, and the infiltration, and blowing people's brains out, and all sorts of things." The problem was that "they would be unloading and we were young and not trained and we didn't know how to put up the barriers and the defenses."

Some Comparisons with Freedom Summer

On the question of degree of activism, two points are clear: the extent of activism among American war resisters who came to Canada varied after they arrived, and presumably still does; and there can be no perfect way of measuring how active individuals were then or are now. Yet it is still possible to learn a great deal about the causes and consequences of activism by assessing its expression in measurable ways. Doug McAdam's *Freedom Summer* provides both a classic illustration of the possibilities and some useful benchmarks for comparison.[1]

The Freedom Summer project brought hundreds of primarily white, northern college students to Mississippi for the summer of 1964 to help staff freedom schools, register black voters, and dramatize the continued denial of civil rights throughout the American South. McAdam followed up applicants and participants in this program nearly twenty years later to assess the personal and social consequences of their involvement. A focus of his study was an examination of the media's portrayal of former 1960s protesters as opportunistic and self-serving, using as examples former activist "stars" such as Jerry Rubin, who later became a stockbroker. "Thus," McAdam notes, "the collapse of the Movement in the early 1970s allegedly triggered a period of wholesale generational sellout that found the lion's share of former radicals embracing the politics and lifestyles of the 'Me Decade.'"[2]

McAdam found few if any "political sellouts" among former participants in Freedom Summer. Indeed, the effects of their Freedom Summer experience were long lasting. Twenty years later the veterans of this movement remained involved in political activism. A comparison of participants in the project with applicants who also had been accepted for the project but did not participate showed that the former were significantly more active than the latter. The comparison with accepted applicants who subsequently chose not to participate in Freedom Summer was a stringent test, because their applying and being accepted into the program identified these individuals as activists to begin with. McAdam makes this point by noting that "the no-shows did not differ significantly from the participants in the values they brought to the project."[3]

The Vietnam war resisters who came to Canada are arguably different. To many observers, including leaders of the organized antiwar movement in the United States, the war resisters who came north seemed to be irresponsibly escaping rather than purposefully confronting the Vietnam war. Todd Gitlin lumped "draft dodging" together with "sex, drugs, and rock 'n roll."[4] Joan Baez implored American youth to come back from Canada and confront the system at home. Tom Hayden and Rennie Davis criticized the Canadian exodus. The American leadership of SDS put pressure on the Student Union for Peace Action in Toronto to disassociate itself from the counseling of draft resisters. As noted in the previous chapter, this pressure ultimately led SUPA to send TADP on its own way.[5] Many on the left doubted the effectiveness and therefore the legitimacy of American participation in a Canadian Vietnam war resistance movement. This marked one of the few circumstances in which representatives of the New Left seemed to agree with Richard Nixon, who put his case against the "draft dodgers" cogently: "Yeah. Sure. These people from the elite don't go . . . And they're all fucking running . . . [Mockingly] This is about the war. What are they talking about? I got no sympathy for them."[6]

The accepted applicants and participants in Freedom Summer, whose commitment nobody on the left seriously questioned, are therefore an interesting standard of political activism against which to compare the American war resisters who came to Canada. Since most of the items in McAdam's study are included in the Toronto war resister survey, it is possible to make systematic comparisons. We can first compare the two groups' prior involvement in civil rights activities. This is shown in Table 4.1.

Although figures are presented by gender for the American resisters, this breakdown is not present in McAdam's Freedom Summer study. Since women previously have been found to be more politically active than men,[7] it should be noted that while half of McAdam's Freedom Summer sample is female, only 30 percent of the American resister sample are women. About half of the American migrants were women overall, but our sample is restricted to those women who came with men who were resisting. The smaller proportion of women in the American resister sample makes the combined comparison of male and female war resister respondents with the Freedom Summer subjects a conservative assessment of war resister activism.

Two further points should be noted. First, as pointed out in Chapter 1, the war resister sample is not intended to represent all resisters who came to Canada, but rather those who were drawn to and settled in metropolitan Toronto, which was a focal point of resistance activities. Second, Freedom Summer took place earlier in the 1960s than the Canadian migration, and there were fewer activist opportunities in the earlier period. Despite these caveats, however, comparisons can be informative.

As shown in Table 4.1, war resisters were distinctively bimodal in their backgrounds. About half had no prior involvement in civil rights, while about a quarter had been highly involved, with the remainder in between. The male American war resisters were less involved in prior civil rights activity than the females. The Freedom Summer participants and applicants who withdrew were somewhat more evenly dispersed in their involvements. The applicants who withdrew were slightly more skewed toward noninvolvement than those who participated. Thus, although the majority of American war resisters had not been involved in prior civil rights work in the United States, a large minority of them—a slightly larger proportion than of the Freedom Summer participants or applicants—were highly involved in civil rights work before coming to Toronto. Furthermore, more than a third of the male and female American war resisters were highly involved in peace activity before coming to Toronto, even though about as

Table 4.1 Levels of prior civil rights and peace/antiwar activism among American war resisters in Canada and Freedom Summer participants and withdrawals

	Civil rights activity					Peace/antiwar activity		
	American war resisters			Freedom Summer participants	Freedom Summer withdrawals	American war resisters		
Levels of prior activism	Male (n = 70)	Female (n = 30)	Total (n = 100)	Total (n = 720)	Total (n = 239)	Male (n = 70)	Female (n = 30)	Total (n = 100)
High	18.6%	43.3%	26%	20%	10%	37.1%	46.7%	40%
Moderate	15.7%	3.3%	12%	25%	19%	17.1%	20.0%	18%
Low	8.6%	16.7%	11%	31%	37%	7.1%	16.7%	10%
None	57.1%	33.3%	51%	24%	34%	38.5%	16.6%	32%

Note: Freedom Summer entries from Doug McAdam, "Recruitment to High Risk Activism: The Case of Freedom Summer," *American Journal of Sociology* 92 (1986), Table 6.

large a proportion of the males were uninvolved in these efforts. The implication is that American war resisters who came to Toronto were split between experienced activists—at least as experienced as those young people who went to Mississippi—and those who previously had been uncommitted.

It might be expected that many of those without political experience in the war resister sample would be military resisters, who typically became politically involved later than the draft resisters. A comparison of draft and military resisters in Table 4.2 confirms this expectation. Military resisters scored less than half as high as draft resisters on a scale of prior activism described in Appendix B (Table B.1).

Table 4.2 confirms a number of other statistically significant background

Table 4.2 Early differences and later similarities between male draft and military resisters (n = 70)

Item	Draft resisters	Military resisters	t-difference
Early differences			
Year of arrival	1968.40	1970.47	2.71*
Father's SES	54.69	46.13	2.10*
Prior U.S. activism	2.85	1.13	2.73*
Ranking of 1969 events:			
Woodstock	.05	.60	−3.26*
Washington demos	.27	.80	−1.97*
My Lai	.35	.93	−2.12*
Use of *Manual*	.98	.33	2.97*
Difficulty deciding	2.87	3.73	−2.02*
Underground contacts	.02	.33	−4.29*
Lived underground	.04	.40	−4.38*
Education	8.67	7.80	2.69*
Later similarities			
Current marriage	.75	.73	.09
Occupational status	59.75	56.07	1.11
Income	64,500.00	64,333.33	.02
War resistance in Canada	6.95	5.80	.62
Ties to early contacts	.31	.27	.31
Current political views	7.67	7.33	.90
Current activism	6.29	3.40	1.66

*$p < .05$.

differences between draft and military resisters. For example, the military resisters arrived in Canada on average two years later than the draft resisters, after having reacted significantly more strongly to the events of 1969, including Woodstock, the Washington antiwar demonstrations, and the revelation of the My Lai massacre. The military resisters also had lower-status fathers, were less likely to have had access to the *Manual for Draft-Age Immigrants,* experienced greater difficulty deciding to come to Canada, and were more likely to have used underground contacts and to have lived underground. In view of all this, it probably is not surprising that the military resisters' level of education was significantly lower than that of the draft resisters. The military resisters on average had some college experience, while the average draft resister completed college. Nonetheless, from the point of immigration on, the lives of the military and the draft resisters began to converge. It is possible that a tendency toward homophily resulting from the respondent-driven sampling method may have enhanced this appearance of convergence, but the shift is nonetheless striking between the differences in background and the similarities in biographical outcome of military and draft resisters.

Since all of McAdam's sample who went to Mississippi were involved in Freedom Summer, his research does not emphasize variation in the degree to which these young people were politically active in Mississippi. In contrast, there were clear differences in the form and extent of the political activism of the American war resisters in Canada. Some of the questions in the interviews were intended to determine whether respondents, once they had arrived in Canada, helped to support other Americans who came, and whether the respondents participated in resistance organizations or activities. Their responses to these questions can be regarded as measures of the extent to which these individuals became part of the resistance efforts in Toronto. As indicated in the lower part of Table 4.2, military resisters were not significantly less involved than draft resisters in war resistance activities after they arrived in Canada.

Nearly three-quarters of the American resisters in some way helped to support newcomers who followed them to Canada from the United States. In order of reported frequency in the interviews, this support consisted of offering counseling or advice, providing temporary housing, sharing food, helping to find jobs or job offers, and (least often) loaning money. While about half offered counsel or advice, only about a third loaned money. Few had much money to lend, although as noted earlier, some who had money did indeed lend it. Mary Rauton, who operated Ragnarokr, was one of the most widely appreciated supporters of draft and military resisters. Rauton and those she lived with often provided shelter to newly arrived resisters. She also provided numerous job offers for use with immigration, and she was involved on numerous occasions in bailing out resisters who were jailed during marches and demonstrations. For several years, she also helped host a pig roast on May Day to satirize the American war effort.

Aside from providing assistance to newcomers, about two-thirds of the newly arrived resisters were also actively involved in the mobilization efforts of the resistance organizations. In order of reported frequency, this participation involved attending organization marches and demonstrations; helping to organize marches and demonstrations; engaging in other forms of community organization work, such as leafleting and mailings; and doing staff work for antiwar organizations, such as TADP and Amex. Nearly 60 percent of the respondents attended marches and demonstrations, while about one-third did organizational work. The latter took many more forms than those mentioned above. Jack Colhoun was perhaps the most tireless of the organizers. His editorship of *Amex* through much of the 1970s was especially important in the effort to get a meaningful amnesty from the American government for military as well as draft resisters. These efforts peaked in 1974 and 1975, when he was not only editing the news magazine but also leading a weekly noontime vigil, regardless of weather, on Fridays in front of the U.S. Consulate on University Avenue.

Although the level of American immigrant support and participation in the Canadian antiwar movement may be higher than many observers have assumed, this activism was not universal. Many resisters in Toronto were politically active in the mobilization of opposition to the war, but a substantial minority were not. The economists' concept of "free rider" is often applied by analysts of social movements to the latter group, even though we have questioned the applicability of this kind of characterization to American resisters, whose coming to Canada was itself a political statement.

Three Decades Later

Apart from the question of how politically active American resisters were before and when they came to Canada, there is the further issue of how active they are now, three decades later. An interesting benchmark for comparison is again the Freedom Summer participants and withdrawals, who were tracked twenty years after their experience in Mississippi. The results of the interviews, as reported in Tables 4.3 and 4.4, suggest that in terms of a number of measures of current activism, the American resisters probably rank somewhere between the Freedom Summer participants and withdrawals. Table 4.3 presents unadjusted comparisons of the Toronto resisters with the Freedom Summer participants and withdrawals. Table 4.4 presents some lower- and higher-bound estimates of current activism among American resisters, with adjustments for possible bias that network connections in the respondent-driven sample might have introduced into these comparisons, as discussed below and in Appendix A.

In unadjusted terms, just over half of the Toronto resister sample is currently active in a social movement, while nearly half of the Freedom Summer participants and about a third of the withdrawals are. The mean number of political organization memberships of the Toronto resisters is about 1.9, compared to 2.1 for the Freedom Summer participants and 1.4 for the withdrawals. More than two-thirds of the Toronto resisters consider themselves to be "leftist" in their current politics, while respectively about 60 and 40 percent of the Freedom Summer participants and withdrawals placed themselves on the left. Finally, the resisters are today markedly more inclined than either the Freedom Summer participants or withdrawals to favor use of the tax system to reduce income disparity. Looking back to Table 4.2, we see that the military resisters are very much like the draft resisters in their current political views, and although they currently appear somewhat less active politically, this difference is also not statistically significant. Overall, the Toronto resisters have turned out to be relatively persistent in their activism.

The respondent-driven nature of the Toronto sample (described in Appendix A) may have inflated the measurement of current activism attributed to American resisters. The political-process theory of social movements suggests that respondents who are currently more politically active will have remained connected to other resisters; such people are more likely to ascribe significance to the factor that they have in common, and this may have led them to be drawn into the sample. Following this theoretical prediction, removal of all such respondents from the sample can provide a lower-bound estimate of current political activism among resisters. This figure will be conservatively biased because a representative sample would include some such respondents. Fortunately for the estimate, an interview item asked respon-

Table 4.3 Levels of contemporary political activism among American war resisters in Canada and Freedom Summer participants and withdrawals

| Measure | American war resisters | | | Freedom Summer participants | Freedom Summer withdrawals |
	Male (n = 70)	Female (n = 30)	Total (n = 100)	Total (n = 212)	Total (n = 118)
Currently active in any social movement	47.1%	70.0%	54.0%	48.0%	33.0%
Mean number of memberships in political organizations	1.5	3.0	1.9	2.1	1.4
"Leftist" in current political stance[a]	62.9%	86.7%	70.0%	60.0%	41.0%
Agree that "tax structure should be modified to reduce the income disparity between the rich and the poor"	81.4%	100.0%	87.0%	56.0%	40.0%

Note: Freedom Summer entries from Doug McAdam, "The Biographical Consequences of Activism," *American Sociological Review* 54 (1989), Table 4.

Table 4.4 Estimated levels of contemporary political activism among American resisters in Canada and Freedom Summer participants and withdrawals

Measure	American resister estimates			Freedom Summer estimates	
	Lower bound[a] (n = 52)	At and below median[b] (n = 58)	Full sample (n = 100)	Participant sample (n = 212)	Withdrawal sample (n = 118)
Currently active in any social movement	34%	40%	54%	48%	33%
Mean number of memberships in political organizations	1.1	1.2	1.9	2.1	1.4
"Leftist" in current political stance[c]	59%	57%	70%	60%	40%
Agree that "tax structure should be modified to reduce the income disparity between the rich and the poor"	79%	85%	87%	56%	40%

Note: Freedom Summer entries from Doug McAdam, "The Biographical Consequences of Activism," *American Sociological Review* 54 (1989), Table 4.

a. Respondents reporting they have been uninfluenced in the direction of their current activism by ties and contacts from war resistance era.

b. Respondents at or below median in number of contacts (n = 0–3) retained from war resistance era.

c. The designation "leftist" was reserved for those subjects who used the numbers 1, 2, or 3 to designate their current "political stance" on a 10-point scale ranging from 1 for "radical left" to 10 for "radical right."

dents if the direction of their current activism was influenced by their ties and contacts from the war resistance era. The first column of Table 4.4 presents lower-bound estimates of current activism when those members of the Toronto sample who affirmed such influence are removed. This lower-bound estimate suggests that resisters are almost identical to Freedom Summer withdrawals, as measured by their involvement in any current social movement; that their level of current membership in political organizations is slightly lower than that of the withdrawals; and that they are more like the Freedom Summer participants than the withdrawals in their current political attitudes.

However, as indicated earlier, purging the sample of *all* respondents with significant prior ties to fellow resisters tilts the sample too far in the opposite direction of the presumptive bias. A truly representative sample would preserve some proportion of resisters who remain in contact and are a source of influence on one another. To provide a further estimate of current political activism, I determined that among sample members the median number of retained contacts from the resistance era was between three and four. The second column of Table 4.4 presents estimates of current activism including only those resisters who have three or fewer remaining contacts. This estimate places the resisters halfway between the Freedom Summer participants and withdrawals in terms of current activity in any social movement, still slightly lower than the withdrawals in mean number of memberships in political organizations, and still more like the participants than the withdrawals in current political attitudes. These estimates, taken together, suggest that the American resisters are probably somewhere between the Freedom Summer withdrawals and the participants in their current activism. Since the 1990s were probably a less activist era than the 1980s, perhaps as a result of being farther removed from the 1960s, and since the Freedom Summer withdrawals are almost certainly more activist than average American citizens, we may conclude that the resisters have, in relative terms, persisted in their political activism.

Explaining Current Political Activism

Of course, to conclude that the resisters overall remain an active group is not to deny that today some choose to be politically and socially inactive. Further explaining who remains politically active, and who does not, thirty years later is a thought-provoking and challenging task. Parents, partners, and peers are likely to influence an individual's level of political activism. These sources of influence stretch temporally from the past through the present, thus having an early and continuing influence on a person's life course.

The "red diaper" theory of political activism, focusing as it does on the importance of parental socialization, puts the emphasis squarely on the past. Todd Gitlin's analysis in his book *The Sixties* emphasizes the linkages and rifts between the Old and the New Left in American politics, and often these linkages turn on family ties. Gitlin writes, "I, for one, was a liberal youth, raised by liberal parents, dreaming liberal dreams, moved by liberal heroes, who threw himself into political activity and moved leftward in the early Sixties."[8] The argument is that parents instill a commitment to activism through their political and social beliefs and through the example of their involvement in political and social movements. The intergenerational conflict between parents and their adolescent children that prevailed in the 1960s presents a challenge to this explanation, but parental and family traditions nonetheless remain an important factor.

A more contemporary explanation might give greater attention to partners, especially to the women who played a major, but nonetheless often neglected, role in the antiwar movement. The frustration of some women over this neglect led to the emergence of the feminist movement. Renée Kasinsky notes in *Refugees from Militarism* that this frustration was expressed at a 1970 Montreal conference of resisters from across Canada, where women protested that "they too were political refugees; they too had made the political decision to leave the United States, whether they came with a draft resister or deserter or whether they came alone."[9] Kasinsky goes on to observe that the women's "desire to work equally in these aid groups led to some concrete changes in the groups' structures and goals." Nonetheless, even in the early 1990s, McAdam could still note that "the sociological study of social movements remains only lightly touched by the 'gender revolution' in the social sciences."[10]

The best substantiated explanation of persistence in political activism is found in McAdam's *Freedom Summer*. McAdam emphasizes the radicalizing influence of peers. The experience of engaging in social and political protest with a group of like-minded peers can build into a lifelong commitment to activism. Social networks formed in one's early experiences of political action frequently set a foundation and offer opportunities that can lead to continuing involvement. Mark Granovetter calls this a process of "social embeddedness" often built on the strength of weak but lasting ties,[11] and McAdam has demonstrated that recurring contacts among the Freedom Summer participants led to their continued high involvement in social and political activism. High-profile examples, such as Mario Savio, who participated in Freedom Summer in Mississippi and went on to work with civil rights veterans in developing the Free Speech Movement in Berkeley, illustrate the power of this explanation. It may not be a coincidence, then, that Mark Satin, who began the work of the Toronto Anti-Draft Program, had his first experiences with political activism working in the civil rights movement in Holly Springs, Mississippi.[12]

Using information collected from the interviews, I constructed a model of the current social and political activism of American war resisters in Canada. This model, summarized in Figure 4.1, is based on the results of a regression analysis presented in Appendix B, Tables B.1 and B.2, and uses the same scale as McAdam's study of the biographical consequences of Freedom Summer.[13] This scale sums the respondents' current involvement in social and political movements. The Toronto resisters' present involvement takes a number of forms. Nearly half the sample reported being involved in neighborhood, community, or tenant groups or movements, including participation in recent efforts to stop the amalgamation of the metropolitan Toronto area into one supercity. More than 40 percent were active in the New Democratic Party, and more than a quarter were involved in other left-oriented political parties at the time of the interviews. More than a quarter reported being active in professional caucuses or groups within their professions, and more than 15 percent were involved in cooperative day-care and alternative

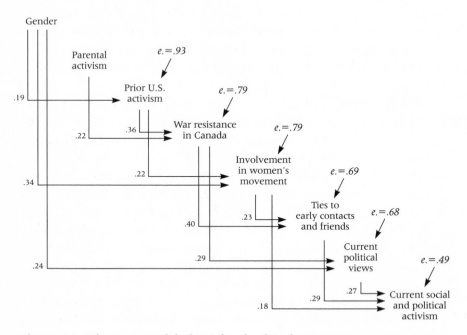

Figure 4.1 Life course model of social and political activism among American war resisters in Canada

school programs. A smaller number said they participate in food and work co-ops.

The analysis summarized in Figure 4.1 indicates three preliminary points about the contemporary activism of war resisters: the female partners of male war resisters reported being more socially and politically active than the males; parental activism had a small and indirect influence on the resisters' activism; and prior involvement in U.S. activism and active involvement with peers in war resistance soon after coming to Canada have had an enduring effect on respondents' social and political activism. Furthermore, how these influences come into play are as revealing as the simple fact of their being an influence.

The tendency of the women partners to be more active in the present is not a product of their being more active when they arrived in Canada. Although the women in my survey, as in McAdam's research, were slightly more likely to have been involved in prior activist causes in the United States,[14] after arriving in Canada the men and the women displayed similar levels of support and participation in war resistance efforts. Over time, however, the men probably became more involved in their careers, while women were more likely to persist in social and political activism—for example, through the women's movement.

Naomi Wall remembers exactly when the women's movement became a conscious part of her life; it happened during the Montreal antiwar conference described earlier.

I thought about gender issues, but I didn't become a feminist until the late spring of 1969, when I went to an antiwar conference in Montreal which was attended by hundreds of people, lots from the States. It was the first time that we felt we were meeting to involve American antiwar activists in our efforts to get guys off the bases and into Canada as an antiwar strategy . . . I think it was May 1969, and American feminists were there . . . There was this long table up on a platform, of Canadian antiwar activists. We were the host organization for the conference. I was the only woman up there . . . because basically by then I was running the show [at TADP] . . . I was very war-focused, but I wasn't focused on the difficulties that women were having being heard in the antiwar movement. It was at that conference that I was challenged by women, American and Quebecois women, from the floor. They stopped the meeting. They were trying to make a point, that there were valid antiwar points that weren't being heard and that they were being shut down. And finally a woman stood up and said, "Until women's issues are dealt with at this conference, we will not allow this conference to go on." And I said, "Oh, excuse me, excuse me, this conference has to go on, we have to deal with the war. We will deal with the women's issues." And I was soundly criticized, and because I was progressive, instead of becoming defensive, I just shut up. After the morning session several of the women came up and invited me to a women's caucus and I have not looked back since. That was my initiation, and I began to approach my antiwar work very differently from that point on. I began to see the specific role of women in the work, I began to look at how I related, I looked at ways of hiring women to work as counselors. That was the turning point for me in terms of my feminism, although I didn't actually work for a feminist organization until 1976.

The impact of the women's movement was lasting, for Wall as well as for others. About half the women in the resister sample participated in the women's movement, and this participation has stimulated continuing and subsequent activism. Today, about 70 percent of the women in the sample are socially and politically active, compared to less than half the men. (Table B.3 in Appendix B makes it clear that the impact of the women's movement is specific to women in the sample.) This finding of the long-lasting involvement of women in social and political activism replicates a similar pattern observed in McAdam's study of Freedom Summer,[15] and it also supports a further argument by McAdam about the importance of organized structural ties.[16]

The activism of some American parents also was a modest and indirect source of the adult activism of their children in Canada. War resisters whose parents were activists were more likely to resist the Vietnam war actively in Canada. Several resisters told fascinating stories that illustrated how politically committed their parents were.

For example, Tom Kane, who organized resistance work on the Purdue University campus as well as with the Union of American Exiles in Toronto, recalled that his parents were both members of the Communist Party in Chicago. Tom's parents did not tell him of their party membership until he was in his twenties, because they feared that if he knew, he would someday encounter problems with loyalty oaths, which individuals were required to take to get jobs at that time in the United States. Nonetheless, Tom certainly learned the attitudes and values of his parents. When his parents later told him about their party membership, Tom remembers his reaction: "At the age of 24 I found out an important piece of history . . . I found out why I had the political beliefs I have . . . My parents were communists. They were thrown out of the party, I think in 1953. They had serious disagreements with the central committee in Chicago." Tom went on to explain, "One doesn't have severe disagreements with the central committee. You get thrown out!"

Hugh Wylie also learned in later life of an incident that placed in bold relief his father's political beliefs and actions. Only after his father's retirement did Hugh find out that his father played a decisive role in the publication in 1972 of the famous photograph of nine-year-old Phan Thi Kim Phuc running down a road in Vietnam, naked, horribly burned, and in screaming panic, fleeing a napalm attack—a photograph that is widely believed to have changed public opinion about the war. Hugh discovered a letter his father wrote to the editor of a local newspaper regarding the publication of a picture of an unclothed child. "His letter said . . . that he knew of a case where in fact a photo was going to be stopped because the child was naked and then the new photo editor came on duty and decided to run it and that it may have had great impact on the ending of the war. And he in fact was that editor. He never told me until this letter to the editor appeared in the Florida paper." It is likely that Hugh Wylie was influenced during his youth by his parents' expression of their political convictions, albeit probably by way of other less extraordinary events and examples.

Yet, while parental socialization probably plays some role as a starting point, the early activism of resisters themselves in the United States is more strongly predictive of their later active support of war resistance in Canada; and peer support of that resistance in turn leading to lifelong continuing contacts was a major factor in the development of the resisters' long-term activism.

McAdam's study documented the lifelong radicalizing effect of involvement in Freedom Summer. Americans' involvement in the Canadian Vietnam war resistance had a similar effect (as indicated in Figure 4.1). This resistance resulted in long-lasting and influential ties between contacts and friends and directed resisters' political views in ways that still encourage continuing social and political involvement. This long-lasting, transformative influence of intense political activism is similar to what McAdam found in the Freedom Summer experience and what Granovetter's conceptualization of embeddedness in social networks of like-minded peers predicts.

Richard Brown recalled how the contacts he made while in TADP continued over time and led outside this circle to his long-term involvement in the New Democratic Party and beyond:

> The people in the Program were the collective, and then we all had a circle of friends who you would socialize with. So there was the collective, and the circle of friends would get together on the weekends to socialize. This was the lifestyle . . . There was also a sort of unspoken, unwritten rule in the Program collective that you had to have some kind of outside political thing that you would be involved in, outside the collective, in the community. For me it was the New Democratic Party. At that time there was the Waffle movement going on in the NDP, and I was on the executive of the riding association. It was known as a Waffle Riding. And so I was involved in that, and there was this expectation, although there was nothing in writing at any point, that people had to be involved in something, somewhere else. But Michelle Sanders got involved in day care, I think she still is to this day, and other people got involved in other things . . . I became president of the Gay Businessmen's Council for a couple of years, in the late seventies and early eighties.

In this way the politically active resisters in the sample became part of a variety of social networks that produced patterns of commitment that have persisted to the present.

Laura Jones's Activism

The life-course model of resisters' continuing social and political activism that is summarized in Figure 4.1 is well illustrated through the life experiences of Laura Jones. The story of how Laura came to Canada with John Phillips and established the Baldwin Street Gallery was told in an earlier chapter. But Laura's exposure to social and political activism began much earlier and is a part of her family history. It began with her mother: "My mother . . . used to carry 'ban the bomb' signs when I was a little kid and was involved in the civil rights movement," Jones recalled. "She was very, very involved." Laura's mother was not unique in her family. "I have a relative who started the first public library in North Dakota. I have other relatives who have a house that was used during the underground railroad . . . So I was always told that we have a duty to help."

This family influence continued during the buildup of the Vietnam war.

By the time the early draft card cases started moving through the courts, Laura and her mother had moved to Washington, D.C. "In Washington it was always far more important to me to be involved in peace activities than any school activities." Laura's mother remains involved in political issues. "My mother still volunteers for a lobbyist three days a week. She volunteers two days a week at the White House. She's very involved in issues. She knows what's going on worldwide far better than I do . . . She's eighty-three and hasn't slowed down a day."

Laura Jones and John Phillips made their decision to move to Canada in 1967. She recalls reading an article in the *Ladies Home Journal* about Mark Satin and his early work on Spadina Avenue with the Student Union for Peace Action and the Toronto Anti-Draft Program: "That article actually had addresses in it and we used the addresses when we got here." Although her mother approved of the idea of coming to Canada, Laura was just out of high school and her mother was concerned: "She approved, but she was very upset because she thought I was really too young to be making such a decision."

Still, Laura and John came to Canada, and Laura remembered immediately feeling at home in Toronto. They became involved in the early work of TADP, helping to put together a new printing of the *Manual for Draft-Age Immigrants*. "We got it when we got here and then we helped to staple it together for other people." By the time Laura settled with John on Baldwin Street, a transformation clearly was beginning to occur in her sense of involvement with her community. "I had moved about every three years as I was growing up, and then when I came to Toronto I really never wanted to move again . . . When I moved to Toronto, and particularly settling into Baldwin Street, where you had such an intensely strong sense of community and people helping each other out, it was just a really positive experience."

Jones traced her evolution as a community activist directly to the Baldwin Street experience: "The original draft dodger community stores were the Whole Earth, the Cosmic Egg, the Yellow Ford Truck, Ragnarokr, and our Baldwin Street Gallery . . . Together we started the day-care center, Snowflake; the women had a consciousness-raising group; we had a La Leche League group. The five stores formed the core close-knit set. Then other people came in." Laura saw this time as transformative because of the sense of community, optimism, and purpose that it inspired. Although the Baldwin Street area was often called the American ghetto, Laura questioned both aspects of this description, first noting the darkness of the ghetto imagery: "It was such a happy time in my life, and a ghetto usually implies some level of poverty and overcrowding and lack of light. It was wonderful. It really was this sense of you could try almost any idea and it might work. So for me, it was more positive." She was particularly impressed by the purposeful, directed nature of the people on Baldwin Street. "Everybody who settled on Baldwin also seemed to have an idea, they wanted to carry out the idea—they wanted to start a store, wanted to be a writer, a painter . . . As a group we were very goal-directed." Jones also questioned whether this community should be called American. She thought of it as "ex-American. I really didn't think of myself anymore as being American . . . There's something about leaving, and at that point we didn't think we were going to be able to go back. So the fact that we were ex-Americans was significant. We had decided to—many of the people—live more of a bit of an alternative lifestyle to the traditional American values." So while the Baldwin Street experience had a very American beginning and involved strong ties among this new group of American immigrants as well as continuing protests against the American war in Vietnam, its residents soon branched out into other causes that stretched beyond American preoccupations.

The newcomers' initial forays into Canadian affairs were not always welcomed. The immigrants were sometimes seen as too American. Jones recalled that her first involvement in the local women's movement resulted in bruised feelings. "In the U.S. I'd always been accused of being too passive, too quiet, and then I came here and I wanted to be involved in the women's movement. I had done so much work—plastering the ceilings and helping set up some women's centers—and then I was told I couldn't be on the board, because I was an ex-American." Instead, Laura decided to start a photography program for women. "By then we had our own [Baldwin Street] gallery and a newsletter. I said in the newsletter that I wanted to meet other women interested in photography. We started our own group, which was Women in Photography . . . Since we were located near the University, there were lots of women who came over." With this success and others, the feelings of exclusion gradually passed, to the point that Jones could say, "I was later so involved in Toronto that I don't think that people were even aware that I was American . . . Now I feel more out of place when I go to the U.S. and I realize I have a Canadian perspective, and I don't ever feel out of place here."

Jones's work was always community-based. During much of the Baldwin

Street period she was a part of the Company of Young Canadians. Later she worked with an occupational health clinic in Etobicoke, a community on the west side of Toronto. Eventually she was drawn to Riverdale, the downtown Toronto neighborhood in which the largest number of the members of the resister sample now reside. Like the others, Jones was drawn to this neighborhood for its community feeling. "Riverdale had a reputation of a sense of community . . . It was the first community to take on the Toronto Transit Commission and win . . . There was also the Greater Riverdale Organization that was really a community-based organization. They could get six to eight hundred people to show up for some of their meetings. I wanted to be a part of that spirit."

For many years, Jones worked on occupational health and employment issues in Riverdale. Her efforts often involved consensus and coalition building rather than confrontation. For example, she described how her work with businesses to develop employment plans eventually contributed to bringing some of the fast-growing Toronto film industry into Riverdale: "When the film industry moved to Riverdale—and they are a huge employer in Riverdale—one of the agreements made was that they would give priority in hiring to people who lived in the neighborhood. So a lot of the people who build sets, and do all sorts of things, have actually been from the neighborhood." Laura's work has most recently been as an elected school board trustee. This brings her into contact with people and groups that she has known since she came to Toronto more than thirty years ago. When I asked how many of the original people she stays in contact with, her response was, "Well, dozens. I'm in contact with an awful lot of people—for all sorts of reasons—so I don't really think of them as being Americans anymore. We never talk about coming to Canada anymore. It's all about what we're involved in now."

The Price of Protest

The literature on social and political activism suggests that activists often pay a personal and economic price for their involvement. McAdam's Freedom Summer study found that twenty years later the volunteers who worked in the program were less likely to be married and were more likely to have a lower income than those who were accepted for the program and withdrew. The implication is that commitment to activist causes adversely affects marriage prospects and earnings. Indeed, one of the few disheartening aspects of the Freedom Summer research is that twenty years later women in particular were more likely to be unmarried, somewhat isolated, and lonely.

There is no evidence in the war resister sample that coming to Canada impaired marriage prospects. To create a comparison group to address such issues I asked the respondents in the sample to provide information about a sibling, if possible of the same sex. Ninety percent of the respondents had a sibling. Seventy percent of the siblings were of the same sex, and because having a different-sex sibling is not systematically related to gender, marriage outcome, or earnings, the presence of different-sex siblings does not bias my conclusions.[17] Siblings form a useful contrasting group because they share genetic and environmental background characteristics with the respondents and thus help to hold background characteristics constant in comparisons.[18]

Comparison of the resisters and their siblings showed no significant differences in their marital and parenting histories. Siblings had been married slightly more often (1.3 times versus 1.2 times), had slightly more children (1.7 versus 1.5), and were slightly less likely to be married at the time of the interview (66 versus 70 percent); none of these differences is statistically significant. Resisting the war by coming to Canada apparently did no long-term damage to this group's marital histories. About three-quarters of the males, both the draft and the military resisters, were currently married; the two types of resisters were not significantly different in numbers of marriages (see Table 4.2). Men were more likely to be currently married than the women who came with them (74 versus 60 percent respectively), but this difference was not statistically significant, and a similar difference appeared among their siblings.

There is, however, a significant disparity in the earnings of resisters and their siblings. Compared in Canadian dollars, on average the resisters earned $60,361, while their U.S. siblings earned $69,055—more than $8,000 more. This difference is statistically significant. The disparity is not linked to whether the person was a draft or a military resister, as the two are very similar in income and occupational status (again, see Table 4.2). Nor is this disparity due to differences in education or occupational status between resisters and their siblings. Resisters are slightly better educated than their siblings, and the occupational status of their jobs is not significantly different; both the resisters and their siblings' jobs tend to be highly concentrated in the social and human-service professions. McAdam found that 54 percent of the participants and 55 percent of the withdrawals from Freedom Summer were employed in a variety of social and human service professions: they were teachers and college professors, lawyers and judges, health practitioners, social workers, clergy, physicians and dentists, nurses, psychologists, writers, and artists. Similarly, just over half of the resister sample work in these social and human service professions, and just over 40 percent of their siblings do so as well. As a comparison, McAdam found that less than one-quarter of the general U.S. population of the same age and educational level as the volunteers worked in these professions. So, like the Freedom Summer applicants and participants, the Vietnam war resisters in Canada have chosen to work in what often are called the "helping professions."[19]

Yet it is not simply the occupational status of these professional choices that accounts for lower earnings among resisters. An analysis of resister incomes (see Appendix B, Table B.4) reveals that active war resistance after arriving in Canada plays a significant part in explaining reduced incomes, even with father's occupational prestige, respondent's gender and occupational prestige, and sibling's income taken into account.[20] The long-term influence of resistance activity on the respondents' current political views helps explain the resisters' reduced earnings. Disaggregating this analysis by gender did not alter this conclusion: women and men alike paid for their politics in diminished earnings. In short, those resisters who came to Canada and continued to protest the American war in Vietnam from Canada have paid a lifelong price in earnings for their persistent activism and political views.

Scenes from a Career

No two careers are alike, so in spite of the clearly discernible patterns just reported, it is impossible to pick any single person's work history as an example of the experience of war resisters in general. Nonetheless, an example can provide a sense of how the people and times helped form the pattern of activism and the resulting lower earnings of resisters who settled in Toronto. John Phillips's story is illustrative.

In addition to starting the Baldwin Gallery with Laura Jones, Phillips also became involved in filmmaking. This involvement grew out of the "social change photography" first shown in their gallery. Work at the gallery featured the Baldwin Street resistance experience, incorporated the women's movement, and spawned a widening network of contacts with Toronto social change activists. In the beginning, Phillips recalled, "it was social change

photography . . . and then later on we got into women's photography . . .
That's how it started." John then became involved in teaching photography
to disadvantaged youth through an alternative school called Point Blank.

Phillips's teaching at Point Blank soon included a mentorship that became
the basis of a long-term partnership with a promising student, Clay Boris. "I
taught him photography and his photographs were great, but he said, 'I
want to make a film,' and I said 'OK.'" John continued, "I went to the National Film Board (NFB) and got a small grant and he shot a film on Super 8,
and I helped him do it. A real low-budget thing, but it was about his life and
everything, and it was called *Parliament Street*." The collaboration continued
to evolve, and in 1980 Phillips and Boris made a feature film together that
generated considerable critical acclaim.

> We did a film together called *Alligator Shoes*—and it was invited to the
> Cannes Film Festival, where it won the Director's Fortnight. It won the
> Gold Medal at the Anaheim Film Festival. It got awards all over the world. It
> was a low-budget feature film based on Clay's family, a docudrama. We pro-
> duced it together: he wrote it, I was the cinematographer, and it never made
> a dime. We were both financially devastated by it, and yet it got awards all
> over the world. I have a thick book of clippings, reviews, but that's another
> long story . . . Businesswise, we were terrible. We did this brilliant film and
> we did another film for the NFB called *Rose's House*—an hour-long film that
> got the Silver Hugo at the Chicago Film Festival. Artistically, we were suc-
> cessful.

Phillips's purpose in life had never been to make a great deal of money,
but he needed a more stable financial base than filmmaking was providing.
So he moved on to a brief career in university teaching at York University.
Later he found a way to match his love of filmmaking with the need for a
stable source of income. He got a job with his former partner, Clay Boris,
making films for a unique youth treatment center called Browndale. The
work was fulfilling and exposed Phillips to advanced video production techniques. He recalled this as "a wonderful training period . . . We got to do documentary films for two years . . . We did a thing called *Sheila's Christmas* that
I'm very proud of. We spent a month in North Bay documenting these disturbed teenagers in this group home." This was Phillips's last job working for
others.

Phillips shifted from this in-house position back to the independence of
freelance work, moving ultimately into the video techniques he experi-

mented with at Browndale. He is clearly proud of his independence. Phillips recalled, "From there on I was a freelance filmmaker, freelance photographer, and eventually got into video in the late eighties, as the technology became very interesting, and I started the business that I'm still doing now."

Phillips's career has allowed him to mix social activism and creativity with a certain financial stability. He is not affluent. Nor is he fully satisfied with the trade-offs between commercialism and social activism that his work demands. Nonetheless, he has achieved goals that have their roots in his resistance experience.

> I'm still in debt to this day. I still owe money based on that feature film. I think I'll go to my grave owing money on it . . . What I've been doing for the last ten years is not nearly as interesting socially as what I did before that—but I'm earning a good living at it. I've become a corporate video producer basically, and I do videos for Levis, American Express, and various other companies. I have all the equipment in the basement. High-end, broadcast-quality, computer-based-editing computer graphics. I slowly built up this business year by year; buy a little more equipment, get a few more clients. I finally gave up the weddings and started doing more corporate stuff. But I still do interesting video projects—they are more attuned to my former life. I did a thing on refugees for the Jesuits . . . The biggest video project that I did was a $70,000, hour-long video on AIDS, which I did through an organization called Second Look, which was a street-based community organization in Kensington Market that was working with street kids. My son was involved and got me involved. They got a grant to do a video about AIDS and . . . so we ended up doing it. I'm very proud of that project.

Resisters like John Phillips often earn less than their siblings, but I heard few complaints about their occupational choices. Rather, most seemed pleased with the values their occupations allow them to express.

The Passage of Time

The decision to come to Canada marked a turning point in the lives of the American resisters who settled in Toronto. Some Americans who came limited their resistance to the act of migration in response to draft and military laws. The majority of the Toronto resisters in my sample, however, actively protested the war before leaving the United States and continued their active protest after arriving in Canada. The persistence to this day of social and political activism in the lives of these American resisters is a measure of the directedness of their migration and the life-determining impact of their decision to come to Canada. McAdam's study of Freedom Summer provides a benchmark for comparison. The social and political activism of the resisters lies somewhere between the activism of those who participated in Freedom Summer and those who were accepted to participate but then withdrew. The American women who came to Canada are even more socially and politically active than the men with whom they came.

The persistent activism of the women is partly explained by their progression from war resistance through the women's movement and the resulting lifelong social connections that have nurtured involvement in various causes. Women resisters were also somewhat more involved in protest activities in the United States before coming to Canada. After arriving in Canada, both men and women were highly involved in the war resistance activities concentrated around Toronto's American ghetto. These involvements, before, during, and after the migration, which operated through social connections and through the encouragement of progressive attitudes and values, radicalized the participants and perpetuated their social and political activism.

Even resisters who reported that they were not currently active in any sort of social or political movement had relevant reasons for not being active, and some were in fact active in less orthodox or more intermittent ways. Several members of the sample, for example, reported that they are now working in legal dispute resolution or mediation roles or as judges, and that these activities require them to give up their political activities to maintain an appearance of impartiality. A few reported that they were at least temporarily "burned out" from prior political involvement. One of these respondents argued in a compelling fashion that after a twenty-year "arc" of political activism, including several years in Nicaragua, he now had a right to his own life, a rewarding job, and a family that he could properly support. Another respondent insisted that he was inactive even though he worked in a field crew that helped set up folk festivals each year and that had evolved into a "brigade" that did volunteer construction work for several summers in Nicaragua. This group is currently inactive, but it seemed likely that the work would resume. This respondent insisted that I code him as inactive, reasoning that "something political grew out of this other thing . . . We weren't donating anything but our time—taking our hands, our tools, on the ground, helping a community directly."

Although prior research has found that activists pay a price for their commitments in terms of marriage and earnings, the Toronto resisters appear no more likely to be unmarried, divorced, or childless than their American siblings. By these conventional measures, the resisters seem eminently responsible exemplars of familism. But they do have lower incomes, probably as a result of their continued political activism. In this sense, they have paid for being socially responsible. Since women in general (and in this sample) make less than men, and since the American women surveyed here are more socially and politically active than the men, they have paid a double price economically.

Denise Bukowski and her work as a literary agent for ethnic and immigrant writers provides a fitting conclusion to this chapter. Hers is an unorthodox form of activism that has links to the women's movement and reflects a choice of career path that is purposefully less remunerative than it could be. She described how she served as literary agent for the former head of the New Democratic Party in Canada:

> I represented Audrey McLaughlin as a literary agent and actually took a cut in my income as my political contribution because we recommended that she go with a smaller Canadian house that offered her less money . . . I like taking people on who are perhaps not part of the mainstream . . . I took on a book written by a Sarajevan writer, about the siege of Sarajevo . . . I had to find somebody who could translate from the Croatian, and find a publisher, and it really was a labor of love—I made almost no money from it, but it was a book that I really felt should be published. I thought we were hearing too much from Western journalists and not enough from the people there about what was really happening. I felt it was my contribution to that issue . . . I've often taken up books like that, that I feel strongly about because of my political bias. But I'm not a joiner of organizations. I just choose the books that I want to help because of my politics, through my work.

While the pre-immigration lives of the military resisters and the draft resisters were quite different, especially in terms of their class background and prior activism, there was, surprisingly, less evidence of difference in their lives following their arrival. The difficulties the military resisters faced in making the move to Canada probably are reflected in their lower rate of university completion. But in other ways the draft and military resisters seem to have become much alike. The military resisters' active opposition to the war once they were in Canada was not significantly lower than that of the draft resisters. The two groups remain about equally tied to their early contacts from this period. And the military resisters are not significantly different in marital and occupational status than the draft resisters; the two groups earn almost identical incomes. A tendency toward homophily resulting from the respondent-driven sampling may account for some of this convergence; but given the differences in the background of draft and military resisters, the degree and uniformity of the convergence is striking.

The military resisters are also very much like the draft resisters in their current political views, and although they currently appear somewhat less active politically, this difference is not statistically significant. Thus, the lives of the two groups now seem more alike than different. Perhaps most notably, their early educational differences have given way to similar marital and occupational outcomes. Apparently the American dualism that distinguished draft from military resisters and that was declared irrelevant under Canadian immigration law also became irrelevant to life outcomes once these immigrants had settled in Canada.

The two efforts the Canadian government made to confirm complaints of disproportionate misbehavior by draft or military resisters failed to find such evidence in relation to either group.[21] The similar experiences the draft and the military resisters shared after arriving in Canada likely had more to do with their later lives in Canada than their different experiences before immigrating. As detailed in the following chapter, the evolution of Canada's legal treatment of military resisters after their immigration ultimately encouraged this similarity in the life course experiences of draft and military resisters.

In short, the American resisters' social and political activism extended beyond the draft and military problems that brought them to Canada, their activism was of lasting rather than of passing duration, and it took collective forms, belying assertions that the resisters were excessively individualistic. Although my findings derive from a Toronto sample whose respondent-driven form could have overrepresented the core of the American war resistance movement in Canada, I do not believe that this sample is different from what would be found in other large Canadian cities, such as Vancouver; there is more evidence of similarity than difference. Nonetheless, every movement has both a core and a periphery, and the processes observed in this Toronto sample, which parallel those observed in McAdam's Freedom Summer research, may prove to be more characteristic of core than peripheral members of social movements generally. Where this core might end and a periphery begin for the overall group of American resisters in Canada is an issue in need of further study. In fact, framing issues of activism in the life course in terms of core versus periphery points of origin may prove more salient than the initiator/spin-off categorization introduced in Chapter 1. Meanwhile, at a minimum it can be said that the majority of the American resisters in the Toronto sample have become committed, involved, and persistent in their social and political activism, and their activism is strong and sustained, not diffused or derivative. The Vietnam-era emigration to Canada was not a marginal social movement, perhaps in part precisely because it proved so difficult to marginalize, as will be seen in the next chapter.

CHAPTER 5

Two Amnesties
and a Jailing

Buses assumed unusual prominence in the late 1960s and early 1970s. The British rock band the Who immortalized their Magic Bus. Ken Kesey's Merry Pranksters insisted you were either "on the bus or off the bus" as they careened from coast to coast in Tom Wolfe's Electric Kool Aid Acid Test. The Beatles' Magical Mystery Tour came to take you away by bus. Buses painted in psychedelic colors symbolized the footloose, free spirit of the age.

So in the summer of 1973, when the Canadian Parliament passed an immigration amnesty for persons who were not yet legally "landed," there seemed one obvious way of getting the word to the several thousand draft and military resisters who could be assisted. The Canadian Coalition of War Objectors signed a $1,400 personal service contract with Dennis Hayward—$400 "to paint and put his bus in running order" and the rest to travel between Toronto and Victoria "informing American war resistors how they can benefit from the government's new immigration procedures."[1] The names, addresses, and phone numbers of participating draft resistance groups appeared along the roofline of the multicolored bus, which in larger lettering carried the message "Last Chance for Landed Immigrant Status."

The coalition hoped the bus would inform resisters in remote areas about the immigration amnesty that would run from August 15 to October 15, 1973. The Canadian Council of Churches added to the coalition's efforts by producing sixty-second radio tapes and television film spots featuring musicians Ian Tyson, Joan Baez, and Jessie Winchester. Winchester was a widely known war resister whose southern baritone voice added poignancy to his message:

This is Jessie Winchester. I've been a Canadian immigrant for a number of years now, but a lot of people here aren't. If you or someone you may know are living underground or are otherwise an illegal immigrant, you now have a last and final chance to apply for legal status in Canada. A recently passed Canadian law enables all of those who arrived in Canada before December 1, 1972 to apply for landed immigrant status within Canada. This new law can apply to everyone regardless of whether you entered Canada illegally, worked without a work permit, and regardless of your present military status. The minister of immigration is quoted as saying, "This is a wide open invitation, but it is also a last chance." And a last chance it is. You must apply before the first of October of this year, but before you do be sure to obtain advice and counseling from the refugee aid center nearest you. In Toronto, it's the Toronto Anti-Draft Program, 920-0241.[2]

Aid centers across the country pressed local stations to play the spots with the assistance of local United Church ministers. This publicity was a reminder that the gatekeeping function of the law had not ended with the opening of the Canadian border in 1969. In 1973, as in 1969, there was a covert dimension to these well-publicized developments.

The Canadian government's willingness to regularize the immigration status of draft and military resisters, along with a much larger group of immigrants in the country illegally, contrasted with the United States government's reluctance to provide amnesty for draft and military resisters in that country. Thus, Canadian and American laws continued to define and channel the opportunities, identities, and life paths of American war resisters who wanted to stay in Canada or return to the United States. If the Canadian approach was an open invitation, the American response was a barring of the gate. The Canadian approach made no distinction between draft and military resisters, while the eventual American amnesty punished those who left military service. The dualistic treatment of draft and military resisters, who had become a symbolic expression of Canadian sovereignty in 1969, persisted in the United States. In this sense the Canadian and American policies of the 1970s became opposing amnesties. Canada's "open invitation" was juxtaposed to the enduring admonition "America—love it or leave it." American war resisters, with vigorous leadership from north of the border, continued through much of the 1970s to be active in the two countries' national developments. The evolving policies established the context in which the war resisters developed long-lasting feelings about both Canada and the United States.

Four Strong Winds

The 1970s began with four salient events. One, perhaps least noticed at the time, involved American antiwar activist Tom Hayden, who in the spring of 1970 encouraged participants at a Montreal conference to fight for an American amnesty for exiled war resisters in Canada. At about the same time, Canadian nationalist Robin Mathews denounced such antiwar activities by American resisters as a distraction from Canadian issues. As an ominous reminder of Canada's own problems, in October 1970 Prime Minister Trudeau invoked the War Measures Act in response to separatist violence in Quebec. Finally, Karl Armstrong slipped into Canada shortly after the August 1970 bombing of the Army Math Research Center in Madison, Wisconsin, and after observing the October crisis in Montreal went into hiding in Toronto. These four events had ramifications for much of the rest of the decade.

Hayden's appearance in Montreal signaled that there were now enough war resisters in Canada to attract the interest and attention of the antiwar movement in the United States. Hayden saw potential value in having American resisters in Canada assume an exile status he had earlier opposed. However, to realize their potential Hayden argued that the resisters would need to frame their positions and focus their energies in relation to the United States rather than as New Canadians. "There's nothing political you can do for Canada without getting Canadians very upset eventually," Hayden urged. "You must oppose the U.S. as American exiles, not as Canadians or expatriates."[3] This call for an exile-led campaign for amnesty did not find a ready audience at the Montreal conference, but it anticipated the long-term struggle that was to follow.

Canadian nationalist Robin Mathews brought the exile-immigrant contradiction into sharp relief by attacking the motives and methods of the American resisters. A May 1970 protest at the American Consulate in Toronto of the U.S.-led invasion of Cambodia and the killing of four students at Kent State had resulted in a clash with the police and ninety-one arrests. Mathews charged that the presence of the American resisters was an extension of U.S. imperialism and that they were taking jobs from Canadians.[4] A milder version of this argument asserted that these new and unexpected symbols of Canadian sovereignty should frame their lives as New Canadians and leave the American antiwar issue behind.

The politics of American war resistance in Canada were further complicated by the Quebec Crisis of October 1970. The climax occurred when members of the Front de Liberation du Quebec (FLQ) kidnapped the British trade official, James Cross, and the Quebec Labor Minister, Pierre Laporte, whom they later killed. The federal Liberal government, led by Prime Minister Pierre Trudeau, responded by invoking the War Measures Act, imposing martial law throughout Canada. This use of the military was an assault on the entire separatist movement and went on to include American war resisters within its widening net.

The mayors of Canada's largest cities used the law in a backlash against American war resisters. Mayor William Dennison of Toronto claimed that "a few hippies and deserters are Toronto's only problem." Mayor Jean Drapeau of Montreal charged that draft and military resisters were part of a "revolutionary conspiracy." Mayor Tom Campbell of Vancouver declared, "I don't like draft dodgers and I'll do anything within the law that allows me to get rid of them." All three expressed a willingness to use the War Measures Act against war resisters. Mayor Campbell was the most explicit, telling the *Toronto Star*, "I believe the law should be used against any revolutionary whether he's a U.S. draft dodger or a hippie."[5] During this period American war resisters understandably became concerned about police harassment and cooperation between the RCMP and the FBI.[6]

Quebec and the United States were now both on fire. Todd Gitlin has chronicled this violent turn in his description of the "days of rage" that swept across the United States in the late 1960s and early 1970s.[7] A connection between the violence in Canada and that in the United States was made when Karl Armstrong fled to Toronto with his brother Dwight following the August 1970 bombing and resulting death at the Army Math Research Center in Madison, Wisconsin. Armstrong lived underground for two years in Toronto before he was arrested.[8] An extradition hearing followed, providing a public forum in which the limits of permissible political protest and crime received a Canadian test. The extradition hearing provided another context in which the feelings of resisters about the relationship between Canada and the United States were played out.

These four strong winds—Tom Hayden's call for an American amnesty movement from Canada, Robin Mathews' Canadian nationalist attack on

American war resisters, the October FLQ crisis and its overlap with political hostility toward resisters, and Karl Armstrong's flight to Toronto and extradition case—opened a fateful decade. It was a decade that exposed an ambivalence in attitudes of and toward American war resisters in Canada.

Of Exiles and Expatriates

As 1970 came to a close, the issue of American exile and expatriate identities came into the broader Canadian consciousness, and *Amex* emerged as a lightning rod for the expression of Canadian concern. Canadians wondered to what extent this news magazine was perpetuating unassimilated Americanism.[9] Under the title "The Ardent Exiles," the *Toronto Star* questioned the motivation of contributors to *Amex*, "who apparently regard themselves as militants temporarily exiled in Canada." The *Star* editorial warned that "unless the young Americans for whom *Amex* speaks revise their priorities . . . , they risk arousing a growing hostility and suspicion among ordinary Canadians."[10]

Increasingly, the exile-expatriate debate focused on amnesty and was divided into its Canadian and American forms. The Canadian immigration amnesty came first, in the form of temporarily relaxed conditions for regularization of "landed" immigration status. The American amnesty effort later produced two partial presidential pardons for selective service and military violations. The challenge of the U.S. amnesty effort was to get the American government to reconsider its dualistic division between "dodgers" and "deserters," the distinction between selective service and military law violation. This dualism was symbolic of the unreconciled differences that made a full amnesty impossible. For some, the American amnesty seemed an impossible dream, while for others it seemed the necessary fight. Sometimes partisans broke into open conflict, with those who saw themselves as exiles tending to identify as Americans, and the expatriates often simply wishing to become New Canadians.

Each Christmas during the Vietnam war reporters would descend on Toronto to write maudlin holiday stories about American war resisters. As the 1971 Christmas season approached, the thinking of Jack Colhoun and others about amnesty was beginning to change. To this point, almost all resisters believed that fighting for an American amnesty was pointless. Colhoun, however, had begun to write pieces in *Amex* arguing that the politics of amnesty in the United States offered an opportunity for exiles to advance American understanding of opposition to the war. Although Colhoun's views were in the minority, during the Christmas season of 1971, with Amex and the Toronto Anti-Draft Program, Colhoun began planning a news conference in which resisters would for the first time speak about this issue publicly and collectively on their own behalf.

Proposals for amnesty had been made in the United States by Senators Robert Taft and George McGovern and Representatives Edward Koch and Bella Abzug, and Senator Edward Kennedy was initiating amnesty hearings. Roger Williams, who had recently published his book *The New Exiles,* wrote to Jack Colhoun from England, where he was pursuing a career in journalism. Williams argued that the time was right for resisters in Canada to speak out: "It wasn't up to us to originally demand amnesty . . . But now that the issue HAS been raised, it is up to us to answer it and come forward, at long last . . . It is finally time for the exiles to be heard."[11]

On January 17, 1972, six representatives of the Halifax, Montreal, Toronto, and Vancouver resister groups met the press at the Religious Society of Friends House in Toronto.[12] Richard Brown of TADP acted as moderator, and Dee Knight of Amex presented a position statement expressing Jack Colhoun's view that discussion of amnesty could serve as a vehicle to attack the war from Canada. This statement made clear what the resisters found unacceptable: "We reject the current 'amnesty' proposals in the U.S. because they serve to mask Nixon's escalation of the war, they do not include the same provisions for deserters from the Armed Forces as they do for draft dodgers, they all have a punitive string attached called 'alternate service,' and they all imply guilt on our part when we were the ones who have refused to commit the crime." The statement also made clear what would be acceptable: "What we are talking about is a totally non-punitive restoration of complete civil liberties for all persons charged or persons who might be charged, and/or persons convicted under any American municipal, state, federal and/or military law due to actions relating directly or indirectly to the Indochinese War."[13]

The resisters' rejection of existing amnesty proposals received broad coverage in both the Canadian and the American press.[14] Robert Fulford wrote with characteristic insight in response to the issues raised in Canada by a prospective American amnesty. "The hard question arises," he noted, "are they here now because they want to be here, or because they aren't wanted somewhere else? Many say they won't go home again, no matter what

Washington offers, and some of us are delighted to hear them say it. For certainly, we would miss them."[15]

Free Karl

Exactly one month after the resisters' press conference, on February 17, 1972, Karl Armstrong was arrested in Toronto. Armstrong had been charged with his brother, Dwight, and two others for the first-degree murder of Robert Fassnacht, who had died from injuries resulting from the August 1970 bombing of the University of Wisconsin Army Math Research Center. Fassnacht, who himself had been active in antiwar activities, was working at the center in the predawn hours of the morning when the blast occurred.

Following the bombing, Karl Armstrong had fled with his brother to Montreal; they then moved on to Toronto, where they were helped to hide out by Naomi Wall, who initially assumed they were draft dodgers. Karl's biographer asserts that Karl and Dwight received a great deal of help while hiding in Toronto: "The issue of violence was debated, but in the end it became a personal matter. The fugitives were there, they needed help, and they were judged to be sincere. And so worries about possible repercussions were set aside and help was given."[16] By the summer of 1971, the FBI suspected a connection between Wall and Armstrong. Yet it took another six months, and the help of an informer, for the FBI and the RCMP to arrest Karl Armstrong.

Armstrong based his defense on a clause in the Canadian–U.S. extradition treaty: "No fugitive is liable to surrender under this Part [of the treaty] if it appears that the offence in respect of which proceedings are taken under this Act is one of a political character." Armstrong's lawyer, Clayton Ruby, argued that Armstrong was indeed a political fugitive. "The question," Ruby asserted, "is how we respond to political dissenters who happen to be American."[17] The defense established that the bombing grew out of many demonstrations and a long and acrimonious dispute between antiwar activists and the University of Wisconsin about work being done at the Army Math Research Center. Prominent American antiwar activists—including Staughton Lynd, Noam Chomsky, and Tom Hayden—came to Toronto and testified for the defense.

Despite the well-mounted defense, York County Judge Harry Waisberg ruled in favor of the extradition of Karl Armstrong on June 30, 1972. On hearing the ruling, Armstrong exploded, shouting, "You are a pig, your honor. You are a fascist pig and an enemy of the people." Waisberg responded, "I see no reason why fugitives should be protected by this country from its jurisdiction on the ground that they are political offenders."[18]

The judge's tone of detachment may have served to mask the influence of recent political events, specifically those related to the Quebec Crisis. Two years earlier, in 1970, an American court had facilitated the extradition of the Quebec FLQ's Pierre Vallières and Charles Gagnon from New York City back to Canada. Vallières, who later called for revolution in French Canada in his book *White Niggers of America*,[19] had fled to the United States after an act of violence that paralleled Armstrong's. A bomb planted in a box in the offices of a shoe factory in May 1966 exploded and killed a sixty-four-year-old woman. This event marked the start of a new wave of FLQ action that led to the October Crisis in Quebec in 1970. Like Armstrong in reverse, Vallières and Gagnon were arrested for illegally being in the United States and were charged by Canadian authorities with murder resulting from the shoe factory bombing.

John Liss, who worked on the Armstrong case while still a law student, speculated a quarter century later about the connection between the Armstrong and Vallières cases. He reflected that the Canadian authorities were probably thinking, "If we don't give them Armstrong, we won't be able to get the next guy." Valerie Johnson wrote in *Saturday Night* magazine, "If we extradite your Weathermen, you have to extradite our FLQ."[20] The *Toronto Star* agreed, drawing a direct connection between the Armstrong case, the 1970 Quebec Crisis, and future cases. A *Star* editorial reasoned, "As the tragic events of 1970 showed, we have our own terrorist movements. Unless we are prompt in handing over fugitive terrorists from other countries, we cannot expect the co-operation of these countries in bringing to justice our own malefactors."[21]

Probably few resisters actually believed that Armstrong would be granted political refugee status in Canada. As soon as the decision was announced, his supporters were passing out preprinted leaflets on Yonge Street. John Liss said years later, "I didn't really think that he was going to convince the federal government not to send him back." Despite their feelings about the killing of Fassnacht, Liss and other American resisters in Canada respected Armstrong for confronting the American war machine and forcing it to pay attention to the war resistance movement; and they fought to protect Armstrong from mistreatment, especially when he was placed in solitary confinement in the Toronto Don jail. Liss recalled, "I did things like challenge his being held in solitary, being denied his rations." The personal contact heightened Liss's feelings of ambivalence. "I got to know him a little bit, respected him, but I don't think he respected me as much—he saw me as something of a sellout, I'm absolutely certain."

Karl Armstrong was returned to Madison, Wisconsin, on March 8, 1973, for trial on murder and arson charges. A "Free Karl Armstrong" parade marched down State Street in Madison when his trial opened. Although he was eventually convicted of second-degree murder and arson and sentenced to a twenty-three-year prison sentence, the sentence was later reduced to seven years. Naomi Wall married Karl Armstrong while he was in prison, in part to improve his chances for parole, and she stayed with him in Madison for about six months following his release. She then returned to Toronto. Armstrong is today a free person, living and working in the Madison area, where he owns and operates a set of fruit drink stands, called Loose Juice, on the campus mall.

Back in Canada, the Armstrong extradition helped justify the *Toronto Star*'s conclusion that violence is a crime against democracy. The defense's tactic of importing American political activists such as Lynd, Chomsky, and Hayden in an attempt to establish that violence can be a form of political protest was probably counterproductive. These witnesses strengthened the objection that Robin Mathews had raised: that the politics of the American left were not viable in Canada.

Meanwhile, by explicitly rejecting the legitimacy of violent political protest and thus drawing a sharp legal line around just what forms of political protest were permissible, either by citizens or by potential immigrants, Canada was able to reaffirm its earlier position of allowing the immigration of more peaceful American resisters. Before this reaffirmation could take place, however, things got worse rather than better, especially for American resisters who were not yet legally "landed" in Canada.

The Border Silently Closes

By 1971, the enforcement of the American draft law was in shambles.[22] With the curtailment of American land-based involvement in the Vietnam war and the emergence of a lottery-based draft, the exodus of draft-age Americans was slowing. This did not mean, however, that the effects of the immigration would suddenly end. Both in Canada and in the United States, public attention was shifting to the POWs in North Vietnam and the exiles in Canada.[23] Conservative politicians sometimes used concern for the former group to vilify the latter. In particular, the Nixon Administration sought to drive a wedge between the symbolic images of heroic soldiers and disreputable dissenters. Liberal American politicians, by contrast, expressed concern about the fate of young Americans in Canada, alluding, for example, to their inability to visit their families.

The National Council of Churches (NCC), acting as an umbrella group for thirty-three Protestant and Orthodox churches, supported efforts to counsel draft-age Americans in Canada. Like the Canadian government, much of the Canadian public, and probably most of the resisters themselves, the churches wanted to re-establish a sense of stability and security in these young peoples' lives. Their mental health and well-being seemed to be of particular concern.[24] This was perhaps a sign that resisters continued to be seen as less than fully rational in their cause and actions. A prominent Canadian psychiatrist, Saul Levine, reported he had assessed twenty-four Toronto resisters in various stages of "emotional disturbance," from "disorganization" and "acting out" through "searching" to "adaptation and integration."[25] He surmised that few of the individuals had moved to the last of these stages, tending instead to remain in a "transient situational reaction."

Levine believed he understood his resister patients' problems. He explained, "The United States engenders in its youth a fierce sense of patriotism; the American young people who have decided to come to Canada usually do so with ambivalent feelings."[26] He suggested that the ambivalence and disturbance he observed were magnified by the inhospitable reaction of Canadians that American resisters were increasingly encountering—a reaction reputedly linked to increased unemployment and petty crimes allegedly committed by resisters. A front-page story in the *Toronto Globe and Mail* in the spring of 1970 claimed "U.S. Exiles Turning to Crime."[27] A similar front-page story in the *Toronto Star* early in 1971 asserted that as many as 200,000 Americans were living in Canada illegally and were occupying scarce jobs.[28]

The Canadian public and American resisters alike were more plausibly preoccupied during this period with the aftermath of the War Measures Act. This Canadian act's resort to military measures shocked the resisters who were fleeing American militarism. Levine observed, "Even though it provided considerable potential for abuse, the Act proved very popular in Canada, and Americans who demonstrated against it were castigated."[29] The Canadian government and most Canadians probably just wanted the American newcomers to settle down and settle in by reframing their identities as New Canadians. Levine joined his fellow citizens in worrying that "assimilation does not appear to be one of the dodgers' top priorities. The whole subject has influenced passions, both supportive and hostile. When one dodger is arrested, the whole group is (metaphorically) indicted."[30]

The National Council of Churches responded to this concern by establishing an Emergency Ministries Concerning the War. Richard Killmer was appointed the organization's director and helped put together a book, *They Can't Go Home Again.*[31] In the introduction, Congressman Edward Koch described a visit to Canada during which he met with war resisters. This visit, which had been organized by Killmer, was a platform for Koch's early promotion of an amnesty bill in the United States.

Meanwhile, the Canadian public had begun pressing the government to slow the flow of new immigrants from all parts of the world as the country was by the early 1970s in an economic downturn. About half as many immigrants were allowed into Canada in 1971 as in 1967, and turnover in the immigration department suggested the turmoil, with five different ministers in rapid succession.[32] The tightening of immigration policy soon created a large backlog of immigration appeals.[33]

In early November of 1972, the immigration minister suddenly announced a suspension of the right of visitors to apply from within Canada for landed immigrant status.[34] The suspension meant that war resisters could no longer get landed either from within Canada or at the U.S. border. The resulting crisis soon produced a clash between TADP and Amex. A meeting was held between the leaders of TADP and Amex to devise a strategy to convince the Canadian government to create a loophole that would still allow entry for war resisters. TADP was reluctant to protest publicly; Amex charged that this acquiescence was facilitating a silent closing of the border. Of shared concern was the fact that the number of resisters living illegally underground in Canada had grown into the thousands, perhaps as high as ten thousand. With the tightening of the regulations, these resisters could not apply from within the country or at the border to legalize their immigration status. Dee Knight and Jack Colhoun of Amex pointed out that this situation put resisters in legal jeopardy in both countries and therefore made the need for a war amnesty in the United States even more pressing.[35] TADP argued that public discussion of amnesty already was responsible for a great deal of resentment among Canadians for war resisters.[36]

An Anxious Ambassador

In the winter of 1973 the Nixon Administration responded to new support for an amnesty for war resisters by renewing its attacks on the antiwar movement. The Nixon Administration's hostility toward the antiwar movement made Canadian government officials nervous about the "harboring" of draft and military resisters in Canada. In the late winter of 1973 Patrick J. Buchanan, "Special Consultant" and speechwriter for President Nixon, became a focal point of Canadian governmental concerns. Buchanan wrote an op-ed piece for the *New York Times* that questioned the sympathetic attention the media was giving to draft and military resisters in Canada and Sweden.[37] Buchanan charged that "some U.S. journalists and politicians have been characterizing as the 'best of our younger generation,' and the 'guardians of the national conscience' a collection of draft dodgers and deserters whose statistical profile and performance in exile show them to contain more than the customary complement of malingerers, opportunists, criminals, and cowards." In case there remained any uncertainty about his point, Buchanan concluded, "Especially as one watches the genuine heroes of our age and time debark at Clark Field, to hear the boys who ran away to Toronto and Montreal and Stockholm lionized as 'moral heroes' is—obscene."

The Canadian embassy in Washington cabled Buchanan's piece to Ottawa with a reminder that Buchanan was a "theoretician" and "chief draftsman" for the Nixon Administration.[38] The ambassador was worried about the escalating rhetoric being used to depict resisters. "I have been considering with a good deal of apprehension the likely course of public discussion, agitation, and advocacy," he cabled two days later, "as well as White House and Congressional interest in the position of the draft evaders and deserters in Canada and in the amnesty question." He noted the president's own harsh comments on "sins to be punished" and a recurring refrain of "peace with honor" and "escape with disgrace," which to him implied a consequent need for punishment.[39]

The ambassador was plainly concerned that Canada might become involved in a confrontation with the Americans, a possibility raised by the recent closing of the border. He worried "that some of the young Americans in question might have to leave Canada under the new regulations in order to apply for regular immigrant entry from outside" and that "this is likely to stimulate the controversy even more, with their sympathizers on both sides of the border agitating against Canadian policy and the USA government and the critics of the draft evaders watching us for any signs of our making exceptions." Even if this scenario was not widespread, "It would take only a few well dramatized cases to create a politically sensitive situation."[40] Since Canada was by then housing about 50,000 war resisters, the ambassador's worries seemed reasonable. Ottawa answered the ambassador a few days later, noting that "your concern over possible effects of new Canadian immigration regulations on this very sensitive issue is well understood." The response promised that discussions would be held with the department of manpower and immigration, with special sensitivity to the "particular need for cases involving draft dodgers and deserters to be disposed of as inconspicuously as possible."[41]

The kind of second-dimension covertness discussed in Chapter 2 was again used to avoid inflaming a potential conflict. The irony was that while earlier covert tactics had been used to undermine the policy of liberalization, it was now too late to turn back this policy—the resisters were already "in country." The feed-forward effects of the liberalization policy now required Canada to reduce the likelihood of conflict with its powerful neighbor by quickly getting the unprocessed resisters legally landed, regardless of whether the earlier standards of the point system would have deemed them "suitable."

So in the closing days of February 1973 the undersecretary of state for external affairs wrote the deputy minister of the department of manpower and immigration about the need to meet to address the issue of the presence of American Vietnam war resisters in Canada. The undersecretary echoed the ambassador's warning that "legal cases in Canada dealing with the right of Americans in these categories to remain in Canada may stir up public controversy and have quite a serious effect on Canada/USA relations." This letter was emphatic about the nature of the problem and repeated the earlier advised solution: "I suggest, therefore, that it would be useful if officials of our two departments could meet in order to discuss various aspects of this issue, including the disposal of cases involving draft dodgers and deserters as inconspicuously as possible."[42]

The Canadian Immigration Amnesty

In the spring and summer of 1973 Canadian support groups pushed the Canadian government to reconsider the situation of unlanded American draft-age immigrants. In May 1973, for example, a Quaker committee in Vancouver implored Prime Minister Trudeau to consider the fact that many resisters remained unlanded. The committee explained that these resisters had "either failed to clear the 50 point Immigration hurdle, or else put off applying for Immigrant status until after November 1972, when 'internal' and Border Immigration was terminated. These young men now find themselves in

'No-Man's Land,' . . . no longer able to gain Landed Immigrant status in Canada."[43]

Richard Brown of the Toronto Anti-Draft Program followed in the early summer of 1973 by requesting a meeting with the immigration minister, Robert Andras. Brown wrote that "the counseling centers in Vancouver, Winnipeg, Montreal, and ourselves here in Toronto estimate there are probably 5,000 to 10,000 unlanded resisters here in Canada who must have the option of getting their legal status or face serious legal problems either here in Canada or in the U.S." He further warned that "the problem will not go away" and that "the longer it goes unresolved, the more difficult it will be ultimately to deal with it."[44]

The Canadian government needed a discreet means of resolving the cases of the unlanded resisters. Fortunately, a solution proved to be at hand, since many other ethnic, national, and cultural groups in addition to the American war resisters were also pressing for an immigration amnesty.

On June 18, 1973, Minister Andras introduced a bill in the House of Commons designed to regularize the immigration status of persons who were in the country prior to the closing of the border the previous November. The bill provided a "once-and-for-all" opportunity for people in Canada to apply for landed status, provided they did so within sixty days of the proclamation of the legislation.[45] When the minister introduced the bill at the committee stage he promised, "If they [the immigrants] have any prospects at all of becoming successfully established in our country, they will be granted landed immigrant status."[46]

Richard Brown of the Toronto Anti-Draft Program realized from the outset that this was a serious initiative. Questions remained about the legislation, especially as to whether the point system would be relaxed. Nonetheless, Brown accurately surmised that "for most unlanded war resisters, it will be either this or nothing."[47] Similarly, the United Church, which in 1969 powerfully supported demands to allow military resisters into Canada on the same basis as draft resisters, encouraged the government's plan for an immigration amnesty. The moderator of the United Church noted that "while the new provisions apply to persons from many countries who are staying in Canada illegally, we are delighted that they apply to American war resisters who, in most cases, have made a fine contribution to Canadian life."[48]

The National Council of Churches now hastily decided to revive its counseling program for American resisters associated with groups like TADP in Canada. The emergency ministries of NCC quickly raised more than $110,000 for this purpose. Killmer convened a meeting of the aid groups in Winnipeg, which included the Toronto Anti-Draft Program but conspicuously excluded Amex representatives. Jack Colhoun had no doubts why Amex was excluded: "This latest incident was consistent with a long tradition whereby the NCC would fund only the apolitical aid centers at the expense of the political exile groups addressing the political roots of the problem."[49]

When the Canadian government established the Immigration Appeal Board Act in the summer of 1973, the director of the program asserted that "it's very generous. We're not using the point system at all." The government initially committed $500,000 just to publicize the legislation in Canada and overseas;[50] this figure later was increased to $1 million.[51] The government and aid groups' efforts to inform and advise war resisters about the immigration amnesty, including Dennis Hayward's bus, were successful. Almost 99 percent of the applicants for landed status were accepted.[52]

The Canadian immigration amnesty was essentially universal and unconditional. It was supported by groups that had four years earlier fought for the admission to Canada of military and draft resisters. The earlier decisions to honor Canadian immigration law by placing its principles ahead of U.S. draft and military laws symbolically reaffirmed the sovereign status of Canada and further affirmed the open and humanitarian nature of Canada's immigration policies. The United States would not do nearly as well in its effort to reconcile the divisions caused by the draft and military laws used during the Vietnam war.

An American Amnesty Movement Begins

On January 1, 1972, Henry Schwarzschild opened an office in New York City for the American Civil Liberties Union's Project on Amnesty. The first *New York Times* article that announced the opening of the office reflected the often hostile but also necessarily symbiotic relationship that would develop between Amex and Schwarzschild over the next half-decade. Jack Colhoun staked out the *Amex* exile position, saying, "We left the United States because we did not want to become criminals of the heart and now feel that a government which has the stain of Indo-China on its conscience has no business passing judgment on our 'crimes' and meting out punishment, no matter how seemingly tolerant and however it may be dressed up." Henry Schwarzschild, speaking for the ACLU Project on Amnesty, was from the outset much more conciliatory: "We must overcome the divisions, hatred, and bitterness built by this war."[53]

The core of the debate that would frequently place Amex and the ACLU at odds was whether an eventual amnesty would institutionalize the persistent American dualism that regarded draft and military resisters—"dodgers" and "deserters"—differently, treating the latter group more harshly than the former. Amex and other exile organizations were adamant that the two groups were morally equivalent, arguing that draft resisters simply tended to be better-educated, advantaged youth who had resisted before induction into military service, while military resisters tended to be less-educated, disadvantaged youth who resisted after induction.

One of the first things Schwarzschild did as director of the ACLU Project on Amnesty was raise funds to keep Amex solvent. He also contacted Colhoun about the congressional hearings that Senator Edward Kennedy was convening in Washington on the issue of amnesty. Schwarzschild testified at these hearings, along with David Harris, who had earlier served twenty months in prison for draft resistance in California. Three Canadian resisters—from Toronto, Winnipeg, and Montreal—also attended.[54]

The Kennedy hearings provided a forum in which the argument was made that draft and military resisters should be treated the same way, and this momentarily seemed to blend the two groups together in the public mind.[55] They also provided a context in which Henry Schwarzschild could begin to connect with Jack Colhoun and Dee Knight of Amex. Schwarzschild wrote Colhoun after the first hearing, "I have as many problems with and reservations about what passes for liberalism these days as you, and I suspect that I have been actively at odds with liberals for longer than you're politically conscious."[56] A week later Schwarzschild wrote Dee Knight, "You are young, and at times irascible (not as often as I), and unduly suspicious, and inclined to doubt the morality or courage of those who do not so readily agree that the currently fashionable rhetoric is the answer to all the world's ills. But you're great guys."[57] Colhoun and Knight were at least happy with the brief Schwarzschild presented,[58] "basically," Knight observed, "because most of it came directly out of the last *Amex*, especially the work that Jack Colhoun has done."[59]

McGovern's Miami Amnesty

Vietnam remained prominent in American minds in the early 1970s, although draft calls and the involvement of ground troops declined. Returning veterans from foreign wars have always captured the public imagination; yet the fact that the United States had not attained victory made this war different. George McGovern initially supported a vaguely defined Vietnam amnesty, saying, for example, a year before the 1972 presidential election, "I urge that when the war ends amnesty be granted to those who, on the grounds of conscience, have refused to participate in the Vietnam tragedy."[60] This kind of statement made Dee Knight believe McGovern and his supporters could be convinced to support total amnesty. Early in 1972 Dee Knight's draft evasion case was thrown out of court on a technicality, thus making it possible for him to travel to the United States and participate in the McGovern campaign for the presidential nomination.

On the way to the 1972 Miami Democratic convention Knight met up with a group called Safe Return, which wanted to highlight the plight of Marine Corps deserter Tommy Michaud, then living underground in the United States. Though the effort was ultimately unsuccessful, it gave Knight, and Amex, experience in political theater. Television cameras focused on Michaud on the floor at the Miami Convention, where he was arrested in full view of the public. The group had expected the California delegation and others to then make a motion calling on the rest of the delegates to support Michaud's call for amnesty, but this action failed to materialize.

Knight worried that Safe Return's surfacing of Michaud was not as productive as it should have been, but he also observed that "we did make a splash, brief though it was, on national television, to get this guy surfaced and to move McGovern a few more meters to the left on the question of amnesty." This movement came when McGovern said in a speech to demonstrators in a hotel lobby in Miami that he favored a "general amnesty" for all who refused to serve in the armed forces because of their opposition to the war.

It was also at the 1972 Miami convention that Dee Knight connected with the organization Vietnam Veterans Against the War (VVAW) and for the first time met Ron Kovic, author of *Born on the Fourth of July*. "They camped out in a place, I forget the name of the park, but they had a campground park and Ron was one of the leaders there. I got acquainted with him there and that ended up being a really valuable connection that we sustained."[61] Knight's comments support Jerry Lembcke's observation that "veterans had enormous credibility, and the anti-war movement avidly sought their involvement."[62] As Lembcke notes, this alliance was crucial because it countered the efforts of the Nixon Administration to weaken liberal support for amnesty by constructing a symbolic conflict between the "evil" of the antiwar movement and the heroic "goodness" of returning veterans. As Lembcke's research on veterans and my own study of American resisters in Canada confirm, there was in reality much more cooperation than conflict between resisters and veterans who opposed the war.

Agnew's Attack

Vice-President Spiro Agnew staked out the Nixon Administration's position on amnesty in a speech to the national convention of the Veterans of Foreign Wars in August 1972. Agnew seized on McGovern's Miami hotel lobby statement in support of a "general amnesty" as the point of attack. "The President has announced that he is opposed to the granting of any general or unconditional amnesty for those who evaded the draft," Agnew asserted. "He believes that, when the war is over and our prisoners are released, anyone who has evaded the draft must pay a penalty before receiving a pardon."[63]

For Agnew and the Nixon Administration, there were guilty parties: not only the resisters in Canada, but also antiwar groups that were supporting an amnesty. The vice-president asserted that a general amnesty "would tear the country apart" and that "it would be a cruel affront to those servicemen who were seriously wounded in battle and who lie now in veterans' hospitals unable to rejoin their families or to resume active lives as civilians." In this way Agnew sought to drive a wedge between liberal and more radical supporters of amnesty, making the liberal supporters more vulnerable to criticism and therefore less willing to fight for a broad and meaningful amnesty law.

Nixon's 1972 landslide election was built around a series of wedge issues and slogans—including "amnesty, acid, and abortion."[64] Perhaps more disconcerting to those supporting amnesty was that although McGovern called for an amnesty a year before the election, by the following September he had excluded military resisters from his plan, and in October he recommended alternative service for draft resisters.

Paths to Paris

Back in Toronto, life went on much as before, in part because little had been expected from the American election anyway. The Toronto Anti-Draft Program continued to counsel resisters, but Danny Zimmerman, who was running the program, noted that most resisters expected to stay in Canada permanently.[65] Jack Colhoun felt that the predominant attitude at TADP and among resisters more generally was "amnesty, who cares, we like it here, but it would be nice to visit parents."[66] The work of TADP and other counseling groups now mainly consisted of reviewing draft cases to exploit the possibility of getting charges dropped and helping deserters to get undesirable discharges as easily as possible.

Colhoun and Amex had taken the lead in maintaining and building support for amnesty in Toronto, which would at best be a long and uphill struggle.[67] Amex hosted small spring and summer conferences on the issue. Dee Knight returned to Toronto after his work in the McGovern campaign. Amex agreed to co-host, with Safe Return, an amnesty conference to be held in early 1973 in Paris.

One path to Paris led through London and Fritz Efaw, who had made contact with Amex before the 1972 Democratic Convention. Efaw had the first glimmer of an idea that would result in his own nomination for vice-president on an amnesty platform four years later. His initial idea was a modest suggestion for the 1972 convention. "I think you in Canada," Efaw wrote from the Union of American Exiles in Britain, "should put a lot of pressure on the Democratic Party to let someone in to the convention to represent exiles in Canada. I don't want to here because there aren't enough of us to claim to represent."[68] Dee Knight was unable to respond to Efaw until after the convention, but he then reported his lobbying efforts for Amex and his work with Safe Return.[69] This marked the beginning of a long working relationship between Efaw and Knight that was to produce dramatic results.

Efaw's assessment that there "aren't enough of us" in England was a reference to organized resistance. The American expatriate community in London was large and affluent. Dee Knight recalled that they "were much more middle-class . . . you know, [Bill] Clinton was one of them . . . He was your basic Oxford draft dodger . . . They tended to be upper-middle-class college kids who went to England . . . and stayed there as draft resisters."[70] Another resister from Britain wrote, "They are made up of wealthy Americans who became involved after the Chicago Convention and were involved through the McGovern campaign. These are the people of the cocktail parties with Paul Newman and Gore Vidal."[71] Nonetheless, by December 1972 Fritz Efaw was able to say that the growing Union of American Exiles in Britain would be represented at the planned Paris Conference.[72]

Unfortunately, at the last minute President Nixon asked French President Georges Pompidou to ban the Paris meeting. Pompidou did so, and the conference was called off.[73] Still, all was not lost. The Amex representatives held underground talks with some veterans and exiles. A group also met with Jean-Paul Sartre, who wrote a letter that was published in *Amex* supporting an unconditional amnesty. Perhaps most important for future developments, Knight and Colhoun met Efaw and established a direct link into European resistance activities. Meetings with representatives from Vietnam Veterans Against the War strengthened a tie to GI groups by establishing that veterans with less-than-honorable discharges needed amnesty too. Against the backdrop of the failed Paris conference, it was easy to overlook the significance of the newly developing ties to Efaw and VVAW, and difficult to imagine how important these ties would prove to be to the American amnesty movement.

Two Meetings in May

What turned out to be a prolonged end game in the struggle for amnesty began in May 1973 with two meetings, set in Washington and Toronto so that both Americans and American war resisters in Canada could take part. The meetings visibly brought together representatives of veteran and resistance groups, again contradicting the Nixon Administration's suggestion that these groups were polarized. Though these groups were not in opposition, they did need to be brought together. Jerry Lembcke observes that "without a script for the occasion, these two parties, whose roles in the war were so different, did not always know what to say to each other."[74] Women emerged from the substructure of the movement leadership to serve as a bridge between veterans and resisters.[75] Gold Star Mother Louise Ransom and Irma Zigas of the War Resisters League and Women Strike for Peace helped organize the conferences and create a national coalition group.

A result of the Washington and Toronto conferences was the establishment of the National Coalition for Universal and Unconditional Amnesty (NCUUA), which would soon become the most important force for amnesty in the United States. A distinctive feature of this coalition of liberal and radical groups was its statement of purpose, centering on two firm principles. First was the link between amnesty and war in general: the purpose of the NCUUA was "to mobilize the American people to work for an universal and unconditional amnesty . . . and . . . to resist any such wars in the future."

Second was a broad definition of whom the amnesty was to be for, including "not only draft resisters, but also deserters, all vets with bad paper discharges, and civilians with 'criminal' records for their opposition to the war and military racism." A significant feature of this second principle was that it redrew the line of what could be considered acceptable forms of war resistance to a point that could conceivably include acts of violent protest. The more liberal members of the NCUUA were uncomfortable with such radical principles, yet they accepted them, probably because of the credibility that the active support of the exile (Amex) and veteran (VVAW) groups gave the coalition.

A Parting of Ways

The period from 1972 through 1973 brought major changes at Amex, the organization that Stan Pietlock had begun in the late 1960s in Toronto. Dee Knight and Jack Colhoun were doing the bulk of the amnesty reporting, while Pietlock continued to do a lot of nonamnesty editorial work. Pietlock acknowledged the need for the amnesty work, but he was more committed to becoming a Canadian. The extent of this commitment became clear when Pietlock published a photograph of his new Canadian citizenship card in the fall 1972 issue of *Amex*. Pietlock was reframing his national identity in a very public way.

Amex thus had a mixed identity that was perhaps characteristic of resisters' lives in Canada. However, the balance of power at the organization was shifting away from Pietlock. The group was always looking for help, and most of the new workers were committed to amnesty work. Steve Grossman and Evangeline Mix were typical of the newer members of the organization. Grossman had left Chicago at the end of 1972 as his trial date was approaching before Judge Julius Hoffman, who had presided over the Chicago Seven Conspiracy trial. Grossman and Mix had done community organization work in Ohio and had met Dee Knight at the Democratic Convention in Miami. Identifying as exiles, the two became major supporters of the exile cause within the Amex collective.

By the fall of 1973 Pietlock felt that the amnesty work of Amex was becoming counterproductive to his own and other resisters' lives in Canada. He acknowledged the relevance of such work, but he argued that "*Amex* is not that crucial to the fight for amnesty, a fight which is ultimately going to be won in the U.S. anyway."[76] Pietlock believed that the work of Amex should come to a close. In contrast, most of the staff saw the organization's aim as balancing the needs of amnesty and assimilation, with the amnesty issue requiring a voice and a collective base that the immigrants' natural assimilation into the Canadian environment did not require. As a letter written to Pietlock in the name of the Amex staff put it, "Amnesty relates to a large portion of the exile community as a general need. It cannot be accomplished individually. Assimilation also relates to a large portion of the exile community. It, however, can be accomplished individually."⁷⁷ Dee Knight also wrote to Pietlock regarding the ambivalent relationship between assimilation and amnesty in resisters' lives in Canada. "Are you an exile, an expatriate, or a Canadian?" Knight asked rhetorically. "Once you've made a choice, each of us has the tendency not only to defend that choice very fiercely, but also to fight over why it's the best choice."⁷⁸ This reframing of national identity was, in the temper of the times, both political and personal.

Pietlock chose to leave Amex permanently and prepared a piece to be published explaining his reasons for leaving. "What disturbs me most," Pietlock wrote, "is the recent but clearly identifiable growth of U.S. chauvinism around the AMEX office." In a handwritten note added to the prepared text, Pietlock raised the issue of a survey that *Amex* had done of its readers on the subject of amnesty, asking, "Whatever happened to the AMEX survey? You shouldn't be afraid, really, of what it showed."⁷⁹ This survey, never reported in *Amex*, is discussed in the following chapter. It exemplifies the continuing doubts that resisters in Canada had about an American amnesty.

Pietlock and the staff of *Amex* finally resolved many of their differences in 1973, with Pietlock agreeing to transfer the magazine into Knight and Colhoun's hands. Twenty-five years later, Stan Pietlock expressed his regret that "those guys never did get real jobs in Canada and always seemed to want to go back to the States." Traces of the conflict were still there, but the parties at the time resolved their differences responsibly, in the interest of the resistance effort. Even at the peak of the conflict, Stan Pietlock had signed his letters, "Yours for universal, unconditional amnesty."⁸⁰

The Ball and the Boycott

It was not until late 1973 and early 1974 that NCUUA, at the urging of Amex, began to move ahead in its amnesty efforts. It did so initially in the form of a U.S. speaking tour by Dee Knight and other American Vietnam war resisters from Canada on behalf of sentence reductions for two imprisoned military resisters, Dick Bucklin and Robert Johnson. The following report by Dee Knight gives some sense of both the growing intensity of the amnesty effort and the unheralded day-to-day leadership that women were providing.

> Sandy Rutherford and I are on the road now trying to drum up support. She and Sarah Clemens in Toronto, and I, were in Wilmington, Delaware, and Philadelphia (30 miles away) early this week, doing radio, TV and press interviews on amnesty, and I go back there this weekend for more of the same, as well as some public meetings on it. There is considerable interest in the issue again, and the media exposure we got this week was just tremendous. We were on four different shows on the same NBC affiliate in Philadelphia in two days, as well as talking to editors and columnists of newspapers in both Philly and Wilmington, and doing public broadcasting service TV interviews and cable, and radio talk shows. We also talked with two amnesty study groups in Wilmington, and I am to be a panel member of a "Perspective on Amnesty" debate in Wilmington this Sunday, as well as talking to two different congregations that morning. Hopefully we will set up "Friends of Amnesty/NCUUA" groups in both cities and in others as we go along. I am told that Dan Zimmerman and Katie McGovern are now ready to do some speaking, as well as Tim Maloney, and the three other women from Vancouver and two more from Toronto, and we are working hard to get dates and fees taken care of so this can get going. AMEX sent out letters to about 50 college contacts in upstate and western New York the first week in March, and hopefully we'll have dates there soon. Sandy intends to stop in Los Angeles, and possibly San Francisco, on her return to Vancouver from the east to get things set up there. In Vancouver she will be working with people interested in participating in the campaign, as will Sarah Clemens and Jack Colhoun in Toronto. This is important work, and all who wish to participate are needed.[81]

There is an echo in this description of Charles Payne's observation in his analysis of black women's activism in the Mississippi Delta that "men led, but women organized."[82] Yet even with further help from congressional supporters such as Pat Schroeder and Bella Abzug, the Bucklin-Johnson initiative did not result in sentence reductions.[83] It did, however, demonstrate that Amex and NCUUA could organize on a national scale.

The summer of 1974 brought the U.S. House Judiciary Committee televised impeachment hearings. Nixon's landslide reelection had made the prospects of amnesty appear positively utopian, but his prospective impeachment again made the impossible seem plausible. Amex planned a Toronto concert provocatively called "The Impeachment Ball." Bill King, then a rock musician and now artistic director of the Toronto Beaches' Annual Summer Jazz Festival, agreed to headline the early August 1974 concert. When Nixon announced his resignation, Amex retitled the event the "Impeachment Victory Ball" and hosted a successful evening of celebration that attracted several hundred exiles and Canadians.[84]

The resignation and subsequent pardon of Nixon by the new president, Gerald Ford, jolted the exile community back to life. In August 1974 they were confronted with the juxtaposition of Ford's "full, free and absolute pardon" of the disgraced Richard Nixon with a proposed "earned re-entry program" for resisters, who, in Ford's judgment, "committed the supreme folly of shirking their duty" and therefore would need to accept "penalties to suit the individual mistakes."[85] This conditional, individualized, punitive program was, of course, far from the demands of Amex and NCUUA.

Within days a paid advertisement placed by Amex in the *New York Times* rejected Ford's initiative by emphasizing NCUUA's two primary expectations of an amnesty program: that all resisters be included and that the error of the war be acknowledged. The ad observed that if Ford's plan was accepted, "we would be separating ourselves from the majority who need amnesty: the half million veterans with less than honorable discharges. The proposal also excludes those thousands with 'criminal' records or subject to prosecution for acts of opposition to the U.S. war in Indochina." The ad went on to call for a more meaningful discussion: "Mr. Ford's position still calls for milder punishment and thus does not even begin to confront the war honestly."[86] Just a week after Ford's August speech, Amex announced that from September 21 to 23 it would host a NCUUA-sponsored international conference in Toronto.[87] Fritz Efaw attended, strengthening the relationship between himself and Amex.

After several delays, and his unconditional pardon of Richard Nixon, President Ford formally announced his conditional clemency program for war resisters on September 16, 1974. The program required up to two years of alternative public service and "a reaffirmation of allegiance to the United States."[88] A spokesman for the American Exile Project in Sweden called Ford's plan "punishment not amnesty."[89] A *Toronto Globe and Mail* editorial observed that "the President of their country offered a better deal to his predecessor who tried to destroy the democratic institutions of their country than he did to them."[90] When the International Conference of Exiled American War Resisters met over the weekend of September 21–22 at the University of Toronto, delegates from Sweden, France, England, and nine cities in Canada voted unanimously to boycott Ford's punitive reentry program.

The Ford Fall

Amex and NCUUA were not the only organizations working on amnesty in the fall of 1974. In late August, Clergy and Laity Concerned (CALC) organized the delivery to the White House of a petition with 50,000 signatures calling for an unconditional amnesty, and Safe Return organized a delegation of parents and families of resisters to lobby Congress and the justice and defense departments. "My son doesn't have to apologize for anything," said the mother of one fugitive. "He was going in the Peace Corps when Nixon cut off deferments. He was willing to perform alternative service then but not now."[91] Attorney General William Saxbe appeared on the *Today* show the same day and conceded that what the parents and families were saying was true: relatively few resisters were likely to enter the program. Saxbe said, "They don't want to have to come back and say, 'we were wrong.'"[92]

Kristine King went to Washington to represent her deserter husband, Bill King, after receiving an invitation to join the Safe Return Amnesty Committee's lobbying group. Kristine recalled that her contribution began when "Safe Return Amnesty called out of the blue and flew me down to Washington with this other girl . . . They flew us down there and they just said, 'You're going to lobby your congressmen for amnesty.'" Kristine was part of a group of three hundred relatives of exiles flown in from all over the country. "We got off the plane from Toronto and literally had all the television cameras and microphones in our faces the second we stepped off the plane. We started doing interviews right there." Next there were meetings with Bella Abzug and others, followed by appointments with congressmen and senators. Otis Pike was Kristine's congressman; she remembered that her mother had worked for his campaign. This connection notwithstanding, Kristine recalls Pike greeting her by saying, "Well, young lady, you can come in; but I already know why you're here so I'm going to tell you right off the bat that I am totally against amnesty and nothing you can say will change my mind." This attitude angered Kristine so much that she launched into her planned speech without stopping to sit down. "I blurted out everything I had to say. When I finished, I shook his hand and said, 'Thank you very much,' turned around, left his office, got on a plane, and went back to Toronto." Safe Return called later to say she was the only person who actually changed someone's mind. King's success may have reflected the beginning of a shift in public and political opinion.

Amex maintained its presence by organizing fall and winter speaking tours in the United States. The Ford clemency program allowed resisters to reenter the country for a two-week period in anticipation of beginning the clemency process. Although they had no intention of pursuing the Ford program, first Steve Grossman and Evangeline Mix and then Gerry Condon took advantage of the two-week periods to travel around the United States speaking about the need for a universal and unconditional amnesty.[93]

Steve Grossman introduced his tour in a speech at the second NCUUA conference in Louisville, Kentucky. The partnership of Evangeline Mix with Grossman helped to underscore the role of women, too frequently ignored in the press. Mix herself saw this issue quite clearly: "The media would come in, ignore the women completely, treat them as nonentities, and center on the men. This is understandable, given the society, but hard to live with, especially when you have shared all the decisions, the work, the pain, the uncertainty, the consequences of exile."[94] Mix went on to conduct her own Indochina Mobile Education Project with a traveling van in 1975 and 1976.

Gerry Condon's tour was introduced by Ramsey Clark, the former attorney general from the Johnson Administration. Condon, who was known as the "Green Beret deserter" and lived in Vancouver and Toronto before beginning his four-and-a-half-month speaking tour, covered every region of the country and did not end until June 1975. His tour attracted the attention of cartoonist Garry Trudeau, who ran four *Doonesbury* strips featuring two resisters speaking with the press. These cartoons highlighted the inequity of Ford's pardon of Nixon and the clemency program, and resisters' indifference and skepticism of the clemency program; they also noted that life in Canada was not such a hardship.

By October 1974 it was apparent that Ford's clemency program was attracting little response.[95] The largest group to go through the program were military resisters already in custody, who were allowed to transfer into the program when it began.[96] By the end of December only 3 percent of those eligible for the program had applied.[97] Vernon Jordan, a former civil rights leader and an early member of the Ford Clemency Board, delivered a telling postmortem. "While most of the public's attention has been focused on 50,000 or so war resisters," Jordan reported, "total amnesty should include the more than 650,000 Vietnam-era veterans who hold less than honorable discharges, which amount to lifetime penalties keeping them from government and many private sector jobs, and from rights and benefits enjoyed by other veterans." Jordan's remarks could not have been better scripted by Amex and NCUUA. He added, "It's time to finally end the war by declaring complete, immediate, universal, and unconditional amnesty. In my year on the board I learned that the case-by-case treatment just won't work."[98]

The original closing date for the clemency program was the end of January 1975,[99] at which point Jack Colhoun pronounced the boycott a victory.[100] President Ford refused to concede defeat, granting two one-month extensions rather than ending the program.[101] Amex, NCUUA, and other groups continued to urge a boycott, however, and when the program finally came to an end only 19 percent of the eligible participants had taken part.[102] The boycott was a public relations victory and paved the way for the final push toward a more meaningful amnesty.

The Fight for Amnesty Continues

Phil Ochs may never have sung his famous song "I Declare the War Is Over" as movingly as he did on May 11, 1975, before the more than 50,000 people who had marched and demonstrated and now filled the Sheep Meadow in New York City's Central Park in celebration of peace in Vietnam and Cambodia. Saigon had finally fallen, or been liberated, depending on your point of view. The event was celebrated by more than a hundred antiwar groups. The *New York Times* described it as "a joyous all-day carnival of songs and speeches in perfect sunshine" in a meadow full of "hugging reunions of people."[103] Paul Simon, Joan Baez, Pete Seeger, and Peter Yarrow joined with Tom Paxton, Richie Havens, Odetta, Harry Belafonte, and others to sing about peace and protest. Anita Hoffman, wife of Abbie, and their child, America, played in the grass. Still, there were reminders of unfinished business, especially the issue of amnesty. Congresswoman Elizabeth Holtzman from Brooklyn established the refrain that echoed through the speeches: "It's finally happened! It's real! The only unfinished business is to bring our boys home—total and complete amnesty for all."

Meanwhile, Fritz Efaw in London was in regular contact with Amex in Canada and with representatives of the Democratic Party in the United States. In the beginning Efaw made both nervous. Dee Knight recalled, "We had very mixed feelings because we knew that Fritz was a little squishy on the politics of amnesty—he was actually closer to the mainstream liberal position on amnesty and war resisters than we were."[104] Efaw made the mainstream Democrats even more uncomfortable. When Efaw cornered Hubert Humphrey and George McGovern about amnesty at a November 1974 Democratic fund-raiser in London, Efaw reported to the Union of American Exiles in Britain that "both senators were non-committal on the subject, insisting that amnesty was an executive issue, and not something to be dealt with by Congress."[105] Efaw added, "A couple of right schmucks they are, too, and the same in spades for all their champagne swilling friends from Hampstead and Belgravia."[106]

Regardless of misgivings or potential cross-purposes, a new set of potentially fateful relationships was emerging between Jack Colhoun and Amex in Toronto, Fritz Efaw and the exile groups in London, and Dee Knight and NCUUA in New York. Amex formed the moral and emotional center of this axis in Toronto, but Efaw's efforts in London and Knight's efforts in New York City were becoming increasingly important. All of the participants also felt bonded to the veterans' groups, especially Vietnam Veterans Against the War.

National Amnesty Week

For the war resisters and amnesty groups, the 1976 presidential campaign began with the declaration of a "National Amnesty Week" in February 1976. The previous spring and summer had seen a shift in public opinion, as reflected in prominent editorials cautiously conceding the case for unconditional amnesty. A *New York Times* editorial in May 1975 concluded that "the danger that full amnesty may absolve some whose motives were surely questionable is a far lesser risk than saddling the nation's conscience with this singular exception to the spirit of the new beginning." The *Washington Star* and the *Boston Globe* adopted similar positions.[107] Amex saw the change in mood as an opportunity to act and urged NCUUA to call for a week of public education and support of a full amnesty. NCUUA agreed, and announced that National Amnesty Week would be held February 22–28, as the beginning of its crucial 1976 program.[108]

Fritz Efaw could feel the shift in mood as far away as England. He wrote jointly to Amex and NCUUA that his group, now called the Union of American Exiles and Concerned Americans, was planning to mark National Amnesty Week at the same time as in the United States by holding a Vietnam vigil each noon hour in the front of the U.S. embassy in London. Efaw wanted to go beyond this, suggesting that he could be nominated by Democrats Abroad as a delegate to the 1976 Democratic Convention. He noted that "there are clear advantages to having an actual draft dodger on the convention floor to talk to delegates, but this clearly would require close coordination with NCUUA people in New York, and I wouldn't consider it unless the idea had full backing from NCUUA and you."[109] National Amnesty Week was still in the planning stages, but everyone, including Efaw, saw the 1976 Democratic Convention looming on the horizon.

Amex and NCUUA were both initially cautious about Efaw's ambitions and responded primarily by encouraging his lobbying efforts in connection with National Amnesty Week and hearings among Democrats to be held in London.[110] Efaw's energies would not so easily or very long be diverted; however, for the moment everyone recognized the importance of making the week-long amnesty event a success. Amex played a central role in developing the concept, the plan, and the publishing of a local community *Organizing Guide* for the week-long observance. The opening day of Amnesty Week was highlighted on the *CBS Evening News* with Bob Schiefer, and featured interviews with several draft and military resisters. Governor Michael Dukakis of Massachusetts and the governors of a dozen other states and many more mayors officially proclaimed National Amnesty Week. More than three hundred activities were held across the nation. In Washington, Senator Philip Hart of Michigan helped organize a Congressional Amnesty Conference held at the end of the week. The conference was moderated by journalist Martin Agronsky and involved a diverse group of participants, from I. F. Stone to Geraldo Rivera from the news media, to Steve Grossman and Gerry Condon from Amex.[111] The events of the week established that amnesty was a national political issue that demanded attention, especially from the Democratic Party, since many party members displayed their support. Even Fritz Efaw was able to report from London that "our demonstrations at the U.S. Embassy during N.A.W. were fairly well-attended, though not huge."[112]

The Primaries and the Platform

National Amnesty Week was barely over when the presidential primaries began. Steve Grossman and Jack Colhoun in Toronto and Gerry Condon in the United States began focusing on the primaries as soon as the week ended. Democratic candidate Jimmy Carter's pledge of a "Vietnam pardon" quickly emerged as a focal point. Carter introduced his pledge by saying, "I think those kids who have lived in Sweden or in Canada or have avoided arrest have been punished enough." Then Carter drew a distinction between an amnesty and a pardon: "In my opinion, amnesty says what you did was right. Pardon says whether what you did was right or wrong, you are forgiven for it." Carter pledged only to give an unconditional pardon to the draft resisters. "For those who deserted due to their opposition to the Vietnam war, I would not issue a blanket pardon, but would treat them on a case by case basis."[113]

Carter's position appealed to liberals by providing an unconditional pardon to draft resisters, while his refusal to use the term "amnesty" and his case-by-case approach to military resistance appeased the conservatives. Canada's immigration policies more fully and inclusively accepted, and indeed welcomed, both draft and military resisters into its midst, making their acceptance a symbol of Canada's own national sovereignty. Carter's war amnesty institutionalized a symbolic and instrumental dualism by more narrowly reabsorbing draft resisters and by selectively, restrictively, and punitively responding to military resisters with less than honorable discharges, which could relegate them to the margins of society by denying them access to many jobs.

The fact that so many Americans still believe that Carter implemented a sweeping amnesty is probably a reflection of how powerful the desire to forget the underlying issues in Vietnam remains today. The desire of Amex and, to a lesser but still significant extent, NCUUA was to put the moral issue of the war and its legacy in the damaged lives of many resisters, especially military resisters, front and center in the American consciousness. Amex and NCUUA attempted to raise this consciousness in the Democratic presidential primaries and party platform hearings, and then at the convention itself.

Despite such efforts, most candidates concluded that taking a position on amnesty did not attract votes. NCUUA's biggest preconvention victory came at a mid-June meeting of Democrats writing the final 1976 party platform in Washington. Former antiwar activist Sam Brown introduced a motion to be included in the platform calling for an unconditional pardon for "those who are in legal and financial jeopardy because of their peaceful opposition to the Vietnam War." This motion narrowly passed, but Brown then accepted an amendment proposed by one of Jimmy Carter's influential aides, Stuart Eizenstadt, saying that military resisters should be treated on a case-by-case basis. Eizenstadt later made it clear in an interview with Steve Grossman for *Amex* that Carter didn't plan to observe the party platform anyway, saying with specific regard to amnesty that "[Carter] has indicated that one of the first things that he would do to implement his position would be to sign a pardon for those who refused to serve and are guilty of Selective Service violations and he hasn't gone beyond that."[114] It was clear that there was a limit on how far Jimmy Carter would go on the amnesty issue, but it was also clear that the Democratic Party as a whole might be supportive of a broader amnesty than previously was apparent.[115]

The Exile Primary

"The Democratic Party comes alive here once every four years," Fritz Efaw reported from London. In the spring platform and primary season, the party mailing list swelled to over 4,000 registered British Democrats. Efaw asked to testify about amnesty at the April platform committee hearings in London and collected enough signatures to be nominated as a delegate to the Miami convention. "Overall, my chance of winning [election as a delegate] is probably small," he wrote, "but also very uncertain, and a few hundred votes coming in from Canada and Sweden could easily tip the scales in my favour." He reasoned that "a war resister is a distinctive, if stereotyped, phenomenon, and it may attract liberal and even centrist votes over the greyer shades of liberals." Efaw asked that members of Amex register and vote for him.[116]

Efaw estimated that he would need about 400 votes to be elected as a delegate.[117] When the results were tallied, Efaw had tied another candidate as the last alternate delegate with 307 votes. The rest of the candidates rallied behind Efaw, and he was included as an alternate with the necessary credentials to attend the convention. He explained that "it's a small delegation and they're anxious to make up for that by becoming identified with the amnesty issue."[118]

The planning began immediately, and it included the idea of nominating Efaw for President or Vice-President. Efaw wrote from London, "There is talk of putting my name in nomination." He went on to explain, "This would be a Julian Bond thing. You remember in 1968 when Bond was nominated and he declined because he was 28 or something? Same idea. I'd get a ten minute nominating speech, a couple of seconding speeches, and a minute or so of prime time on national telly while I decline from the floor or wherever I am." The idea was said to have originated with Ronald Dworkin, then a law professor at Oxford and the overseas delegate with the largest number of votes. Efaw realized that if this was to be done, "It has to be done with planning and in a way that is serious rather than a stunt." Efaw also pledged that his first commitment was to amnesty, NCUUA, and Amex, rather than to the delegation. "I won't commit myself to something like the VP nomination unless it has been cleared with you all. The same thing goes for everything I do at the convention."[119] He had already booked his flight before putting the letter in the mail.

An Unconventional Arrival

Within a week of Efaw's electoral coup, Jack Colhoun wrote to Efaw from Amex with a preliminary plan that he had developed with Irma Zigas, who was now playing a key bridging role at NCUUA, connecting Efaw with Colhoun, Knight, Grossman, and others. The aim of the plan was to maximize public visibility of the amnesty issue. Colhoun explained, "This includes massive leafleting, meeting in caucuses with supporters in various state delegations, and utilizing you in the best way possible. Irma probably has relayed to you our plans with respect to an airport press conference." Colhoun went on to say, "We believe the fact of your being nominated for Vice President could also be very valuable in that you'd be able to give a speech . . . Our basic concern is to build visible support within the Democratic Party for an amnesty broader than Carter's in order to put pressure on him in terms of the actual 'pardon' that he would grant."[120]

Members of Amex, including Dee Knight, Steve Grossman, and Gerry Condon, played major roles in preparing for Efaw's arrival in New York City. Dee Knight recalled, "I was charged with the challenging task of making sure that the process of bringing Fritz back galvanized the universal and unconditional piece of our amnesty demands, and we mobilized a lot for him. We had two or three other people in our Amex group come down for the convention."[121]

Knight issued a press release explaining that Fritz Efaw was the first indicted American war resister to run for a delegate seat at an American political convention, and that it was also the first time that Americans living abroad were being allowed to send delegates to the convention. The press release further described Efaw's work for five years as president of the Union of American Exiles in Britain, explained that he was still facing charges for failing to report for induction, and noted that he was still a "fugitive from justice." It stated, "Now that he is voluntarily returning to this country, he hopes the judge will not be vindictive," but added that "Fritz hopes his presence will give the other delegates a sense of urgency about amnesty."[122] When Fritz Efaw walked off the plane he was immediately seized by law enforcement agents.

Dee Knight recalls the scene at the airport and the following events, all of which were well planned to maximize public attention to the amnesty cause.

> I had coordinated a press conference and we had mobilized the reporters to come to the airport to be there for his arrival, and so he was seized on . . . local television. It was splashed in the news, which was part of our tactic. And then the next day he had to show up . . . in federal court in Brooklyn, so we organized another media event for then, as well as organized petitions on the floor of the convention, you know, calling for him to be let out of jail, so he could carry out his role as an alternate delegate—and it was tremendously effective. The fact that he had gotten nabbed meant that our people could go to the delegates on the floor with petitions . . . So we presented a petition to the judge and the judge let him out. He released him. Like it was just a string of victories that we had with him. We did it through mobilizing when he went to court and effectively using publicity to get him out. As soon as we saw that we had him sprung, we said let's keep using these petitions and get him nominated for Vice President. But it was always part of our vision that we had to do petitions to have him nominated for Vice President. That was the whole point of the exercise.[123]

On the Friday following his Thursday arrival, Fritz Efaw went to court in Brooklyn, where his court appearance on the draft charges was postponed until July 26 in Oklahoma City, leaving him plenty of time to attend the convention.

Kovic and Efaw's Convention

NCUUA opened its office in the Statler-Hilton Hotel on Sunday and began its petitioning for Efaw's vice-presidential nomination.[124] The momentum behind this effort was building quickly, and the Carter forces saw it coming. On Monday they first offered Efaw five minutes of speaking time on an amendment to open floor debate of the party platform in exchange for his giving

up the vice-presidential nomination. As soon as he refused this, he was offered ten minutes. On Tuesday, a Carter aide appeared before the Democrats
Abroad delegation to say that Carter did not want the nomination of Efaw to
happen and that if it did NCUUA would be denounced on television as "self-
indulgent publicity seekers." By Wednesday objections were being raised to
Fritz Efaw's age, and NCUUA forces countered by beginning a second petition for Gold Star Mother Louise Ransom as a back-up nominee in case Efaw
was ruled out of order.

One week following Fritz Efaw's return to the United States, the day of
the vice-presidential nomination arrived. Two pivotal decisions were made:
Louise Ransom, as a Gold Star Mother, would give the first nomination
speech; and Ron Kovic, the disabled Vietnam War veteran and author of
Born on the Fourth of July, would give the seconding speech. Twenty-five
years later, Dee Knight commented that Kovic's involvement was essential
for at least two reasons. First, Kovic's role in the nomination symbolized the
joining of war resisters and veterans in support of amnesty: "To forge a bond
between the war resisters and the veterans, to completely obliterate the
main argument against amnesty . . . and then to combine this with having
Louise Ransom . . . was, I think, a political, theatrical achievement that we
can be proud of." Second, Kovic further symbolized the goal of the amnesty
effort to reach far beyond the draft dodgers: "to make it clear that it wasn't a
handful, a relative handful of draft dodgers abroad who needed amnesty
nearly so much as it was America as a whole, and an enormous number, half
a million military veterans, who were suffering significantly more than the
draft resisters."[125] The major elements of the event were in place, but there
remained significant obstacles to be overcome.

Late Thursday afternoon Harold Ickes said that Kovic would not be able to
speak because the podium in the convention hall could not accommodate
a wheelchair. NCUUA countered that they had managed to let Governor
George Wallace speak, so they had better find a way to let Ron Kovic speak.
"He will speak, even if we have to carry him up and hold him on our shoul-
ders to the microphone," the notes of the day report.[126]

Louise Ransom's nominating speech was a perfect example of bridge
building. She began with a promise to campaign for the Carter–Mondale
ticket, then moved into her own painful message, which combined the personal and the political. Ransom said that she had earned her credentials to
address the convention in the hardest possible way: "My oldest son was
killed in Vietnam on Mother's Day, 1968." She expressed her concern for

the more than one million Americans, the largest portion of whom, she said, are poor and black and in special need of amnesty, and asserted, "Total amnesty would be a fitting memorial to the sacrifice of my son." She concluded that it was "with pride I put into nomination the name of the exiled war resister, Fritz Efaw." When Louise Ransom finished her speech, the crowd came to its feet, applauding in a prolonged, cresting wave of emotion.

Ron Kovic was next. Many will recall the image of Kovic wheeling to the podium at the Democratic National Convention, either from their memories of the television coverage of that day or from its reenactment by Tom Cruise in the film version of *Born on the Fourth of July*. (The film included only parts of Kovic's speech and did not explain that it was given to second the nomination of Fritz Efaw for the purpose of bringing the issue of amnesty to the full attention of the convention.)

Kovic's speech, delivered to an audience that had fallen into rapt and respectful silence, told the story of his two tours of duty in Vietnam and his resistance against the war since returning. He described his early feelings of patriotism and his growing disillusionment with the war. Kovic then told of mistakenly killing one of his own men and how his squad accidentally shot a group of innocent civilians, including two young children. He went on to describe his experiences as a paralyzed war veteran in the slumlike conditions of American VA hospitals and his ultimate radicalization when students were killed at Kent State. Kovic noted the hostility his opposition to the war had aroused, recalling that "once in front of the Re-elect Nixon Headquarters in Los Angeles in 1972 I was thrown out of my wheelchair— my medals torn off my chest—and kicked and beaten by the police. I was arrested numerous other times with other Vietnam veterans, and spent five days sitting in my wheelchair in the Los Angeles County Jail. I was cursed at, spat at, threatened, and called a traitor." None of this diminished Ron Kovic's conviction that the war was wrong and that amnesty was right. He announced to the convention that "tonight, nearly four years later, I now have the proud distinction of nominating Fritz Efaw for Vice President of the United States. Welcome Home, Fritz."[127] Efaw was now on the podium too, embracing Kovic before a crowd that was again on its feet, many now in tears, most cheering, with amnesty banners criss-crossing the convention floor and twisting through the various delegations with their demands for universal and unconditional amnesty floating above the crowd.

Finally, Efaw had the floor and the opportunity to make the case for universal and unconditional amnesty that Carter had ignored. Efaw began by explaining to the convention, and a television audience that may have included as many as 60 million Americans, who he was and why he was speaking.

I am an alternate delegate from Democrats Abroad. I am also an indicted Vietnam War resister who has returned to address this convention after seven years in exile in London, England.

The Democratic Party's platform has taken an important step in calling for the full and complete pardon for all of those persons in legal and financial jeopardy because of their opposition to the war in Indochina. If I had waited until early next year to come home, Governor Carter's promised pardon would have included me.

I have not waited. I have chosen to come home at the risk of imprisonment to tell you more about those Americans in jeopardy because we must insure that all of them are included in next January's presidential pardon.

I have come a very long way to be here tonight, and I still have a long way to go. The Democratic Party has come a long way in understanding the issue, but we too, have a long way to go.

For seven years I have watched this country from afar, as it was shaken to its roots by a Republican administration that vilified people like me. They spoke of law and order, but these men—men like Spiro Agnew, John Mitchell, and Richard Nixon, have shown themselves willing to violate the law far more violently than I ever was. I left America at the beginning of that administration. Now I have returned at what, I hope, will be its end. But the legacy of the war remains.

Over one million Americans continue to be punished for their acts of opposition to the war and to the arbitrary nature of the military system during the war.

Although I came from a fairly poor family, I was able to attend college because of a scholarship. This meant that when I went to England I could expect to find work. My brother, no less opposed to the war, couldn't go to college and couldn't get a job after high school. He joined the Navy, rather than be drafted into the army in Vietnam.

The great majority of draft-eligible American men were never drafted, by virtue of deferments, loopholes, privileges—and luck. Hundreds of thousands of less privileged men only came to understand the unjust nature of the war after they experienced it first hand. There were over 432,000 war-era desertions. Some people object that the deserters left their units on the battlefield. But less than one percent of Vietnam war era desertions were under battlefield conditions.

There is no justification for tying up the lives of tens of thousands in lengthy legal procedures in order to weed out those few. A case by case review is a provenly slow and inefficient mechanism.

The great majority of these men came from poor families; they often had little education; a disproportionate number of them are black—victims of a war that Governor Carter has rightly called racist.

Dissent within the military took forms other than desertion. Less than honorable discharges were often the result of anti-war activities—the great majority for actions that are not crimes in civilian life. Ninety percent of these discharges were imposed without trial. People with such discharges are virtually unemployable today. They are still paying for opposition to a war that most members of this party have come to realize was unjust. These people must be included in the pardon of a new Democratic administration.

Eight years of Republican administration have exacerbated divisions in our society that are deeper than at any time since the civil war. The Democratic party can now confront the divisive lingering problems of the Vietnam era with a truly broad amnesty which includes all of the war's victims: civilian and military resisters, deserters, and veterans with less than fully honorable discharges—over one million in all.

My family in Atlanta had grave reservations about my coming home—they were afraid for my sake. But I was not afraid, and I believe this Party will stand with me.

The burdens of the war fell unequally on different people in our nation. The wounds of war can only be healed if President Carter proclaims an equal amnesty for all the war's victims.

I am proud to come to this convention to represent war resisters. The risk involved in coming before you was certainly worth taking. I respectfully decline nomination for Vice President of the United States. I seek no office, and no further recognition.[128]

All three television networks carried the speech live, allowing an enormous viewing audience to experience vicariously first the pensive hush and then the thunderous ovation generated by Efaw's remarks within the convention hall. Kovic and Efaw embraced again, and then Efaw pushed Kovic in his wheelchair back and forth across the convention hall, followed by a parade of supporters carrying banners for universal and unconditional amnesty.

The next morning, newspapers across the nation carried pictures and stories about the event. The *New York Daily News* perhaps best captured the moment with its headline, "Hero Asks Amnesty for Viet Deserters." Jack Colhoun and others watched the events unfold from Toronto, where they knew that although they were in another country, they were very much a part of it all. Colhoun wrote, "The 1976 Democratic National Convention was the amnesty movement's stage. It was the dedicated core of amnesty activists, working day and night at the convention, who injected some reality into an otherwise banal political celebration. But without similar tireless efforts by amnesty activists throughout the U.S., none of it would have happened."[129]

Carter's Anticlimax

The amnesty movement had put all of its knowledge and resources to work in the several months leading up to National Amnesty Week in February 1976 and then over the six months following, leading into the Democratic Convention in July. Dee Knight felt that by this time, "We understood the political dynamics, Fritz had the guts and clarity of mind to not only come up with the idea but to stay focused . . . The relationships that we had forged and developed through those years really came into play—most importantly that we had forged with Ron Kovic, and I think that the experiences of what we had learned about how to intervene effectively in the political arena came into play as well."[130] Still, the work was not finished.

Amex now undertook a radio talk-show campaign in the United States.[131] Steve Grossman and Jack Colhoun did most of the interviews over the phone from Toronto. Grossman also led a segment of the War Resisters League Continental Walk for Disarmament and Social Change across the Peace Bridge that linked Ontario and New York at Niagara Falls. The symbolism of the potential return of American Vietnam war exiles to the United States was unmistakable.

Fritz Efaw also helped kick off a national week of support for amnesty between January 8 and 16, 1977. In his press release, Efaw wrote, "It is time for politicians to stop shifting the blame for the death and destruction of the Vietnam War back and forth between resisters and vets, and to place responsibility for the war and its consequences where it belongs—with the policy makers who led us into war and vindictively seek to punish those opposed to the war and to ignore and exploit veterans of the war."[132]

But as much as it might have seemed to those involved that the amnesty movement was maintaining momentum, it was not. Jimmy Carter was now the Democratic presidential nominee, and his challenge was from the Republican right rather than from the Democratic left. Carter's election that fall did not improve things. Charles Kirbo, a "white-shoe" Atlanta lawyer, became the point person with whom amnesty representatives met. Ron Kovic and Gerry Condon joined a nine-member delegation that met with Kirbo in Atlanta on December 8, 1976. Kirbo was stubborn on the "deserter" issue, stressing the need to support military discipline.

President Jimmy Carter had his press secretary, Jody Powell, announce his oft-discussed pardon on his first day in office, January 21, 1977. The unconditional pardon covered indicted and convicted draft resisters and non-registrants, but it excluded deserters and less-than-honorably-discharged veterans. A Pentagon study was commissioned to consider remedies for the latter groups. The public and Congress's response to Carter's pardon was resoundingly negative. Politically, amnesty was a "nonstarter" for the Carter Administration. Consequently, and in contrast with the Canadian government, which had widely publicized its immigration amnesty and made special efforts to inform and include war resisters, the U.S. Congress denied funding for Carter's pardon program, and the administration did little or nothing in response.

President Carter had his secretary of defense, Harold Brown, announce the second step of the program on April 5, 1977. The plan allowed Vietnam-era deserters with no other military charges pending against them to return to "military control" to be discharged "less-than-honorably." It soon became clear this was the best deal the amnesty movement was going to extract from the Carter Administration, and for the next six months Amex served as a counseling service. Jack Colhoun now went through the amnesty program and wrote about the experience in *Amex*. Amex believed that they should publicize the second phase of the Carter program while attacking its moral and political bankruptcy.[133]

The Bus Stops Here

This chapter began with the image of the Who's Magic Bus, which may have inspired real-life efforts to find "unlanded" American war resisters who needed help in legalizing their immigration status during the 1973 Canadian immigration amnesty. These efforts overcame differences of wealth and background in extending landed immigrant status to American war resisters in Canada. The contrasting image in the United States hearkened back to a more distant, mean-spirited memory of some citizens being relegated to the "back of the bus," to use Jack Colhoun's words in an article he wrote for *The Nation* about the Carter pardon's punitive mistreatment of military resisters. Colhoun's frustration with the pardon was reflected in his conclusion: "For a President who has become a world-wide advocate of human rights, Mr. Carter has a long way to go in restoring the civil and political rights of those who resisted a war that was itself a crime against humanity."[134]

In the spring of 1977 the Carter Administration grew steadily cooler in its treatment of amnesty supporters. Initially, Amex and NCUUA worked with limited success through back channels into the White House to achieve minor concessions in the treatment of military resisters. Ultimately, however, the Carter Administration wanted to leave the amnesty issue behind. In a final act of desperation, Colhoun wrote a letter to Sam Brown, who had been an antiwar activist and was then serving in the Carter Administration.

Colhoun reminded Brown that although they both worked in the same antiwar movement, it was Brown's compromise amendment to the 1976 Democratic platform plank on amnesty that had resulted in the insertion of a "case-by-case" clause for the treatment of military resisters. Colhoun was writing Brown just after seeing him on television being sworn in by President Carter as director of a new White House program. Carter had applauded Brown's earlier work in the antiwar movement. Colhoun, outraged, wrote, "I spent ten years in that same antiwar movement both in the States and in exile, but according to the Carter pardon my antiwar commitment is not recognized at all. I'm still out in the cold. I want you to do your utmost right now while the decision-making process is still ongoing with respect to amnesty for deserters and vets." Colhoun went on to emphasize the class and racial dimensions of the pardon issue and closed by telling Brown, "I and all other deserters are counting on you to go to bat for us."[135]

Brown's response was prompt, polite, and profoundly pessimistic: "the President's position prior to the platform hearings and since then has been more limited than my own . . . I can assure you that I have raised the issue in every forum where I have had that opportunity with the President or with senior staff. Consequently, I think that my influence on that subject is exhausted."[136]

Sam Brown, the "dodger," and Jack Colhoun, the "deserter," personified the American dualism about Vietnam war resistance. It was a dualism that Canada had surmounted in its immigration policy and amnesty, but that the

United States would never overcome, despite the election of a president who acknowledged the wrongness of the war.

Americans' belief in "my country, right or wrong" caused a division in the way Vietnam draft and military resisters were treated in the United States, and this division could never be bridged; yet appeals to sovereignty served to overcome this dualism in Canada, first in 1969 when the American military resisters began to arrive, and again in 1973 when an immigration amnesty legalized the status of the remaining "unlanded" resisters. Canada too had drawn a line between permissible and impermissible protest, but the line in Canada had been drawn differently.

The Canadian line was drawn when that country allowed the United States to extradite Karl Armstrong from Toronto for his role in the death that resulted from the bombing of the Army Math Research Center at the University of Wisconsin. This decision was made in response to Canada's own problems involving separatist protests in Quebec and the extradition of Pierre Vallières from the United States in connection with a death following a factory bombing in Montreal. Although the prosecution of Vallières was eventually overturned in Canada, Canada was in principle nonetheless able to justify its division between criminal and legal forms of political protest by drawing on more broadly shared values that define violence as criminal. This allowed the final opening of the legal gates of immigration to the remaining unlanded war resisters.

The attempt to achieve a universal and unconditional Vietnam war amnesty in the United States reached its peak at the Democratic Convention in July 1976. By then the 1960s were long gone. From the 1976 convention on, Americans became increasingly disinclined to be reminded of the war and lost interest in amnesty. The failure of the United States to offer an unconditional and universal amnesty contributed to the long-lasting feelings of resentment that most war resisters would harbor about the United States for the rest of their lives.

Still, by any reasonable measure, the Canadian Vietnam war resistance was an extraordinary success, especially the persistence of the Toronto Anti-Draft Program and Amex. The exile movement was based on the belief that individuals could make a powerful, collective statement against the Vietnam war by refusing induction and military service and by leaving the United States in large numbers. The resulting migration was the largest political exodus since the American revolution. TADP initially provided counseling and helped American war resisters settle in Canada, and later lobbied the Canadian government to provide an inclusive and effective immigration amnesty that included military as well as draft resisters. This amnesty was thoroughly successful, and allowed more Americans, some disaffected and disadvantaged, to become responsible and productive New Canadians.

Meanwhile, Amex increasingly turned its efforts to the seemingly intractable task of making Americans confront the wrongness of the Vietnam war and the need for a universal and unconditional amnesty. Overcoming the American inclination to punish and forget was an unlikely prospect from the start, and it consumed the attention of Amex for more than six years. Over time, American public attention was focused on these issues in ways and to an extent that never would have been possible without the extraordinarily persistent and well-organized efforts of Amex in Toronto. These efforts made the concept of resistance through exile a reality, and it helped achieve an unconditional amnesty in the United States for draft resisters. While the same result could not be achieved for military resisters, Amex was able to mitigate the mistreatment of this group of resisters in ways that no other organization could or would. Amex organized a cross-national, cross-class, and cross-race movement that was remarkable in its unwavering resoluteness and responsibility of purpose.

Jack Colhoun has written his own eloquent epitaph for this movement: "If *Amex* can leave a legacy, we hope it will be as pioneers in developing the political utility of exile as a form of war resistance, and that our experience will serve as a historical model for future generations of Americans who may need to resist similarly unjust U.S. wars against Third World national liberation movements."[137] In 1978, Lawrence Baskir and William Strauss, who had worked for the Ford clemency program, published a book about the Vietnam war resistance that testified to this legacy. These two veterans of a program that most resisters found reprehensible were forced to concede that "perhaps more than any other single aspect of the Vietnam war, the exiled draft resisters and deserters symbolized the conflict over the morality of the war and the values of those who refused to fight it."[138]

CHAPTER 6

Choosing Canada

On Christmas Day 1976, about a month before President-elect Jimmy Carter announced his Vietnam pardon, the television show *All in the Family* aired an episode entitled "The Draft Dodger." Resisters watched from Canada as one of their own was portrayed through the lens of this popular show to a large audience in both the United States and Canada. Norman Lear's production company had developed the episode with input from Gold Star Mother Pat Simon. Originally the plot had featured a military resister, but a draft resister was later substituted.[1] This decision reflected the difficulty Americans had in overcoming the differing attitudes toward "deserters" and "dodgers"; but several sentences of dialogue dealing with the distinction served to prejudge the issue before most viewers would have realized it had been introduced.

The draft dodger, David, was originally from Chicago, a friend of Archie Bunker's son-in-law, and had been living in Canada. He dropped by the Bunkers' unexpectedly on Christmas Day. Archie was suspicious when he heard where David was living, and after a few insults about logs and whale meat, he demanded, "What have you got in Canada that we haven't got here?" David answered, "Freedom," and Archie's mood darkened. David was momentarily defensive, announcing, "I'm not a deserter, I'm a dodger." The ground then shifted so swiftly to Archie's demand for further explanation of David's decision to resist that the validity of the deserter-dodger dualism was implicitly conceded. David explained that he resisted and went to Canada because his draft board "couldn't come up with as many reasons for killing people as I could for not." Archie simply concluded, "What he did was wrong."

Archie's protests notwithstanding, David was invited to stay for Christmas dinner. Archie had invited his close friend Pinky, whose only son had been killed in Vietnam. Archie was not just angry about David's politics, he was distraught in anticipation of upsetting and insulting his friend. When Pinky arrived and was introduced to David, Pinky instinctively called him "son." This only made Archie more uncomfortable, and he became more upset as David's identity as a war resister became apparent. It was all Archie's wife Edith could do to get Archie calm enough to sit down at the dinning room table.

Archie was frustrated by his inability to resolve what he took to be a grievous insult, in the form of David's presence, to the memory of Pinky's lost son. He finally turned in desperation to Pinky for guidance. Archie was astonished when Pinky responded, as many Gold Star parents like Pat Simon did, by saying, "My kid hated this war too, but he did what he had to do. And David here did what he had to do, but David's alive to share Christmas dinner with us. And if Steve were here, he'd want to sit down with him. And that's what I want to do too. Merry Christmas, David." David replied in kind, "Merry Christmas, sir." The spirit of the season prevailed.

"The Draft Dodger" is still an emotionally wrenching show to watch today.[2] The plot movingly raises central issues involved in the amnesty movement. The choice to make this the Christmas program of such a popular series demonstrates how by 1976 the exile movement in Canada had captured the attention of Americans. Yet the show made its case in favor of amnesty for draft resisters while ignoring military resisters. That is, like Carter's pardon, the program addressed the draft resisters' situation while, and perhaps by, obscuring the plight of the military resisters.

Many draft as well as military resisters who watched this dramatization of American feelings about war resistance and amnesty from their exile in Canada doubtless sensed an ambivalence in the show's message. The program's moral inferences, like the pardon, were conditional, uncertain—laden with misgivings. The ambivalence of the well-meaning but half-hearted plot dramatized a mentality American war resisters had chosen to leave behind by making their lives in Canada. The show's thinly developed characterization of David revealed how little Americans knew, then as now, about the lives of American war resisters in Canada. How did the resisters feel about their relationship to the United States then? How do they feel now?

The *Amex* Amnesty Survey

Amex, the antiwar news magazine most widely read by war resisters in Canada, undertook a mail survey to assess the feelings of its readership in August 1973. Emotions and tensions were rising at Amex. The Canadian government had announced, and would soon implement, its immigration amnesty for "unlanded" individuals who were living without legal status in Canada. The early wave of American war resisters were starting to become Canadian citizens, after a mandatory five-year waiting period. Stan Pietlock, the founder of *Amex* magazine, had recently become a Canadian citizen and believed that it was time to begin winding down organizations and magazines like *Amex* so that American war resisters could get on with their lives as new Canadians.

Dee Knight and Jack Colhoun at the same time were increasing their roles in Amex and wanted the magazine to focus more heavily on the amnesty movement in the United States. Knight and Colhoun soon assumed editorial control of the magazine, but first they undertook a mail survey to assess what their readership wanted from the magazine. Although the results of this survey were never published, the fifty-five responses are preserved in the archival records of the magazine.[3] Reader surveys characteristically are uncertain in their representation, and this one is no different. Nonetheless, it produced an array of responses that provide insights into the thoughts of those readers of *Amex* who chose to respond in the summer and fall of 1973.

A key question was whether resisters saw themselves returning to the United States within the next three years. Only four of the respondents expected to return, only eight more thought this was even a possibility, and the overwhelming majority, forty-three, said they did not expect to return, although many wanted to be able to visit. Typical responses were:

> "After living in Canada, I have found it is so much better than the U.S. that I feel the U.S. government did me a favor in forcing us out."
> "The only return would be for the purpose of visiting."
> "No, but would like to visit with no hassle."
> "There is enough in Toronto, what with friends, political parties, demos to go to, school, radio stations, bookstores, to fill up a life."
> "I have never felt lonely, marooned, stranded, or deserted here."
> "I have never planned on or oriented myself to going back to Nixon land."
> "Only if it's legal. Life is too good here to risk it even a little."
> "I'm not lusting to touch the home sod. I would not rush back on the occasion of amnesty. I like Canada."

Some indicated they might like to return at a later point in their lives, but the majority wanted to stay in Canada for the foreseeable future.

Despite the disinclination to return, only about half the readers responded to a question about whether they saw themselves as political exiles in the affirmative. A striking feature of answers to this question was that even those who thought of themselves as exiles usually did not believe this was the most prominent part of their identity. The half who did not think of themselves as political exiles often wrote to explain why.

"I used to [identify as a political exile], but I beat the draft rap after I was here."

"I am here partly because of the U.S. government, but I am not an exile."

"Not really. After I came they decided not to draft me after all."

"That's what got me here, but I don't think of myself that way now."

"Because I'm here: yes. Why I stay: no."

"I'm more interested in Canada than the U.S."

"I would probably have stayed in Canada whether drafted or not, and certainly now, when I am free to return, I cannot call myself any kind of exile."

"Seeing yourself as a political exile means to me that you're still seeing yourself as a displaced, in-limbo American. Seeing yourself as a New Canadian is the beginning of an adventure."

"Seeing yourself as a person in exile is the continuation of a sad time I think most of us would like to leave behind us . . . What good was it to leave if all the heartache comes with you?"

The sense one gets in reading these responses is that this was a time of rapid change for the resisters, when many, if not most, were becoming New Canadians, reframing their identities in these terms. Still, they had not forgotten where they came from, and why they had left.

So while even though most of the responding resisters did not plan to return to the United States, and while most were probably rapidly assimilating into Canadian society, most also remained politically concerned and psychologically involved with the antiwar movement. This is why amnesty continued to be an issue of interest to war resisters. When *Amex* asked, "Do you think we are giving too much coverage to the amnesty movement in the U.S.?" the answer was overwhelmingly "no." Still, the indication of interest was, as in relation to exile identity, qualified. Andy Barrie, now the host of the *CBC Metro Morning* radio show in Toronto, put the matter eloquently in his response to the *Amex* survey in 1973:

> I think there has to be an Amnesty movement, if for no other reason than to exonerate all the criminals of conscience. But with everything else in the past, it's too hard to admit that there's anything I'd want to go back to. It would be nice to have an amnesty, but it's something I'd like to see just happen, without the people here taking part in the demands for it. First of all it's political, which makes compromise likely. And any amnesty which isn't unconditional will be worthless in that it will still allow those politicians who want to make distinctions and pass judgment . . . I see a picture of guys here defending and explaining themselves to a country which may or may not let them back, and it saddens me . . . I think too that Canada, as a people, deserves from us something like appreciation for providing us with an alternative to war or jail. In a global sense, I guess they did only what morality demanded and therefore don't deserve to be praised for it. But in a personal way, I've learned to love this country a little, just for being so "there" when I needed it.

These words captured feelings surrounding amnesty that for years would consume war resisters in Canada and concerned citizens in the United States. In the meantime, no matter what their broader thoughts and feelings about exile and amnesty may have been, individual resisters had to make their own decisions about how to live the rest of their lives.

Arrivals and Departures

Even basic facts about the migration of American war resisters to Canada remain obscure. The number of American war resisters who came to Canada, as well as the number who subsequently decided to return to the United States, is uncertain. In 1972 Russell Nye, a Michigan State University professor of English, characterized conflicting press reports of the number of resisters who immigrated to Canada as "sloppy journalism."[4] Nye noted that in a period of just over six months in 1969, the *New York Times* raised its estimate of the number of American resisters in Canada from several thousand to over 60,000. An account thirty years later inexplicably raised this estimate nearly tenfold, suggesting that "a safe estimate for the number of men and women who went to Canada during the Vietnam War would probably be 500,000."[5] However, the 60,000 figure is probably the most frequently cited

estimate. After surveying the range of estimates, Nye concluded that between 1970 and 1972, "Newspaper and television reports on draft evaders
and deserters in Canada have . . . varied from 10,000 to 100,000, a margin of
error that ought to have stirred a twinge of doubt in some newspaperman's
breast somewhere." He concluded that the actual numbers were unknown
but important.

Patrick Buchanan, as speechwriter and adviser to Richard Nixon, took up
the issue of the erratic statistics and the politics of amnesty in a February
1973 *New York Times* op-ed piece. He noted that the U.S. government estimated there were 4,000 "verified" draft and military resisters in Canada by
1973, while he concluded that the actual number might be 7,000 to 10,000.
Buchanan's argument was that "because of an ideological bias, otherwise
competent American newsmen have engaged in inexcusably sloppy journalism, swallowing whole without inspection bogus statistics fed them by
Canadian-based anti-war groups."[6]

Buchanan did not say how he calculated his own estimate, but he did suggest a method that Renée Kasinsky adopted in her book *Refugees from Militarism*.[7] This involved subtracting the average number of draft-age Americans
who annually came to Canada in the years before the Vietnam war from the
number who came each year during the war, with the annual difference being the estimated number of draft-age Americans who came in opposition to
the war. The number jumped abruptly upward in 1965, peaked in 1970 (see
Table B.5 of Appendix B), and dropped sharply in 1975. The period 1965–
1975 included the years between the Gulf of Tonkin Resolution and the fall
of Saigon, when almost 26,000 men and 27,000 women resisters are estimated to have come to Canada. Since at least another 10,000 men and
women probably came as visitors and returned without becoming "landed"
immigrants, the 60,000 *New York Times* figure may be a relatively good guess,
even though it was premature when first cited.

Buchanan and others might argue that since they were not subject to the
draft women should not be included in estimating the size of the resistance.
But Denise Bukowski convincingly argues that for women, "a double layer
of conviction and commitment came into play . . . We had to believe our
country was wrong and our men were right, and that one was worth giving
up for the latter."[8] Even restricting the number to men and to the period
1965–1972 (before the Paris Cease-fire Agreement of 1973) results in an estimate of over 20,000 American male resisters coming to Canada (see Table
B.5): more than double Buchanan's estimate.

It is more difficult to calculate how many of the Americans who came in opposition to the war have remained in Canada. This may explain why in 1978 Lawrence Baskir and William Strauss reported that "no more than one-fourth of the original forty thousand exiles remain in their adopted countries" and then later indicate with regard to the same population that "most decided to stay in Canada or Sweden."[9] The latter statement is almost certainly more accurate than the former.

The 1996 Canadian census can be used to estimate the number of American Vietnam war resisters who have stayed in Canada. This can be done most accurately for the years 1967–1972, when the largest numbers came (see Table B.6 in Appendix B).[10] In contrast to the years before 1965, when less than a third of Americans who immigrated to Canada stayed for twenty-five years or longer, more than half of the American Vietnam war resisters stayed. At least 56 percent of the women and about 53 percent of the men resisters remained who came between 1967 and 1972.

The fact that slightly more female than male resisters stayed in Canada is striking, in part because many of these women are no longer with the men they accompanied. This tendency adds further weight to Bukowski's assessment of the commitment of the women. Her further thoughts about what it means to have stayed, no longer living with the man with whom one came and in a country where there is often no other family member, is striking. "It means," Bukowski writes, "being an invisible immigrant to an invisible country, but nevertheless standing firm in the conviction that, under the circumstances, you are in the best of all possible places, and that by staying here you have made a political statement about your old country and your new one."[11] Sandra Foster put it differently. "If the old notions of women as nesters have any credence," she reasoned, "then that would lend itself to staying—I mean, how many nests can you build?"

The estimate of resisters who stayed is likely conservative because of undercounting and underreporting. Within the years 1967–1972 is a U-shaped trend, with about 58 percent of the resisters staying who came in 1967, followed by a steady decline to about 47 percent of the 1970 arrivals, and then building again to 65 percent in 1972. Recall what was happening within Canada during these years.

Pierre Berton sets the stage for the first wave of American resisters in the title of his book *1967: The Last Good Year.* This centennial year was a time of optimism, symbolized by Montreal's Expo 1967. Canada was in an expansive, welcoming mood that included record levels of immigration, with young Americans among the most numerous new arrivals. The Pearson and Trudeau governments made Canada a safe haven for draft-age Americans during these early years. The American war resisters became unexpected symbols of Canadian sovereignty with the support of such prominent groups as the United Church. The resisters who came during these first years were among the most likely to stay.

Of course, good times never last forever, and, as noted in the previous chapter, the Quebec Crisis and the imposition of the War Measures Act in 1970 marked a low point. Unemployment was growing, and the war resisters became scapegoats. The mayors of Montreal, Toronto, and Vancouver voiced new complaints about the rebelliousness they associated with the American war resisters, and the *Toronto Star* editorialized against war resisters who remained focused on "American" or world problems rather than on becoming Canadian. The resisters' idealized images of Canada gave way to the specter of martial law and prejudice. Relatively few American war resisters were directly affected, but the backlash led larger numbers of arriving resisters to leave Canada. Still, nearly half stayed.

If the middle to late 1960s was a time of renewal, and 1970 a time of reappraisal, then 1972–1973 was a time for reaffirmation. Canada reaffirmed its commitment to American war resisters by implementing the Canadian immigration amnesty. The government not only relaxed immigration requirements for those in the country by 1972, it also allocated substantial government funds to publicize and undertake the immigration amnesty. War resister groups found the Canadian government receptive to their needs and, again, prominent groups like the United Church were supportive. Nearly two-thirds of the war resisters who came to Canada in 1972 responded to the warmth of this attitude by staying.

These were the changing social contexts in which American resisters came and made decisions about staying in Canada. During 1970 and the War Measures Act, there was an increased rate of return migrations to the United States. Yet even then most resisters stayed, and larger majorities stayed in the earlier and later periods. In comparison, before and after the Vietnam war only about a third of immigrating Americans stayed in Canada.

Of course, the resisters' choices and circumstances were unique, and more complicated than census numbers alone could possibly communicate. Some of the lasting implications of these choices and circumstances are reflected in the hundred interviews I conducted with resisters who stayed. The interviews help us understand why the resisters made the decisions they did, and provide insight into their long-term significance. Choosing to stay in Canada, to reframe one's identity as Canadian, and perhaps most of all to become less American, was a more complicated, deep-rooted, and long-lasting process than most resisters anticipated. Physically leaving the United States and coming to Canada proved far easier for most resisters than psychologically leaving the United States and shedding its influence.

Families Disrupted

The transition to adulthood is often a turbulent period. Most of the resisters were in their early twenties, and in this period of their development, when they came to Canada. Many had already left home for their postsecondary education, but were still closely tied to their parents and families. These young Americans were not just leaving home, they were leaving their country. Sons thought they would never be able to return. Daughters chose to join their loved ones. The war was literally tearing families apart. Family and national feelings collided in unexpected ways. Individuals suffered major disruptions in their lives.

Some families openly opposed their sons' and daughters' plans to come to Canada. Stephen Strauss, now an editorial writer for the *Toronto Globe and Mail*, remembered that his parents argued in different ways against his decision to emigrate. "They were unhappy. My mother's suggestion was 'Don't go to Canada, go see a psychiatrist,' because she was sure that he would find me crazy and that I could get off on some kind of mental deferment . . . My father was a refugee from Germany. He'd fought in the U.S. army and felt a very strong loyalty to the U.S. They didn't like . . . my decision." These same parents later helped Stephen to enlist Colorado congresswoman Pat Shroeder in a successful effort to get charges against him dropped.

Janice Spellerberg had a more difficult experience, perhaps partly because she had already left home on less than ideal terms. At the time she decided to move to Canada, Janice was modeling for art classes. "Somebody from that class called my parents, told them first of all that I was modeling for art classes, and that I was leaving for Canada . . . So when I called my parents they already knew and they were really upset with me . . . They wrote me off for a couple years." Janice later reconciled with her parents and went back to live with them for a period before returning to Canada.

Sometimes members of extended families became involved in conflicts about decisions to come to Canada. Carol Ricker-Wilson, who is now an educator in Toronto, recalled a Christmas celebration that rivaled the *All in the*

Family episode described at the beginning of this chapter. "This . . . relative went on about 'these damned hippies,' and the whole number, and my Quaker aunt was just furious because she was totally antiwar . . . and we were even more so. Everybody walked out without speaking to each other." Carol's father helped her husband solve his draft problems, but Carol recalled a lot of family tension.

Some parents encouraged their sons and daughters to leave. Stephen Handler, now a high-level administrator with a home health care organization, was relieved when his father concluded, "I'd rather you go to Canada than come home in a box." Michele Sanders was just out of high school when she told her parents she was marrying a man who was in jeopardy of being drafted. Her father "just looked at us and said, 'You can't go to Vietnam.' I mean, he just looked at this guy . . . and said, 'It's going to ruin your life.'" Michele and her partner took this warning to heart and left for Canada.

Steven Burdick, now a labor leader, found that his father at first opposed his going to Canada and then changed his position, saying, "Well, if you are going to do this, why don't you do it before they draft you." Steven's mother responded more instinctively: "I could probably have held up a bank and my mother would have said, 'I'm sure there was a good reason for it.'" In the end, "they were not happy to see me go, but I think they felt that they understood what I was doing and they were supportive."

The most common parental reactions to sons' and daughters' departures involved mixtures of approval and disapproval, probably because parents were no better prepared than their children for the decisions they were pressured to make. Devastation and resignation are the terms that Susan Bowman-Krongold, a social services professional, uses to describe the reactions of her and her husband's parents to their decision to come to Canada. "Rob's dad just about had a heart attack . . . I think the people in my parents' generation who fought in the big war, they really had a lot of trouble with this concept that you don't serve your country." Father and son reconciled when a grandchild was born, but the process was difficult.

Jon Caulfield, now a sociology professor, found his parents divided. His father supported his position "because I made the decision and that was what I was doing . . . If I'd decided to do the other thing, he would have supported that too." Jon's mother wouldn't commit herself. Jon concluded that this was a "split decision" and soon followed his own conscience. When the FBI came to his home, Jon's father told them he would not be intimidated.

Lisa Steele and her first husband received regular reports about visits of the FBI to her and her husband's parents' homes. The husband's parents "were much more politically conservative than my father and my step-mother, who were a little bit more loose about things. They weren't, you know, proud of it, but they weren't humiliated by it. They would just tell us if the FBI had been there . . . But I think his parents were really humiliated by it. It was quite awful." Some reconciliation had been achieved before Lisa's father-in-law died, but the experience left its mark.

Both of Steven Bush's parents were opposed to the war, but their opposition led them to different conclusions about Steven's decision to come to Canada. His mother "mostly approved," even if she didn't completely un-derstand her son's reasons for his decision. His father felt that the more hon-orable thing would be to go to jail. Steven had already gone to jail twice in connection with demonstrations and protests and wasn't persuaded of the utility of spending more time there. He says that, in the end, "my father's opposition was principled . . . We didn't have a big fight over it."

Hugh Wylie's father served in the navy during World War II and his ship was attacked by a kamikaze. Ironically, Hugh eventually became the curator of the Japanese collection at the Royal Ontario Museum. At the time of the Vietnam war, he recalled, his parents "thought I should go into the Coast Guard, and I said . . . that wasn't a strong enough statement. So they were not overjoyed with my decision." Nonetheless, Hugh's parents visited him in Toronto.

Gloria Shookner is a social worker and helps newly independent women learn how to manage their finances. Decades after making the decision to come to Canada with her then-husband, Gloria was reminded recently of the mixed feelings generated by her emigration. She returned to the States to help celebrate her parents fiftieth wedding anniversary. "This aunt said to me, 'Why did you move to Canada?' My mother was on the other side of the kitchen and she was across it like a shot, standing between me and my aunt, and before I could get my mouth open, she said Malcolm [then Gloria's hus-band] got offered a better job." Gloria noted that there was a time when she would have gone to battle on the issue, "but, you know, I thought I'm going to let this pass, this is what she needs people to think."

Robert Simpson, like many resisters, found that his parents did not really seem to want to confront the issue of the war and his decision to come to Canada. "We didn't talk about it much, and it's funny, because my father was an Elksman, not only an Elks member but an Exalted Ruler of one of the lodges. So he was really into this pretty patriotic organization." Taking this into account, Robert interpreted his father's silence as support. "He kind of supported me by not confronting me about it."

Perhaps the families most torn by the war, and most troubled in their silence, were those in which children made opposing decisions about service. Carolyn Egan, now a health counsellor and educator, reported that her husband's brother was in Vietnam at the time they decided to leave for Canada. "We kept in touch with his parents," she recalled, although "there was an awkwardness in that." In the end, "It's one of those things that just became unspoken."

CBC talk show host Andy Barrie concluded that his father "just felt helpless." Andy's older brother had gone to Vietnam. "It had taken them years to somehow accommodate my brother's odd ideas about going to Vietnam, and just as they finally tried to internalize that, I was going in the opposite direction."

Clearly, these families in turmoil had difficulty finding the right words of wisdom to pass on to their children—young people who were no longer adolescents, but adults making life and death decisions about war and nationality. And once the decision to relocate was made, these young people faced the still-harder process of identity formation and reformation.

An American Ambivalence?

The background of family discord, uncertainty, and silence that accompanied the departures of American war resisters often prompted, and probably frequently intensified, the resisters' early feelings of ambivalence about leaving the United States and coming to Canada. Marginality is a common feeling among immigrants confronted with the prospect of living their lives in a new country. Even when the decision to immigrate is made rationally and responsibly, feelings of doubt and uncertainty often follow, at least for a time.

Neil Smelser has explained how ambivalence can expand our understanding of social processes, including particularly relationships formed between citizens and nation-states, arguing that ambivalence and rationality are not contradictory but interconnected processes.[12] Smelser notes that American culture tends to favor univalent understanding and downplays dualistic or ambivalent aspects of social and national life.[13]

Smelser uses the perspective of Albert Hirschman's book *Exit, Voice, and Loyalty* to introduce a reconceptualization of the ambivalence surrounding citizens' reactions to leaving their native land. Hirschman suggests that a kind of "splitting" process often follows decisions to move to another country: "In leaving his [or her] country the emigrant makes a difficult decision and usually pays a high price in severing many strong affective ties. Additional payment is extracted as [s]he is being initiated into a new environment and adjusting to it." Hirschman reasons that a predictable result is to bond strongly with the new country: "In retrospect, the 'old country' will appear more abominable than ever while the new country will be declared to be the greatest, 'the last hope of mankind,' and all manner of other superlatives."[14]

Smelser acknowledges that Hirschman's "splitting" process may be common, if not typical. Nonetheless, he argues that a more valid explanation of how citizens form and renounce their allegiances to past and present nation-states should acknowledge that deep-seated feelings of ambivalence also are involved.[15] Hirschman's splitting process is apparent in the accounts of American war resisters. Given that the attitudes of Canadians themselves toward the United States are full of ambivalence, mixing open admiration of things American with more than occasional distaste and disdain, it is not surprising that the arriving Americans would also have felt some ambivalence, at least initially. Denise Bukowski remembered an expatriate American university professor once telling her that "to be an American in Canada is to constantly abrade, to rub the fur the wrong way." Many young American resisters felt this unexpected dissonance when they arrived.

Stephen Strauss has a writer's comfort with words; yet he found it hard to articulate the nature of his feelings when he first arrived in Canada. This much he remembered: "I was an American who didn't know what it was to be a Canadian. Self-exile is not a place; it is a state of mind." Terri Hope, who works now in social services, felt her national and ethnic roots very strongly: "I think being from New York and Jewish is ingrained. It's a way of being and thinking." Leaving, at least for Terri, wasn't simply a matter of moving from one location to another. "At first I spent a lot of time trying to actively reject being an American . . . I left America, and that was me at that time. I'm different now." Similarly, Alan Guettel, a CBC producer, could not forget his roots in the United States: "As much as I didn't want to, I was constantly reminded that I was American . . . it was always on my mind."

In the beginning, many resisters found that it was the holidays that most reminded them they were now living in a foreign land. The fact that Canadians celebrate Thanksgiving a month earlier, and that American

Thanksgiving is a classic family holiday, produced strong reactions. Malcolm Shookner found his first Thanksgiving with his wife in Canada especially disconcerting. "November of 1970, that was the year that we missed Thanksgiving. I always think of it that way because we got settled about a week before American Thanksgiving up here, and we were so grateful and thankful that we decided that we were going to celebrate and we were going to have a really great holiday." Then Malcolm realized Canadians weren't celebrating. "We didn't realize that Canadians celebrate Thanksgiving six weeks earlier . . . It was such a strange thing. It was one of the first cultural conflicts. You know, 'What's going on here?' We're in a different place."

Pam Oxendine now works as a psychotherapist. Then she was trying to hold her family together and felt a need to observe this classic American holiday. "It was funny because . . . it was Thanksgiving, we [celebrated] American Thanksgiving . . . Priscilla must have been about four or five. We had a dinner and Tom and I were there, and we looked up and down the table, and it was all the American exile community."

Susan Bowman-Krongold felt that more than the holidays weren't right. "The wrong identity was a really good way of describing it. I don't think I had my identity secured at all at that point. I didn't know who the heck I was . . . Was I an ex-American? Was I a New Canadian? I didn't feel any of those things." At the same time, Susan was also experiencing the transition to parenthood. "I was young, I was twenty-two, and I was pregnant. I mean I was like, 'Oh my God,' you know, who the hell am I, and now I am having a child. It was a strange time."

Martha Friendly was also a new mother and had not yet begun her career researching the problems of urban children. She too felt adrift, searching for bearings in a foreign, suburban Toronto setting. "I had this baby and I lived in Willowdale in the suburbs and I didn't know anybody. It was a long winter. I remember it was cold and it snowed in April . . . I hadn't figured out how I was going to make out." Martha felt isolated. "I attributed some of that to having moved to this stuffy country where you couldn't get the *New York Times* and people didn't talk to you in elevators." Both male and female resisters experienced a culture shock, which was reflected in ambivalent thoughts about national differences and identities.

Despite their initial feelings of discomfort, all of the resisters quoted stayed. Whether in spite or because of their early feelings of disorientation and ambivalence, all began a process of reframing their identities to accommodate their new situation. Lee Vittetow described how this process of change began with his efforts to suppress an ambivalence that proved longer lasting than expected. Comparing then and now, Lee said, "I guess I think of myself in kind of hybrid terms . . . I sort of dropped a lot of my identity as an American when I got here. I sort of blended into the environment and really didn't allow myself to pay a lot of attention to my American background. And that probably changed kind of progressively over a period of time, so that now I identify as a Canadian citizen who's an American expatriate of some fashion."

Lee's account is especially revealing when he describes changes that he consciously initiated and has since internalized:

> I think I was absolutely traumatized by my move here . . . I lost all traces . . . of my American accent, which was a pronounced kind of Missouri accent— because that's my family origin. I'm good with languages. It's something I can do. I can kind of listen to somebody and in about five minutes I'd have it down pretty good . . . I used to listen to CBC all the time—"I'm going to sound like Stanley Burke [a CBC newscaster]," right? I listened very carefully to how he pronounced things. I wound up saying things like "aboot" and "eh?" And I talked that way for years. Then it sort of dropped off about ten years ago. Presumably at that point, I think it was just my own atti-tude—I felt progressively more and more comfortable. And, of course, by that time, my accent, because I lived up here, was more and more interest-ing. I have in fact changed, so I think I have a kind of hybrid—there are elements of several different places where I have lived or my family has lived—people I affiliate with or whatever. It's quite interesting. I think I identify more as a Canadian than anything else, but there are certainly as-pects of my American background that are more evident, more active.

Lee's efforts to make his accent fit his environment were reflective of the en-ergy that American resisters invested in making Canada home rather than just a place to live. As Vittetow's comments reveal, and as Hirschman's anal-ysis suggests, making the transition often involves downplaying one na-tional identity in order to develop another.

Deepening the Difference

My interviews included questions that asked the respondents to rate them-selves on a scale from zero to ten in terms of how strongly they identified with being American and Canadian, both when they first arrived in Canada and at the time of the interview. Such questions might invite retrospective reinterpretation of past feelings. Eviatar Zerubavel, in discussing the distinction between autobiographical and sociobiographical memory, points out that "exiting a group or a community typically involves forgetting its past."[16] A selective repression of feelings of being American may be a reason for the findings reported next, but if this is so this selectivity is variable and interesting in itself as a source of real-world behavior.

The most striking pattern in Table 6.1 is the overall reduction over time in feelings of American identity and corresponding increase in feelings of Canadian identity. This pattern obtains whether the respondents are female or male, draft or military resisters. All cross-time comparisons yield significant differences. The only significant variation from this general trend is that military resisters identify more strongly as Americans in the present than draft resisters do. Nonetheless, the military resisters are now more notably Canadian than American in their national identification and substantially lower in their American identity than when they came.

The overall pattern of change in respondents' national identity is most easily seen in Figure 6.1, where the findings are graphed by respondents' year of arrival. The figure illustrates that, regardless of year of arrival, American resisters now identify much more strongly with Canada than with the United States. Furthermore, no matter the year of arrival, the level of identi-

Table 6.1 Feelings of U.S. and Canadian identity among male and female draft and military resisters, on arrival and at contemporary interview (1 = identifying very little; 10 = identifying very strongly)

Identity	Female resisters (total)	Male resisters (total)	t-ratios	Male draft resisters	Male military resisters	t-ratios
American identity						
Then	7.10	6.11	−1.75	5.96	6.67	−.91
Now	3.63	3.43	.71	3.07	4.73	−2.31*
t-ratios	6.30*	7.23*		6.70*	2.76*	
Canadian identity						
Then	2.67	3.26	1.08	3.13	3.73	−8.5
Now	8.03	7.86	−.36	8.00	7.33	1.02
t-ratios	−9.76*	−13.11*		−12.38*	−4.85*	

*$p < .05$

National
identity

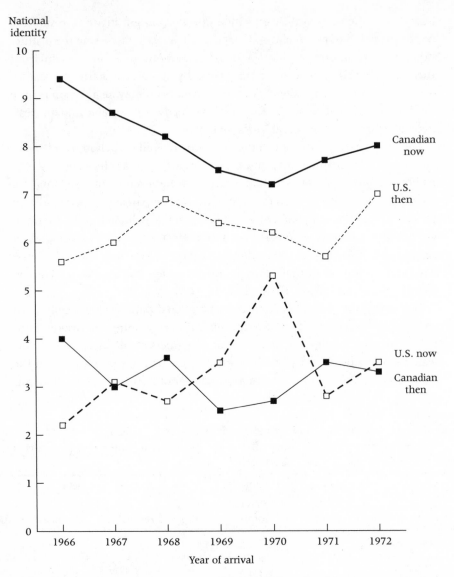

Figure 6.1 Feelings among resisters of U.S. and Canadian identity, on arrival
and at contemporary interview

fication with Canada has increased dramatically over time, while the level of identification with the United States has declined. With a single exception, 1970, the differences in levels of identification with Canada and the United States are greater now than they were at arrival. This reflects Hirschman's notion that the American resisters have reframed their feelings of national identity by becoming more positive about Canada and more negative about the United States. In general, the American resisters have reframed their identities as expatriates from the United States and now identify strongly with Canada.

The temporal pattern in Figure 6.1 is consistent with that observed earlier in this chapter with the Canadian census data. These data indicated that re- sisters who came to Canada in the earlier and later years of the migration were most likely to stay in Canada, while those who came in 1970 were least likely to remain. From the interviews with resisters who stayed in Toronto, we again see that those who came early and late identify most strongly with Canada, while those who came in 1970 identify least strongly with Canada. As noted previously in this chapter, the early and later years were the periods in which Canada welcomed the resisters most warmly, while 1970 was the year of the Quebec Crisis and the War Measures Act. The interview rankings reveal that even the American resisters who arrived in 1970 bonded with Canada strongly enough to score 7.2 on the 10-point scale; in addition, however, Americans who came in 1970 remain uniquely high in their identification with the United States. The War Measures Act seems to have kept the resisters who arrived that year from lowering their identification with the United States as much as resisters who arrived in other years. These 1970 resisters on average retrospectively ranked their identification with the United States on their arrival at 6.2; this number has only declined slightly to a score now of 5.3, which is high relative to those who arrived in all other years. A strong identification with Canada and cor- responding move away from identification with the United States is the overwhelming pattern in these data.

Becoming Canadian

Many of those interviewed spoke of how long it took for them to feel at home in Canada and to acquire a sense of being Canadian. Many, however, emphasized that this period was not entirely depressing or distressing for them. In fact, for some it was more exhilarating than traumatic. Stephen

Strauss recaptures a sense of the excitement, pride, and adventure that accompanied his decision to come to Canada. "You have to understand it was the sixties," Stephen recalls. "It was exciting: to take hold of your destiny and go off to a foreign country and start your life again." The circumstances gave him a feeling that what he was doing was significant: "I've never, before or since, felt so much like I was riding a wave of history. I could see myself in magazines and newspapers, and hear things about me, not me personally, but me the collective, and doing this was such a political act." Lisa Steele echoed the feeling of excitement: "You know, I really wanted to be here. I was very excited . . . The people we knew increased in numbers, and mostly it was very young people . . . who were bold, . . . doing interesting things."

Allan and Karen Kazmer stopped to reflect on their future at the moment they crossed the border, which followed on the heels of their getting married. After crossing the bridge in Windsor, they literally stopped their car to reflect on what these joined events would mean for them in the foreseeable future. Allan recalled:

> We bonded, physically, spiritually, mentally—coming together—a crisis occurs, and you have to deal with it. We went through the crisis together. We fled our country. It sounds dramatic, but it is. Karen did a poetic thing. When we crossed, the two honeymooners off to Canada—she said after we crossed into Windsor, "Allan, point the car towards Detroit, say goodbye to Detroit. Allan, you may never be able to go back to Detroit, to the USA again—I can, but you can't." With tears in my eyes I said goodbye. And off we went to Toronto. We lived in a boarding house for six months, slept in one twin bed, and stayed in this room for six months. All the anxiety of being underground, criminals. Would we find employment? Would we be accepted as landed immigrants? Having survived all of this was truly a bonding experience. It was such a strong start for us. For us, Canada was such a wonderful country and Toronto was such a beautiful city. We got off to a really strong start.

Yet, at the same time, none of this was simple or without complication. Lisa Steele lived at first in the Baldwin Street area and initially felt overpowered by her Americanness and her Baldwin Street surroundings. "I was steeped in the American ghetto," Lisa recalls, "you couldn't get away from it. Also . . . I read American publications at that point a lot . . . I remember having to find the *Village Voice*, which was really hard to find in Kansas City, let alone in Toronto in 1968. But I really felt desperate to find it . . . because you didn't necessarily trust the papers here to tell you what was going on, in particular, the political stuff." Similarly, Steven Bush commented that "for several years I related primarily to U.S. politics rather than Canadian politics, as probably most immigrants do. You carry the homeland with you." Malcolm Shookner felt he was "an American expatriate, you know, and it took me a while to put on the Canadian identity."

Tom Needham also spent much of his early time in Toronto among American resisters. During this period, he worked with the Union of American Exiles and Amex. His perspective a quarter century later is that "it was my social scene for a while, while I was finding my way here, 'cause I didn't know anyone here. But gradually I knew more and more people." There was no specific time or place at which Needham became Canadian, not even the eventual ceremony of becoming a citizen, although it was memorable: "It has nothing to do with the day you get your citizenship, although that was important to me. I wore a white suit and a maple leaf on the pocket . . . As it turned out, [in] a room full of one hundred people from all over the world at the swearing in, . . . the guy standing next to me was another draft dodger. We went out for coffee and talked." Needham felt that the experience of becoming a Canadian was a slow but natural process: "my life got shaped when I was here and I became a Canadian . . . almost the same as my father became an American instead of an Irishman."

Andy Barrie perhaps felt the effect of becoming a citizen more immediately than Tom Needham, but he also said that becoming Canadian took some time, even in a country that is as welcoming as Canada can be to immigrants: "The communalism of Canada really attracted me . . . If you believe in the community of communities, what a wonderful country to be in . . . So I've always thought of myself as a Canadian, almost immediately, but I wasn't one, I was becoming one." When the time came for Barrie to become a Canadian citizen, he was ready. "Certainly . . . when I got my citizenship, I was a Canadian. I bought a Canadian flag and I hang it outside my door one day a year on [Canada Day] the first of July."

Like Lisa Steele, Steven Bush also lived in the Baldwin Street area, but his involvement in acting soon pulled him toward Canadian culture and issues of Canadian nationalism. "There were many people who influenced me," he recalled, thinking especially of people in the arts community. "Canadian nationalism became fairly directly connected to war resistance and anti-imperialism, and that was a fairly easy jump to make. And so I became involved in looking at, and listening to, and watching Canadian culture . . . This was happening at a time when I . . . had made the decision to put down roots here and not to keep looking backward over my shoulder longingly toward the U.S." To keep from looking back, some resisters separated themselves from other Americans. Michael Sutton, who is today a management consultant in the computing field, said, "I distanced myself from the American exile community—on purpose."

Some resisters found the reorientation more difficult than others, and for many, if not most, the process involved a conscious effort. Jennifer Glossop was born in England and moved to the United States as a child. "I think I made more of an effort when I came to Canada to be Canadian than I ever did in the States to be American . . . I think it was a real effort to pass as a Canadian and not to live as an American in Canada." In the beginning, many resisters commented that they felt like they were "passing." One resister noted that "early on I learned to convert like a fox or a wolf, and just not address my nationality. Some people guessed, some people didn't."

Richard Brown emphasized the crescive and yet unfinished nature of the transition. He felt the cusp of adulthood was late for a new beginning. "It's been a slow process over the years. There are still a number of things about me that are still uniquely American, and I recognize that." Nonetheless, he felt he had managed to change. "To the extent that an adult can assimilate the culture of a new country, I feel that I have, and that I'm very comfortable with it." Brown added that he is especially conscious of the cultural change when he travels between Canada and the United States.

Even though Karen Lawrence was an adult when she came here, she felt Canada was where she came of age. For Karen, "This is where I grew up . . . I had just turned twenty-three . . . so I hadn't really fully grown up . . . I had lived in New York City for the year and a half before, and other than that I had been in a protected environment of a university which was also a religious school . . . So all of my adult friends are here, you know, the people I have met over the years." She feels that these people really helped her form her identity. Kevin Vrieze expressed a similar sense of change, which his family recognizes. "My parents still introduce me as their Canadian son— they now know that even though I was born in Wisconsin, culturally I am Canadian . . . Given the sort of 'start over,' and the age at which it happened, it had a strong cultural influence, and in almost every respect for the better. That stays with you. My formative years, if you like."

Most of the resisters found Toronto to be a different place than they imagined, and this hastened their desire to assimilate. Allan and Karen Kazmer are struck by this point when they travel to the United States. Allan said, "My business takes us away quite often and people ask us where we're from and we say 'Canada.' We were born in the States and emotionally it's caught on that we really are Canadian." Allan then explained the background to these feelings, using an incident from the night they arrived as an example. He and Karen started out for a walk and stopped to ask another young person for advice. "'Where shouldn't we go?' That was the first question . . . He said, 'Well,' he looked at us rather stunned, 'like how athletic are you?' And we said, 'No, you don't understand, where shouldn't we go, what parts of the city shouldn't we walk in?' And he said you can go anywhere you want, and that was such a novel thought." Allan and Karen felt this was part of why they developed early bonds to the idea of being Canadian.

Alan Guettel was astonished at how open the politics of the city were. "We had never seen a city like this . . . The politics were becoming open and there was a . . . level of democracy . . . you couldn't see in places like New York or Chicago." Jack Colhoun found that the politics of the city and country were an invitation to action that also required restraint, "because Canada was more a kind of sleeping giant and we'd just come from the States with this great intensity and you had all this organizing experience . . . and there were empty spaces . . . so you pull into those spaces, then all of a sudden . . . you know, you gotta learn to walk a little slower, talk a little slower—so it was easy to get in and become too dominant." Jack Colhoun found his place by focusing on the politics of Amex and the resister community, and he eventually returned to the United States.

Others, like Sandra Foster, jumped into the political fray of Toronto municipal politics. Sandra felt strongly about the opportunities this new environment offered. "If the country had opened its arms to me, then I felt an obligation to put my roots down here and eventually to build a life, and to eventually put something back and to be very clear that I was not just a kind of displaced American." Sandra Foster has since worked in city and provincial government and held numerous elected and appointed offices over a quarter century of public service.

Many resisters are today unabashed in their identification with Canada. Philip Marchand is seldom as positive about the books he reviews for the *Toronto Star* as he is about his adopted country: "Some years ago, it might have been in the late seventies, early eighties, I saw the maple leaf and I thought 'God, I really like this, I really like this.' I felt patriotic toward Canada, and it struck me . . . what a good feeling. I realized how much I loved Canada." Stan Pietlock recalled a television interview from his days in founding Amex: "When Norm Perry was interviewing somebody, and I was mentioned, I was called more Canadian than the average Canadian, and I think that's true of many of us." Robert Simpson added an only slightly cautionary note to his enthusiasm when he observed that "by 10 [on the Canadian identification scale] I mean I'm not a raving nationalist . . . but I feel strongly Canadian." Stephen Handler put the matter succinctly but sincerely: "I'm very grateful to this country. It has provided me with wonderful opportunities. I've had my ups and downs in life, but I do not believe that I would have had a better life in any other place in the world. For me Canada is the best place in the world to live, and I have no intention to move back to the USA."

Canada simply became home for most resisters, and this coincided with their feelings of becoming Canadian. Most came to identify with Canada as they lessened their identification with the United States. Allan Kazmer described how his feelings changed. "I'm proud to be a Canadian, a 9—a booster. Right up there. Just after I came to Canada we didn't feel Canadian, but we were really impressed and we were so angry with the United States. So I think it was a strong reaction. I strongly identified with Canada, but a lot of it had to do with my reaction against the United States."

There is a strong sense in the interviews that the resisters felt forced, but in the end felt they had made a good choice. Tom Kane says, "I got pushed and it was a good thing!" John Wolfson says of his roots in New Jersey, "It's not home anymore. It just isn't." Most resisters feel they were pushed by circumstances early in their adulthood and voted with their feet—more on the basis of hope than knowledge. Laura Jones said, "We didn't think we were going to be able to go back. So the fact that we were ex-Americans was significant."

Resisters now vote more knowingly, and with their hearts, for a life chosen in Canada. Carolyn Egan captured the sense of change when she noted that sometime during the early to middle 1970s "I watched the U.S. news and I remember that I stopped." On the Canadian side of the 10-point equation, "I took out citizenship . . . I know that that's my identity, like a 7. My life is going to be here, my life is here." On the American side of the equation, "It's not off the table, but it's mostly, maybe, a 3. I live here."

The gap Carolyn Egan reported in her feelings of national identity is typical, with the notable exception of those who came in 1970. But there is perhaps as well a note of ambivalence in Egan's references to the two countries. The resisters often expressed lingering feelings of Americanness, especially feelings of being culturally (rather than politically) American, and concerns about how different Canada will be politically in the future. John Liss, a Canadian-trained lawyer, still feels more strongly Canadian than American, but he worries about his Canadian identification: "I'm afraid it's about a 7 now. What I used to take as being a Canadian . . . I'm still there but Canada has left . . . It's not that I don't want to feel strongly Canadian, it's that I'm afraid that Canada is losing its ideals and becoming much closer to the United States, which I left, and I would leave again if need be." These comments raise contemporary concerns that hearken back to issues that were and still are significant, especially in the minds of many resisters who came to Canada in 1970, a time when social and political differences between Canada and the United States suddenly seemed vulnerable and demonstrably tentative, when attractive aspects of Canada seemed in doubt and even in serious danger.

Echoes of the War Measures Act

Most probably think of the War Measures Act as having left a lasting mark only in Quebec, but as noted earlier in this chapter its effects were broader in their significance and prominently included American war resisters. War resisters in many cities of Canada were tarred by politicians with the same brush used to vilify the FLQ in Quebec. In a time of rising economic as well as political uncertainty, some politicians and pundits scapegoated resisters as malcontents, revolutionaries, and criminals. The media disseminated these charges, and an atmosphere briefly developed in 1970 that was hostile and threatening to the well-being of resisters in Canada.

These political developments influenced the resisters' national feelings. As Stephen Cornell and Douglas Hartman note, group identities are products of "specific relationships, evolving over time; of specific events, their interpretations and justifications."[17] Those resisters who came in 1970 were most likely to return to the United States; and, as discussed earlier, though they displayed the same tendency as other resisters to have changed their national allegiance, increasing their identification with Canada and diminishing their identification with the United States, they also lowered their identification with the United States to the smallest degree, less than 1 point on the 10-point scale, and they scored lowest in their identification with Canada. In short, this group was not as quick to reject the United States as were those respondents coming to Canada in years other then 1970, and they are not as intense in reframing their identities as Canadians.

The resisters in the sample elaborated on such feelings in the interviews. Fred Reed, now a freelance writer, was in Montreal when the War Measures Act was imposed. He recalled having the same kinds of feelings then that he had experienced in the United States during early stages of the Vietnam war. "When the Canadian government brought in the War Measures Act, and was arresting people into the small hours of the morning, people whose only crime was to have spoken publicly in favor of Quebec independence, I said, 'I want no part of this.' That was for me as galvanizing an event with regard to Canada as the Vietnam war was for the United States." Reed stayed in Canada, but he has not forgotten the War Measures Act.

The events of this period confused many of the resisters. John Liss said, "I reviled Trudeau . . . during the War Measures Act," but in retrospect he has had to balance this feeling with his equally strong respect "for the fact that he was prepared to tweak the nose of the beast to the south." The imposition of the War Measures Act forced Sandra Foster to reappraise Trudeau's Liberal Party. "I was attracted to the Liberals, the Trudeau leadership, but then, of course, what does he do, he declares the War Measures Act. I was outraged. I was among those who sent telegrams of outrage to Ottawa . . . That sort of ended the Liberals as far as I was concerned." Barbara Dresner and her friends were shocked that Canadians so easily accepted the suspension of civil liberties under the War Measures Act. "We couldn't believe it, in the States there would have been fires everywhere . . . That was our first shock about Canada and Canadians . . . How much they trusted their government." Katie McGovern was similarly surprised when she attended a demonstration against the act. "There was a demonstration and it was at Nathan Phillips Square and I went . . . There were about twenty-five people, of which probably twenty were over fifty, and most of them were from the Communist Party." Katie McGovern found that her outrage about the War Measures Act was easily mistaken by Canadians for American arrogance and that her expression of outrage was impolitic and unwelcome.

A telling incident during this period was an event that did *not* happen, for fear of its potential repercussions. This nonevent would have involved a coup for the exile groups in Toronto—a high-profile appearance for the exile movement by Jane Fonda. Fonda was then supporting the Coffeehouse movement around U.S. military bases, which was sending military resisters to Canada. Jack Colhoun, who by October 1970 was a leading force at Amex, recalls that "Fonda . . . did come to Toronto during this period. We were working with TADP. We both agreed that she would do some public stuff and raise some money . . . She came up in October. We met her at the airport and talked . . . She agreed it wasn't a good time and she was going to come back, but she never did." This missed opportunity reflected the tension that surrounded the War Measures Act in English as well as French Canada.

The War Measures Act left a lasting impression on American war resisters. It was another factor, in addition to that of the ties to people and places left behind, that caused feelings of ambivalence, particularly for those who arrived in 1970. These feelings persisted alongside the resisters' new and strengthening sense of Canadian identity. To ignore these lingering feelings is to ignore an important part of the later lives of American war resisters in Canada.

Baseball, Bourbon, and the Blues

The resisters I interviewed have lived nearly all of their adult lives—more than half of their lives—in Canada. Yet many, if not most, retain some ties to the United States. These residual ties may reflect feelings of ambivalence. For while American war resisters living in Canada today have overwhelmingly strengthened their feelings of Canadian identity, and correspondingly lessened their feelings of American identity, they also express mixed feelings about their nationality. Smelser warns that survey measures often miss these feelings.[18] He noted, "Because ambivalence is such a *powerful, persistent, unresolvable, volatile, generalizable, and anxiety-provoking* feature of the human condition, people defend against experiencing it in many ways."[19] Such ambivalence is reflected in the resister sample; however, these feelings may more accurately be seen as residual ties to the United States than outright ambivalence. For ambivalence denotes a sense of being torn between contradictory states or feelings, rather than simply accepting their coexistence.

Perhaps the most striking evidence of continuing ties involves citizenship. While about three-quarters (73 percent) of those interviewed have become Canadian citizens, three-quarters (75 percent) have remained American citizens, and nearly half (49 percent) are today citizens of both countries. In earlier years, before a U.S. Supreme Court decision allowed the possibility of dual citizenship, many resisters did not want to risk losing their American citizenship by becoming Canadian. At the same time, landed immigrant status in Canada granted nearly full rights of citizenship, with the notable exception of federal and provincial voting privileges. A member of the sample who has not become a citizen of Canada explains: "There is absolutely no pressure to become a citizen . . . even though I feel a lot of kinship for the country . . . I wonder if I ever will [become a Canadian citizen]. I always keep mumbling about it, becoming a Canadian citizen, . . . but I don't know."

Meanwhile, most of the respondents remain in frequent touch with people and places from their American past. Almost all reported that they have traveled in the United States in the previous year (89 percent) and are in communication with family members (92 percent) and friends (78 percent) in the United States. Nearly a quarter (23 percent) lived for a time in the United States since originally coming to Canada, and a majority (54 percent) would consider doing so in the future. Of those who have children, more than half (59 percent) have obtained U.S. identity cards for their children and nearly two-thirds (66 percent) would consider sending their children to college in the United States. So while the majority of the American war resisters have stayed in Canada, and most have no current plans to go back to the United States, most also have not cut their ties to the United States, and in fact they mostly keep open the option of returning for themselves and their children. These are objective indicators of residual ties to the United States.

There are also subjective signs of residual ties. John Wolfson articulated the feeling of many resisters when he said, "I feel like a New Canadian, but I also feel like an American." Tom Kane made the same point in a more critical way: "Americans are very chauvinistic . . . I'm still one. I'm both, I'm a Canadian and U.S. citizen." Laura Jones feels she must be more a combination of national ties than she realized, because, she said, "I'd been here all these years and thinking that I was Canadian and I find myself married to another American." Jim Brooks reflected on something distinct but intangible that led him to conclude, "Of course I'm Canadian, but there's something in me that is not Canadian, whether it's energy, whether it's humor . . . Not to say Canadians don't have it too, because they do, but it's something you associate more with Americans." Meanwhile, Kristine King finds that her New York roots are always close to the surface: "There's certainly a part of me that I can't deny . . . I . . . find myself always saying, 'Well, I'm from New York.' I guess that sort of gives me the idea that though I might feel quite Canadian, I do—I have a certain amount of pride in being from New York; it's a great place to come from."

Eric Nagler recognizes a bipolarity in his feelings: "I feel far more Canadian when I'm in the U.S., and I can see my differences when I'm here. I can see myself—my Americanisms, when I'm here." Karen Lawrence said, "When I go to the border, I'm an American when I go that way, and I'm a Canadian when I come the other way . . . Yes, I'm a Canadian, you know, glad of that, but I'm also an American. Like I can't really deny my heritage because my first twenty-three years were a significant part of my life, but also the other part is very significant too. So both." James Smith admitted, "There's . . . a part of me that I'm still discovering that's more American than I expected." Fred Reed put the matter in fundamental terms: "If you ask me, inalterably, what I really am, I would have to say 'an American' . . . You see, I'm in this place, but not of it."

Most resisters at some stage have been discomfited by the duality of their national feelings. Katie McGovern found in her earlier years that she felt uncomfortable with her Americanness: "I had a problem identifying with being an American. I'm sorry, I really did . . . I think I would have preferred to say 'yes, I'm from another planet.'" She realized that although she felt American culturally, "Politically, I felt completely alienated." But over the years, Katie reported, "I've accepted the fact that being American is who I am. I'm just another immigrant, my background is American . . . I feel like a hyphenated Canadian and the hyphen is American." Passage of time and middle age may be helping some resisters to come to terms with such lingering feelings of Americanness.

Andy Barrie, who feels much more Canadian than American, provided insight on the way Americans, resisters included, acknowledge their country of origin to Canadians.

When someone says, "I'm originally American" it means "No, we didn't go to high school together and maybe I didn't play hockey as much as you did as a kid, understand that, but also understand that I don't still think of myself as an American" . . . I have never tried to pass in the sense that if people asked me, I'll always tell them my story, the whole story, by the way. I used to do an open line radio show, and someone would say, "Where you from?" And I'd say, "The States." "Why are you here?" I'd say, "I deserted from the Vietnam war" . . . They're never sure, is that a major revelation? It may be to them, but it's never been to me. But on the other hand, like a million other immigrants, if there's a way for me to merely state my case about any particular issue without necessarily having to refer to being an American, I'll usually try to find a way to do so, because there's among Canadians a "that explains it" attitude, for better or worse. Someone knows you for six months—and likes you or dislikes you—and they'll find out you're an American, as people by the way have found out after knowing me for ten years, and didn't know this, knew me casually, and then they get this "Oh, that explains it."

Barrie regards the issue of national origin as more of a distraction than a provocation. Still, and even though he feels much more Canadian than American, Barrie insists that Americans have a distinct voice that is a valuable addition to the Canadian chorus. He feels he can see this in his own work in radio. He finds, for example, that his work on radio is more self-revealing than is expected in Canada. "That's not something that comes particularly naturally to Canadians. So we have what I'm saying, a voice, and we disclaim that voice for all the reasons that ought to be obvious about Canadian–U.S. politics, about cultural imperialism, and everything else. We disclaim that voice and we disown that voice and we hide that voice, but it is a voice." Barrie concludes that disclosure works best for him; but adds, "I completely understand other people's wish to submerge it, if not hide it, just submerge it, because it becomes an issue, it gets in the way, you get the 'that explains it' syndrome, and you don't want to hear it. You just want to be heard. You don't want to be told 'of course you'd say that, you're . . .'" Still, Barrie argues that disclosure makes more sense since, in the end, "I am what I am and so there are qualities that are for sure in my soul that are American." His position is that it is better to acknowledge this and move on.

Denise Bukowski feels strongly that American ambivalence is actively provoked and reinforced by Canadian attitudes. She notes that in Canada, "It is perfectly acceptable in many quarters to discriminate openly against Americans, and Americans are sensitive to this; most of us hide our place of birth from others as long as possible; we confess it in confidence and mutual relief to each other after the second glass of wine at a party, like children whispering a naughty secret behind the garage."[20]

Some residual American feelings can be traced directly to families of origin and the circumstances and consequences of the separation of resisters from their parents. Steven Bush alluded to the connection in a somewhat abstract way when he said, "Part of me will always be American . . . It's not just the Canadian–American dichotomy that I have carried around in my brain, but also that my parents were both southerners, and I lived for a very important part of my life in the south, but I also had many of my ideas formed by the north during the civil rights movement." Gloria Shookner also feels a family connection to the south: "I still identify with my American roots, those are my roots. I go down to visit my parents and hear a little bit of a southern accent . . . so melodic, and there are still things I identify with being an American, that I'm proud of being an American—that—part of it's my family identity, that sort of fight and stubbornness, and all that, but part of it's my American roots too."

For others, the residual tie that derives from connections to family is more concrete and explicit. Carol Ricker-Wilson links these feelings to being an only child of aging parents. "My elderly parents have seen very little of us, like two or three times a year we go down. So I think that's been very difficult on them, and I feel a lot of guilt around that. Certainly since we didn't get along all that well sometimes, and once the children were born . . . we just put down roots here. So that's where the regrets are." Sarah Miller mentioned that return trips associated with the loss of family members rekindle forgotten feelings. She said, "I've had a lot of back and forthing over the last three years—in my work, but also personal stuff because of family dying, closing up various households, and coming to terms with all that. I really enjoy the time I spend in the States."

Feelings of family also figure in metaphors that resisters used to understand their mixed identities. For Rob Winslow, the idea of rejecting his American identity would be like rejecting his family: "It would be silly to say that I'm anti-American, then I'd be anti my family, anti my culture, anti my roots, anti my whole—my whole point of reference is American. I see myself as transplanted. I'm a Canadian, but I see myself as American and Canadian—I don't see myself as one or the other." Robert Johnson uses the apt analogy of adoption. "I do feel an identification with others who come from the same kind of background . . . It's like being an adopted child—I feel a very strong allegiance to this country that took me in and made me welcome, but I also feel an identity coming out of my youth, my childhood, of the country where I grew up."

Resisters' residual feelings about their national identities also are expressed in their relationships with their children. Pam Oxendine addressed the issue of intergenerational change in national identification. Her daughter, who was born and has grown up in Canada, sometimes complains about her mother's way of interacting with others. "She says, 'Mom, you're so loud.' And I'll say, 'We have a cultural difference. You are Canadian and I'm American. You know what it's like when you go home and see Grandpa.' And she'll say, 'Oh, yeah.' And I'll say, 'And your Uncle.' And she'll say 'Oh, yeah.' And then I say, 'Well, that's who I am. I can't tell you to be loud and you can't tell me to be quiet, because that's a part of who we are and we are different.'"

Lisa Steele's thoughts about national identity, particularly citizenship, were affected, perhaps unknowingly, by her husband. "I finally realized . . . I was getting older and we'd go down and watch my husband vote and . . . I felt like one of those elderly Italian ladies [dressed traditionally in black]. So I thought, this is stupid . . . people who live here should vote . . . I was really in this quandary of my own making." Lisa became a Canadian citizen, but this did not put an end to her residual feelings of national identification.

Finally, there is simply the residual power of the American experience that is in part nostalgia and is recalled and expressed in various ways. Stephen Handler offered a restaurant metaphor to communicate his sense of the lingering power of an American upbringing. "In a Canadian restaurant you have to wait to get the attention of the waitress, because she is elsewhere doing other things; and in an American restaurant you have to wait to enable the waitress to share her life story with you. The waiting time is the same but it's that openness that I miss. After almost thirty years I still miss it . . . I just miss what I knew was America—even if it doesn't exist anymore."

Allan Kazmer began with a disclaimer that wound up leading in a different direction. "We don't feel American at all," he said. "We really enjoy our decision to become Canadian. This feeling has evolved. We miss the openness, brashness and directness of Americans . . . We miss that . . . I miss American blacks too . . . There's a spirit and an attitude and a joy about them, and I go back to Detroit and I say, 'Yeah . . .' That's part of our background culture. It's a walk, an attitude, it's a giggle. I say to myself, 'I really miss this.' I miss just seeing that spirit."

John Phillips was reminded of his American roots when he recently traveled with a group of Americans for whom he was making a corporate video. He recalled, "I got such a charge out of being with these sixty dyed-in-the-wool southern Americans. It really reminded me of how different Americans are from Canadians. The spontaneity, the friendliness, comfortable with you, interested in 'what's your story,' open-minded, ironically, unprejudiced in terms of being open to ideas and who you are—a tour with sixty Canadians would not have been the same." He concluded, "I've never gotten over being an American in that sense."

Tom Needham occasionally remembers the basics, simple things that make him think fondly of the United States. "I have lots of things I still like about the USA: baseball, bourbon, and the blues . . . Here you can get an Italian sandwich, there you can get the Italian-American blend in its purest form . . . Baseball, bourbon, and the blues are still my favorites—and you should see my Canadian wife. She always loved the blues too, and I hate hockey." Such American heresy is seldom openly confessed in Canada.

We're Not in Kansas Anymore

Nostalgia and ambivalence aside, the overwhelming feeling of American resisters is that coming to Canada was a turning point in their lives—in the vocations they have chosen, in the way they see the world and their place in it, and often in their social and political activism. John Wolfson is not atypical in the sharpness with which he draws the picture. "I don't want to overplay it," he began, "but I think it's affected just about everything I've done—it stands out—the whole time, the whole situation, it just stands out . . . quite simply my life just divides between before that and after that."

Many felt when they arrived in Canada that it was simply "the right place"—probably a place they would have belonged better from the start. "I think it's Robert Frost who talked about 'being homesick for a place you've never been,'" Andy Barrie recalled. "I mean, when I came to Canada I'd never been here, and I thought I had arrived home. In fact, all these years I might have imagined I was being socialized as an American in the States—it seems like I was in fact, in some way I couldn't know, being socialized as a Canadian—like what transsexuals say, 'I'm a male trapped in a female body,' I was a Canadian trapped in the body of an American."

Dennis James remembered a similar feeling. "I consistently had a feeling of alienation and a kind of 'what planet do I come from?' Because I felt so—I played sports, I was on teams, and I was accepted, and I had friends, but as I looked at my peers, I just felt odd, out of it. After I came here and I kind of got acquainted, it really felt like home, and I had this feeling of 'no wonder I felt so odd,' because at some level I felt odd because I was in an alien culture. This is my culture. I feel at home here."

Canada's open immigration policy for draft and military resisters was the initial opportunity that changed these former Americans' lives, and once in Canada they often found political and occupational opportunities that were nonexistent or limited in the United States. Steven Burdick became involved in Canadian union activities and said, "Clearly it was transformative." Dennis James observed, "I've been able to find really fulfilling jobs, jobs that I really like. I've liked working in the mental health field and I've really liked working in the addictions field. It's just so wonderfully rewarding. I'm not so sure that that's the kind of career track I would have taken in the States."

Stephen Handler also pointed out the impact of coming to Canada on his work in health care administration. "I probably would have left social work and returned to school. The opportunities here, professionally, wouldn't have existed in the States." Malcolm Shookner echoes this theme: "I was able to develop my career in social work . . . I think the social environment here is much more positive and enabling of those kinds of things, like community work and that kind of stuff to happen. That's not to say that it doesn't happen in the United States, I'm sure it does, but it was such an alienating society, you know, because of the war and other things going on that I couldn't imagine having been able to do those things there."

The sense of expanded opportunities probably was even greater among those in the arts and cultural fields, and these opportunities extended to the possibilities of mixing work with a progressive political agenda. Steven Bush said of his early years, "I found in Toronto Workshop Productions a theater where I liked the work artistically, but it was also much more progressive politically than any theaters that I encountered in the States. It was much farther in the direction of the kind of social changes that interested me."

Alan Guettel stated bluntly, "My life here is entirely different." He realized this a few years ago, when he returned to the States. "I went to New York with a bunch of stuff—records I had produced, and shows I'd written . . . I've run a little record company, I've written plays that have been on stage . . . I've written television shows . . . I've done a bunch of stuff." Alan took samples of his work to a person he knew who was well positioned in the entertainment industry. "He just looked at me and he said, 'What did you come to New York for? In New York you get one chance to do one thing in your whole life' . . . He said, 'This is ridiculous. There's no such experience like this in the USA' . . . That made me realize, it's much more democratic here, much more open to getting started in things." For Guettel the issue also had to do with freedom of political expression. "I felt comfortable. Actually, I was very surprised that there was not such a stigma about being a leftist. I met different kinds of leftists. I met trade union kinds of people, older people, and immigrant people . . . where in the USA most of my friends were university types. I felt very much at home here."

Martha Friendly also felt that she was exposed to a broader cross-section of people in Toronto than she was or would have been in the United States. She concluded, "I never would have known people who are in trade unions, you know, or there isn't the whole sort of social advocacy, social justice kind of thing." She also felt her children were exposed to a better social environment. "The United States is much more class compartmentalized, and racially and ethnically compartmentalized, and my kids never had to endure that . . . I mean I'm not saying it's absent, but . . . I realize all the time how polarized and divided the U.S. is." Don Holman had the same feeling. "Sure there's racism here," he said, "but my kids have grown up with their friends being Chinese, Vietnamese, from Peru, from Senegal, from all over the world, a much richer experience for them." Friendly acknowledges that things won't necessarily stay as she prefers, but she also blames the American influence for this. "I see lots of things in Canada that I really dislike . . . When I put a tag on them I think it's the Americanization of Canada."

Sandra Foster has pursued a successful career in politics that is mainstream and progressively oriented, a combination that she believes would have been unlikely in the United States. "My political involvements were extreme in the States," she recalls, "and I just don't know if I would have moved to more mainstream politics in the way that I did here." Foster found different possibilities in Canada. "I think the opportunities for me with my interest in the public sector, the public and the nonprofit sectors, and public service in its broadest context, not necessarily limited to bureaucracy, the opportunities for me were here and they were closed in the States." She found a place for herself within the mainstream of Canadian politics. "The appreciation of the role of public-sector intervention to make life better for people, the leavening, I think it is pretty strongly established here, and certainly very strong when I came to Canada, and unheard of in the States."

Ann Pohl found that a better health care system and a more progressive tax structure for many years made Canada a place where she could better afford to be a political activist. "I know that I wouldn't have been able to live the life I've lived in Canada in the States. Basically I've been a social justice advocate and political activist my whole life."

Other resisters who have pursued activist goals are conscious that they have paid a financial cost in diminished earnings. None complained, but many were conscious of it. Katie McGovern observed, "I'm not financially stable at all, despite having been in this job [school-community worker] for a while, because it's not a high-paid position . . . But it's been a very interesting life and very fulfilling, and being able to do this kind of work is very creative. So I'm happy." Peter Milligan passed up an opportunity to go to Columbia University and likely could have chosen his American law school. He commented, "Had I gone to law school at NYU or something like that I probably would have been a very different person . . . Who knows. I mean, my dad's a businessman. I certainly would never have met the people that I met when I was involved here in land-use planning and urban development in social housing. Who is to say? In any case, I find Canada to be a very special place for me."

There have, however, been some disadvantages. Sandra Foster noted the cost of leaving family behind. "I haven't been close to my family, so I lost the closeness to my family that I might otherwise have had—and in particular the closeness to my sister that I might have had." Jennifer Glossop mentioned similar feelings about leaving friends behind. "I think probably I ended up cut off from people—I think certainly if I'd stayed in Chicago, stayed with my parents as opposed to coming here, I probably would have been more involved with the group of people I grew up with—I think in some ways it cut me off from friends." Neither Foster nor Glossop thought these were reasons enough to regret emigrating to Canada. "I didn't like it when I was there," Glossop recalls. "When I went down to visit my parents, I was always glad to get back to Canada."

Eric Nagler said that the move to Canada "helped fashion me, it helped give me tools to survive, to be an independent person, to be who I am. It was like an annealing process, when you take iron and heat it up to a temperature so it becomes steel, that kind of process." John Wilson said, "Coming to Canada has allowed me to be myself, to be true to myself in a much easier sort of way. I mean, I feel that if I had stayed in the States I would have probably ended up not that dissimilar, but . . . there would have been both religious and political and social pressures on me, which I would have had to spend too much time and more energy combating to get where I am now." Wilson in mid-life returned to school and now is a fund-raiser for an environmental group in Toronto.

Charlie Diamond also said that coming to Canada helped him mature and gave his life autonomy and direction. "It made me grow up real fast. It made me mature very fast, because I came from an upper middle class Jewish family and I was somewhat spoiled . . . I had to learn to make a life for myself emotionally, socially, every which way. It was a very good experience for me." He believed that making the move helped him realize the importance of taking an ethical position on an issue, even if it had financial and emotional costs, and this conviction has led him to devote most of his adult working life to helping the homeless.

Many resisters emphasized that coming to Canada was a turning point in their construction of their view of the world. Sarah Miller saw her move to Canada as the source of her work in the environmental field. "It's very responsible for who I am . . . what I do . . . It very much gave me a perspective that I didn't have when I was living in the States." The move to Canada, followed by her exposure to a feminist perspective on the environment, changed her way of relating to her surroundings. "I think women don't take ownership all that seriously—I think that the stewardship approach to . . . your relationship to the land . . . is a really important part of it for me." Coming to Canada led to her being introduced to a feminist environmental perspective, and this in turn shaped her work as well as her life on the Toronto Islands.

Fred Reed emphasized the narrowness of the American view he feels he escaped. "Well, Americans . . . tend to be kind and generous, welcoming . . . not impolite, but lacking in curiosity . . . As soon as you are exposed to what goes on at the periphery of the universe, as defined by them, you get a different perspective on life, on the way society could operate, or might operate, and so on." Reed was one of the first American resisters to come to Canada, but his experience of acquiring a wider worldview was often repeated among those who came later.

Denise Bukowski put the issue of world vision even more strongly, from the vantage point of her career as a literary agent. She said that the move to Canada "made me have a completely different worldview than I would have had if I'd stayed in the States and absorbed its monolithic view." She found this was even true in the relatively sophisticated world of publishing. "It is a very isolated place that's totally turned inwards, so even canvassing the publishing community, you're not going to find a wide variety of worldviews, even though they are the New York City intellectual community, so to speak . . . I'm glad I escaped that." Denise Bukowski also feels that by developing her own niche in Canadian publishing, she has been able to accommodate her political interests.

Michele Sanders came to Canada when she was only eighteen. She commented that she felt that her youthfulness, combined with the fact of the migration, was especially influential in shaping her worldview and, in turn, her lifelong involvement in social and political activism, an activism that was given direction by her early experience as part of the mobilization of the Canadian Vietnam war resistance:

> Just my sense of what the world . . . how the world perceives the United States, for one thing, was tremendously expanded, within three weeks of being in Canada, and has just continued to grow. I think my sense of other cultures, my awareness of the value of diversity and embracing that, instead of trying to melt it all into one big shiny flag . . . I think I developed a critical sense of patriotism, which I never would have had had I not come to Canada. I think I developed a humanitarianism and a stronger sense of social responsibility because of what I went through. I would say that this is in relation to the politics with a critical eye to the United States, but also in relation to the helping that went on as a result of coming here, being helped to come here, and then continuing to help others to come here. So all of that . . . TADP is all about that, and so was the free clinic, an extension of that, and then the child-care program. I think all of that was laid out in part because I was able to follow through on prioritizing. Social contributions, which I never would have done had I stayed in the U.S., I don't think. It would have been like beating your head against a wall. Plus, I don't know . . . I just had a different vision there.

Sanders summarizes her experience of choosing Canada this way: "I think it opened up a whole new world to me that was impossible to have imagined when I was living in the United States."

John Moore also felt that Canada changed his life trajectory. "I'm sure I was on my way in the States," he said, "for a life in 'whatever,' you know, in the sixties you could get a job doing anything, so, selling insurance, even military service in some modified capacity. There were all sorts of possibilities in my life until Bobby Kennedy got assassinated, and it all just disappeared." Moore continued, "I don't think I'd be as politically aware if I'd stayed down there. I think the draft created a certain political awareness inside of me . . . I moved from a political person to a politicized person . . . It made me realize that all life choices have a political component and that very much carried over into my work . . . That wouldn't have happened if

I'd remained in the States." John Moore spent many years in legal aid work and now does labor adjudication.

Carolyn Egan said that she felt her life was affected as much by the 1960s as it was by coming to Canada. She also mentioned the women's movement as being of central importance in establishing a lifelong trajectory of social and political activism.

> I'm still a very politically active person—I'm still involved in the pro-choice movement. I was involved in the women's movement within a year after coming here. I'm involved in the trade union movement, so I'm pretty politically active, and I don't think there's any doubt that having been radicalized in the sixties and the Vietnam war and the effects of all that was going on in the sixties, I think it did have quite a dramatic effect on the way I live my life, and I think if I was brought up or had come of age in a different period, it would have been perhaps different, so I don't think there's any doubt that it had a major effect.

Egan is emphatic about the place of the women's movement in her personal political trajectory: "Certainly the role of women was changing at that time, so I think a lot of people who were involved in those movements later went into the women's movement because they said, 'Well, there's a struggle for liberation here.'"

Richard Brown now works in the field of stress management and counseling. He made a direct connection between his present career and the work he did soon after coming to Canada at the Toronto Anti-Draft Program with resisters who were in distress. As he put it, "I was one of the lucky guys . . . I was able to do a lot of good to help people at the time because I realized when I got up here that I was doing a lot better than a lot of these guys. I figured, 'Hey, I got off easy on this, why not help some of these guys who aren't having it so easy.' I've got a direction now that couldn't have happened if that had not occurred, and I'm very content with the direction my life has gone."

Thirty years later most resisters said they felt good about their decision to oppose the U.S. selective service and military laws and the Vietnam war by coming to Canada. These positive statements contrast with the less sanguine predictions of the older normative life-course and collective behavior theories, as well as with present-day depictions of war resisters in films and in critically acclaimed best-selling novels. The account provided in this book of the lives of draft and military resisters who settled in Toronto is consistent with the premises of the political-process theory of social movements and the perspective it offers on the potential role law resistance can play in the life course.

Advocates of political-process theory may have been overly cautious in their reluctance to extend their perspective to more "marginal" or "peripheral" movements, restricting their premises to more "central" or "established" social movements. There is a risk of chauvinism and parochialism in this position. The evidence presented in this book indicates that the decision of American war resisters to come to Canada was, in the political-process terms, a rational and productive response to the opportunity that immigration to Canada presented. I found considerable evidence that these decisions were not just rational actions; they were positive turning points in the lives of the young people who made up the largest political exodus from the United States since the American Revolution.

Some resisters wonder if they could have contributed in different ways if they had stayed in the States, some have gone back because they feel that the United States is where they more naturally belong, and many have continuing residual ties to the United States; but few doubt that their lives were made more meaningful by their decision to move to Canada. Most do not feel like exiles today, but they were exiles when they came, and even those who were critics of the resisters' decision then, such as Tom Hayden and Joan Baez, eventually were convinced that this form of resistance was an effective means of opposition to the Vietnam war. The Toronto Anti-Draft Program and Amex became important mobilizing structures in galvanizing resistance against the Vietnam war and in supporting amnesty, and in doing so they influenced the lives of many of those who were involved in these organizations.

The Canadian government, with the leadership and encouragement of concerned citizens, defended the sovereignty of its immigration policies by making both draft and military resisters welcome in Canada, overcoming a dualism that remains in the United States, in the form of President Carter's final Vietnam war pardon, which was available for only a short period and subjected military resisters to the indignities of restrictive case-by-case reviews. The defense of Canada's immigration law in the face of the challenge of American selective service and military laws opened the gates of opportunity for what was to be a historic migration. The Canadian Vietnam war resistance proved to be a turning point for Canada as well as for the Americans who came. It was a part of the formation of a post–World War II humanitarian role that Canada continues to play in international development and peacekeeping, a role that allows it to maintain independence from the United States while encouraging respect for the sovereignty of other, less powerful nations. Contemporary examples of a more benign and autonomous Canadian foreign policy, which had its beginnings in the sanctuary given to American Vietnam war resisters, include Canada's establishment of independent trade relations with Cuba and its leadership in international efforts to eliminate land mines and to create a permanent international criminal court.

American war resisters have given something back to Canada, especially in cities such as Toronto. "One of the things that's interesting," Lee Vittetow remarked, "is that in that period of time, when you look at what happened in education, child welfare, the arts . . . in the downtown core of Toronto, not the office towers, but in the neighborhoods, all those kinds of things . . . we were a piece of that—in a quiet, blended sort of way. Well, not always so quiet!"

The sights and sounds of Toronto still reflect an American presence. American war resisters were the most numerous immigrants to Canada and Toronto in the late 1960s. Baldwin Street still reverberates with the energy of its communal rebirth as an American ghetto. Many contributed to the renaissance then and have continued to do so. Peter Milligan and Sandra Foster played a prominent part in imposing a height limit on new buildings, and this action helped preserve older neighborhoods in the city core. Mary Anderson, Sarah Miller, and Penny Lawler guided the development of the land trust that preserved the Toronto Islands residential community. Bill King became the artistic director who made the Beaches Jazz Festival one of the city's most joyful celebrations. Andy Barrie has given an articulate new voice to public radio. Michelle Sanders developed a citywide child-care network, Eric Nagler became one of Canada's best-known writers and performers of children's songs, Laura Jones became an influential school board trustee, and Charlie Diamond still looks after the city's homeless. Denise Bukowski established her own agency for immigrant writers; Jim Polk worked through the provincial government to nurture and maintain a Canadian writing and publishing presence. Gregory Kolesar and Stephen Handler helped to develop and now oversee community health care for two of the largest boroughs in the city. John Thompson contributed to the design of the recent streetcar corridor that connects the Bloor Street subway line with the new Harbourfront and historic Union Station, while James Smith assisted in the design and construction of the CN Tower.

These are only a few of the contributions of the thousands of American war resisters who have lived their adult lives in Toronto. Some have come and gone, others will yet return, but the majority have stayed. Over time most of these American immigrants have lost contact with one another, becoming more a part of the life of the larger city than a part of one another's personal lives. Nonetheless, each day many of their paths unknowingly cross in numerous and unnoticed ways, one more group of citizens in a city that is among the most diverse in the world. Who today would notice? That they are unnoticed is probably an indication that the resisters have found their natural place. Still, Toronto looks and sounds different because they have been here, and they remain a presence, maintaining an enduring pride in their cause, in their adopted country, and in their life decisions.

APPENDIXES

NOTES

INDEX

Appendix A:
The Respondent-Driven Sample and Interviews

The respondent-driven sampling (RDS) methodology, developed by Douglas Heckathorn, is a variant of snowball sampling[1] in which the members of the sample become actively involved in subject recruitment.[2] In addition to supplying subjects who are difficult to locate, one function of this active involvement is to overcome the need to make "cold" (i.e., unanticipated and unintroduced) calls to prospective respondents, by enlisting each new member of the sample in a chain referral process. Each respondent not only proposed further names, but also contacted the freshly nominated respondents and prepared them for the forthcoming call, while also encouraging participation in the research.

RDS begins with a set of "seed" respondents. I began with contacts I had formed over nearly thirty years of living in Canada; but, like most of the respondents, I knew only a few likely participants. I was able to supplement my list with more plentiful sources: the results of advertising in a national newspaper,[3] the records of a producer of a CBC documentary,[4] the files of two war resistance organizations,[5] and an oral history project on what was sometimes called the American ghetto in Toronto.[6] The oral history project included interviews conducted in 1978 with twenty-one former members of this American enclave; of this group I was able to relocate fifteen. I fanned out from the above sources and identified a diverse representation of the population of resisters that had settled in Toronto. Nearly 90 percent of the sample immediately settled in Toronto on arrival in Canada, and 95 percent of the original Toronto residents were still living there. The incentives I used to motivate respondents were simple expressions of appreciation for their own interviews and for helping to enlist others in constructing a social and historical record of a population (i.e., American Vietnam war resisters who had come to Canada) otherwise at risk of disappearing.

I let respondents know I was also an American who had come to Canada to resist the Vietnam war, and I volunteered to undertake the interview at their convenience. One- to two-hour interviews were conducted with one hundred respondents from June 1997 through May 1998. The interviews took place in my law school office, in respondents' offices and homes, in restaurants and coffee shops. Only four potential respondents refused to participate, and I ultimately received more names of potential respondents than I could follow up.[7]

The location of the study in Toronto and the chain referral process involved in the sampling could have overrepresented interconnected and atypically politicized respondents. The description and analysis of the RDS sample given below explain the efforts I made to diminish this risk, albeit within the limited context of the city of Toronto. In brief, the study began with multiple Toronto seeds who varied in their political origins and outcomes, the succeeding respondents were pursued through multiple waves of referrals, and the referrals quickly branched in a dispersed pattern of recruitment across the city of Toronto. Comparison of patterns in this sample with other studies and with contemporary census data (see Chapter 6) offers evidence that the respondents are not atypical of American resisters who came and stayed in other Canadian cities.

Still, it should be emphasized that this is a sample of resisters who settled in metropolitan Toronto, the largest and probably most highly organized site of the migration of American resisters to Canada. I chose Toronto *because* it was a place where the political process of collective resistance among American Vietnam exiles took place. So the interview sample for this study is not representative of all resisters who came to Canada, or all resisters who stayed in Canada, or perhaps even of all resisters who settled in Toronto, since, for example, the borders of Toronto now stretch further than when this study began and even then included surrounding suburban areas that I did not penetrate. Nonetheless, as shown in this appendix and discussed in the text, particularly in Chapter 4, the interview sample is diverse in background and experiences, similar in characteristics to samples of American resisters drawn in other urban Canadian settings such as Vancouver, and by all appearances representative of American resisters who initially settled in the metropolitan center of Toronto. As described in Chapter 4, Toronto attracted Americans who were bipolar in their degree of background experience with social and political movements. In subsequent years, many of these resisters have remained socially and politically active in Canada. My interest is particularly in the processes by which this did and did not occur. The diversity of the sample allows analysis of such issues. However, in the interest of exploring the sensitivity of the findings to the respondent-driven sampling strategy and also of offering some basis for speculation about the broader experience of American resisters, I employ some lower- and upper-bound estimation procedures in Chapter 4 to establish ranges within which the most provocative findings of this study might apply.

The Methodology

Acting as the sole interviewer, I adopted the following strategy:

1. I called resister A to request his or her participation in the study.
2. I described to A the limited information that exists about resisters and expressed gratitude for his or her considering participation.
3. After conducting the interview with A I requested the name of resister B (and others) for subsequent interview.
4. I then asked A to contact B to encourage participation in the study.
5. After an agreed time interval, usually a day or two, I recontacted A to confirm and express gratitude for A's contacting B.
6. I then contacted B to express gratitude for considering participation in the study and to schedule an interview at a convenient time and place.
7. After interviewing B, the chain referral process recycled with my asking B for names of further resisters, with whom I repeated this process.

Heckathorn's RDS method is intended to mitigate concerns about possible sources of bias in chain referral sampling. The use of the dual incentive system and multiple waves of respondents is intended to increase randomness and resulting representation. Heckathorn argues that following referral chains through multiple waves can overcome dependence on initial seeds; and that the dual-incentive system of enlisting seeds and succeeding members of the referral chain as sources of peer pressure to help in the recruitment process is more likely to draw uncooperative or reclusive respondents into participation.

To assess the extent to which representation was achieved with this method, I compared the distribution of father's education by draft and military resistance status in the Toronto war resisters sample with the same cross-classification of variables in the largest earlier published study of resisters conducted by Renée Kasinsky with a focus on Vancouver. This comparison is shown in Table A.1. Both samples reveal a similar tendency for the fathers of military resisters to be less highly educated than the fathers of draft resisters, suggesting that both samples may be representative of the population of resisters. To assure that inclusion of women in my sample did not introduce bias, Table A.1 also presents results for males only, with no significant change in pattern.

Heckathorn demonstrates that when the RDS method is followed through multiple waves, it is possible to diagram recruitment networks, as shown in Figure A.1, which illustrates the most productive seed in this study. This particular network is tracked through ten waves of recruits. Knowledge of the characteristics of the seeds and the resulting membership of the sample can then be used in cross-tabular form to assess the attainment of independence in recruitment. This independence is assumed to have been achieved when the sample reaches a stable composition with respect to the characteristics on which the research rests. The cross-tabulations just described and presented below provide the information that is necessary to compute the number of waves of recruitment that must be completed before the sample approximates the equilibrium distribution that indicates that the sample has become independent of its starting point. As Heckathorn predicts, for all the characteristics of respondents we considered, equilibrium was reached quite rapidly.

A major threat to independence in chain referral samples is the tendency of seeds to recruit sample members from within their own groups. For example, it might be expected that men would be more likely to recruit other men rather than women. This possibility seemed to be indicated in the initial recruitment pattern shown in Figure A.1: all of the first-wave recruits by this seed were men. However, Heckathorn's point is that when the respondent-driven process is followed through multiple waves, such patterns tend to break down. This breakdown begins in the very next wave of Figure A.1, when three of the next six recruits are women. By the tenth wave of this network, 22 women and 28 men have been recruited.

Table A.2 indicates that male seeds actually recruited more female respondents than did female seeds, with women constituting about a third of the

Table A.1 Parental educational attainment of draft and military resisters in Kasinsky and Hagan samples

Educational attainment	Kasinsky sample (males only)			Hagan sample					
				Males and females			Males only		
	Draft resisters	Military resisters	Total	Draft resisters	Military resisters	Total	Draft resisters	Military resisters	Total
Four years of college or more	46.8% (22)	27.8% (10)	38.6% (32)	51.4% (41)	15.0% (3)	44.0% (44)	47.2% (26)	20.0% (3)	41.5% (29)
Some college or university	14.9% (7)	11.1% (4)	13.3% (11)	12.6% (10)	15.0% (3)	13.0% (13)	12.8% (7)	20.0% (3)	14.3% (10)
High school graduation	38.3% (18)	33.3% (12)	36.1% (30)	18.8% (15)	40.0% (8)	23.0% (23)	23.6% (13)	40.0% (6)	27.1% (19)
Less than high school graduation	0.0% (0)	27.8% (10)	12.1% (10)	17.6% (14)	30.0% (6)	20.0% (20)	16.3% (9)	20.0% (3)	17.1% (12)
Total	100.0% (47)	100.0% (36)	100.0% (83)	100.0% (80)	100.0% (20)	100.0% (100)	100.0% (55)	100.0% (15)	100.0% (70)

Source: Kasinsky data from Renée Kasinsky, *Refugees from Militarism: Draft-Age Americans in Canada* (New Brunswick, N.J.: Transaction Books, 1976).

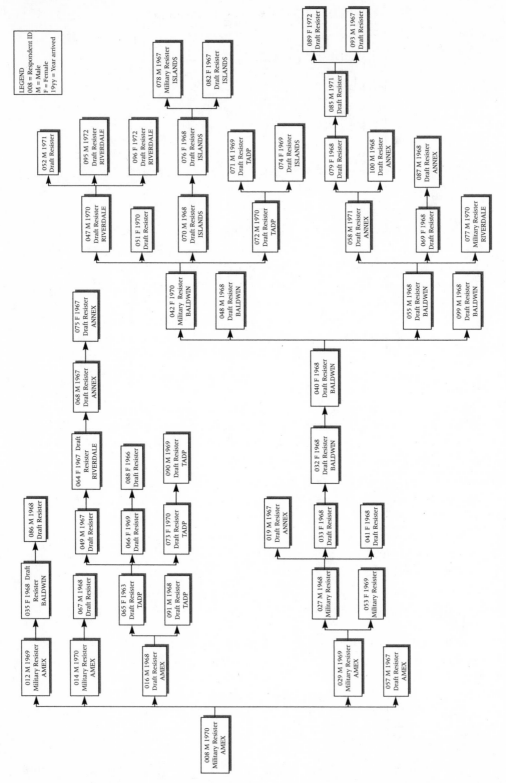

Figure A.1 Diagram of recruitment network for most productive seed (008) in respondent-driven war resister sample

Table A.2   Recruitment by gender

Gender of recruiter	Gender of recruit		Total
	Male	Female	
Male (16)	66.2%	33.8%	100% (71)
Female (4)	77.8%	22.2%	100% (9)
Total distribution of recruits	67.5% (54)	32.5% (26)	100% (80)
Equilibrium	69.7%	30.3%	100%

men's recruits, and a little less than a quarter of the women's recruits. Heckathorn's procedure estimates that equilibrium could be reached across just one wave of seeds, with an independent sample consisting of 69.7 percent men and 30.3 percent women. Our final distribution of men and women in the sample is nearly exactly that distribution. While an equal number of men and women in the sample might have been desirable, this possibility probably was prevented by a requirement in the sampling that the women recruited originally have come to Canada with a male war resister. A significant number of American women who immigrated during this period came on their own.

Table A.3 presents a further cross-tabulation of seeds and recruits in terms of draft and military resister status. Military resisters constituted only 25 percent of the seeds for the sample, with draft resisters forming the remaining 75 percent of the seeds; both kinds of resisters recruited almost exactly the same proportions of draft and military resisters into the sample, with military resisters forming about 19 percent of the recruits and draft resisters about 81 percent. Overall, the sample consists of about 20 percent military and 80 percent draft resisters. More military resisters initially entered Canada, perhaps as many as one third of all resisters, but they probably also were slightly more likely to encounter immigration and settlement problems and return to the United States. The ratio of draft to military resisters in our sample probably approaches an accurate representation of those who stayed.

Additional cross-tabulations were done by age and year of entry into Canada. These tables also revealed only modest differences in recruitment within groupings; Heckathorn's estimation procedure predicts an approximation of equilibrium within one and two waves of recruitment by age and year respectively. The year of entry in the present study appeared to take an

Table A.3 Recruitment by resister status

Resister status of recruiter	Resister status of recruit		Total
	Draft resister	Military resister	
Draft resister (15)	81.5%	18.5%	100% (27)
Military resister (5)	81.5%	18.9%	100% (53)
Total distribution of resisters	81.3% (65)	18.8% (15)	100% (80)
Equilibrium	81.4%	18.6%	100%

extra wave to reach equilibrium because age was recoded into two categories, with year of entry allowed to vary. The cross-tabulations by background characteristics were consistent with Heckathorn's prediction that independence of seeds and recruits in RDS sampling usually can be efficiently achieved through the use of the dual-incentive RDS methods.

Further examination of Figure A.1 reveals clues as to how independence and representation are achieved through Heckathorn's approach. As the waves of this recruitment network unfolded, the respondents brought into the sample could be identified as members of key groups in the Toronto resister population. For example, the original seed in this network was a major figure in Amex. All five members of the first wave of recruits were also involved to various degrees in Amex. However, the second wave of this recruitment network broke out of Amex and entered into the Toronto Anti-Draft Program and the Baldwin Street American ghetto. The third wave brought in further members of these groups and also representatives of the arts and cultural scene associated with the Annex neighborhood. The fourth wave included individuals from Riverdale and the Islands residential communities. Although today American resisters are spread throughout Toronto, this immigrant group of resisters, as described in the text, initially was concentrated in the center of the city around the University of Toronto. The waves of this recruitment network and others included in the RDS sample brought a wide array of resisters into our study—enough to suggest in quantitative and qualitative terms that representation of this group was achieved within the central metropolitan area of Toronto.

The Interviews

I began the interview by ascertaining demographic information, date of migration to Canada, with whom (if anyone) the migration occurred, and draft or active military status. I then asked respondents to rate thirty-five events placed on a time line from 1960 to 1975 as determinants of their decision to leave the United States. These events stretched from the election of John Kennedy in 1960 to the fall of Saigon in 1975, peaking in hypothesized importance with the Martin Luther King and Robert Kennedy assassinations and the Chicago Democratic Convention riot in 1968.

The interview instrument also included a life history calendar of dated personal events.[8] This calendar was organized from 1960 to the present, with the years listed horizontally in rows. Respondents developed chronologies in vertically arranged columns, charting sequences of changing status, including draft classification, immigration, education, marriage, children, place of residence, and occupation. This life history calendar was an important vehicle for establishing when critical events occurred in the respondents' lives; specific events could be used to establish sequence and timing of other events. For example, respondents typically had no trouble recalling the date of their immigration to Canada, sometimes pulling out a copy of their Landed Immigrant Card to make the point. Educational degrees, marriages, and births of children were also easily recalled. These benchmarks helped respondents recall changes in place of residence and occupation. Within the first thirty minutes of the interview, respondents were able to recall the time and place of many of their most significant life experiences.

Still, and despite their best efforts, it cannot be claimed that their recall was total, correct, or complete. We live in what Zerubavel usefully calls "remembrance environments" and "mnemonic communities" that shape our recall of events.[9] Events such as war and migration may be especially significant in shaping not only the actual recall of facts but also the particular light in which we recall them. Zerubavel writes, "We usually learn what we should remember and what we can forget as part of our *mnemonic socialization,* a process that normally takes place when we enter an altogether new social environment, such as when we get married, start a new job, convert to another religion, or emigrate to another country."[10] Zerubavel goes on to warn that we must be particularly careful not to mistake manifestations of a mnemonic community's collective memory, or "social mindscapes," for genuinely personal recollections.

We see in this book that most American resisters have chosen to assimilate and identify strongly with Canadian society. The experience of assimilation is a selective social filter that is associated with powerful feelings of national ambivalence among the American resisters. The methodology employed in the interviewing process used state-of-the-art techniques such as the life history calendar to objectively date life events and factually establish changing social statuses such as citizenship, education, marriage and occupation; but the *perspectives* of the respondents on these social facts are obviously more socially determined and subjective, and as such they are especially interesting.

In another part of the interview I attempted to develop objective and subjective aspects of the respondents' life stories by using Daniel Bertaux's method for constructing "social genealogies."[11] Bertaux notes that the basic idea of this methodology is to "define the unit of observation so as to include several generations (at least three), and to have roughly as many persons/ couples on each generation; in short, to define 'rectangular' genealogies."[12] Each respondent was represented by this method as a point in a genealogical tree where two inverted pyramids touch each other at their vortex. The tree included the war resister and (ideally) a same-sex sibling, their parents and spouses, and their respective children. The special value of siblings in this methodology is their availability as a unique comparison group for war resisters that holds family background relatively constant. These siblings were incorporated as comparison points to assess hypotheses about the disruptive effects of war resistance and migration to Canada on educational, marital, and occupational life outcomes.

Bertaux emphasizes that the development of these social genealogies is valuable not only for the collection of quantitative data about life outcomes, but also as a means of stimulating qualitative accounts of the family life stories that "fill in the blanks" of the respondents' lives. Bertaux notes that in contrast with more conventional data, these genealogies can be especially valuable in revealing the central role of women in shaping the trajectories of life stories. He emphasizes how crucial this kind of information can be for populations that have experienced long-distance migrations, noting that "the further away lineage trajectories are from . . . ideal-typical reproduction or 'immobility' patterns, the more family stories are needed to help understand what were the 'real stories' behind the observed mobilities and discontinuities."[13] Much of the qualitative material in this account of American resisters in Canada derived from the interviewing surrounding these social genealogies.

Other parts of the interview focused on the role of the war-related migration to Canada in shaping respondents' subsequent involvement in social and political movements and activities. The interview instrument was explicitly designed to allow the collection of closed-ended, quantitative sources of information about social and political activism and its impact in the form of life outcomes, while at the same time incorporating open-ended probes intended to elicit more qualitative discussions of the issues involved. I found that it was particularly helpful to ground the latter discussions around key life transitions, such as the first several months of life in Canada, marriages and marital breakups, choice of occupational careers, and decisions about having children. Far from being distant background issues in these respondents' lives, events and activities related to decisions to leave the United States and come to Canada remain lively issues that have continuing, if not daily, relevance in terms of the respondents' personal efforts to make sense of their evolving life experiences.

Appendix B: Tables

Table B.1 Inventory of variables for activism analysis

Variable	Measures and values	x	SD
Gender	Female = 1	.300	.461
Parental activism	Activists = 1	.320	.469
Prior U.S. activism	Sum of: civil rights activity (0 = not involved; 3 = very involved) Peace/antiwar activity (0 = not involved; 3 = very involved)	2.790	2.284
War resistance in Canada	Sum of: Helped others come = 1 Counseling/advice = 1 Housing = 1 Food = 1 Money = 1 Job offers = 1 Organizational involvement = 1 Joined staff = 1 Active on campus = 1 Direct action projects = 1 Community organizing = 1 Membership = 1 Fund-raising = 1 Marches/demonstrations = 1 Mobilization efforts = 1 Strike efforts = 1 Media forums = 1 Contributed money = 1	7.150	6.264

Involvement in women's movement Involvement after coming to Canada (0 = not involved; 3 = very involved)	.560	1.067
Ties to early contacts and friends Were personal contacts or friendships you established when you came to Canada influential in your deciding to become involved in current political activities? (Yes = 1)	.380	.488
Current political views Which of the following best characterizes your political stance? (1, radical right; 5, moderate; 10, radical left)	7.890	1.254
Current social and political activism Sum of current involvement in: Any current social movement = 1 New Democratic Party = 3 Other left party = 3 Neighborhood, community, or tenant group = 3 Progressive caucus in profession = 3 Consciousness-raising group = 3 Self-help group = 3 Food co-op = 3 Work co-op = 3 Commune = 3 Day-care co-op = 3 Alternative schools = 3 Full-time activist work = 5	7.500	7.481

Table B.2 Life-course determinants of social and political activism among American
war resisters in Canada

Variable	Bivariate correlation	Total effect	Direct effect	Indirect effect	Multiple correlation
Gender	.372*	.375*	.104	.271	.375
Parental activism	.193*	.153*	−.005	.158	.405
Prior U.S activism	.383*	.302*	.105	.197	.500
War resistance in Canada	.434*	.315*	.100	.215	.572
Involvement in women's movement	.442*	.272*	.176*	.096	.621
Ties to early contacts and friends	.559*	.326*	.291*	.035	.678
Current political views	.544*	.274*	.274*	.000	.714

*$p < .05$

Table B.3   Direct effects of life-course determinants of social and political activism among male and female war resisters

Variable	Males (n = 70)		Females (n = 30)	
	β	SE	β	SE
Parental activism	−.09	1.38	.12	2.38
Prior U.S. activism	.17	.28	−.02	.67
War resistance in Canada	.12	.12	.12	.25
Involvement in women's movement	−.03	.81	.37*	.92
Ties to early contacts and friends	.29*	1.50	.28**	2.82
Current political views	.34*	.54	.32*	1.47
Constant	−8.92		−23.23	
R^2	.40		.62	

*p < .05
**p < .10

Table B.4 Determinants of current income (n = 90)

Variable	Eq. (1)			Eq. (2)			Eq. (3)		
	b	ß	SE	b	ß	SE	b	ß	SE
Father's occupational prestige	−30.00	−.01	229.11	−141.51	−.062	209.85	−3.06	−.01	201.43
Gender	−14703.13*	−.21	7196.18	−13562.86*	−.19	6546.96	−6184.51	−.09	6518.44
Respondent's occupational prestige	670.78*	.20	350.86	464.59	.14	322.47	427.99	.13	303.52
War resistance in Canada	−1130.79*	−.22	531.40	−832.00*	−.16	487.94	−127.57	−.02	502.26
Sibling's income				.32*	.41	.07	.28*	.36	.07
Current political views							−9421.81*	−.35	2727.71
Constant	35494.82			28616.81			93436.78		
R^2	.17			.32			.41		

Note: Equations estimated with OLS regression.

*$p < .05$

Table B.5 Estimated numbers of men and women aged 15–29 who immigrated from United States to Canada to resist the Vietnam war, 1965–1974

Year	Total male arrivals	Male resisters[a]	Total female arrivals	Female resisters[b]
1965	1,922	656	2,592	625
1966	2,447	1,181	3,329	1,362
1967	3,032	1,766	3,750	1,783
1968	4,076	2,810	4,330	2,363
1969	4,405	3,139	5,112	3,145
1970	5,510	4,244	5,714	3,747
1971	4,778	3,512	5,477	3,510
1972	3,980	2,714	5,278	3,310
1973	4,120	2,854	5,356	3,389
1974	4,255	2,989	5,536	3,569
Total, 1965–1972		20,022		19,846
Total, 1965–1974		25,865		26,804

a. Arriving number minus average annual migration of American men, 15–29, for preceding five years (1,266).

b. Arriving number minus average annual migration of American women, 15–29, for preceding five years (1,967).

Table B.6 Estimated proportion of American-born men and women Vietnam war resisters who stayed in Canada, circa 1996

Year of arrival	Arriving immigrants of American origin		Arriving resisters of U.S. birth[a]		Remaining resisters of U.S. birth (1996)[b]		Proportion of U.S.-born resisters who stayed (1996)		
	Men	Women	Men	Women	Men	Women	Men	Women	Total
1967	3,032	3,750	1,622	1,712	1,048	878	.65	.51	.58
1968	4,076	4,330	2,510	2,204	1,408	1,278	.56	.58	.57
1969	4,405	5,112	2,789	2,869	1,373	1,643	.49	.57	.53
1970	5,510	5,714	3,729	3,381	1,698	1,648	.46	.49	.47
1971	4,778	5,477	3,106	3,179	1,533	1,698	.49	.53	.52
1972	3,980	5,278	2,428	3,010	1,508	2,008	.62	.67	.65

a. Respective preceding columns multiplied by estimated proportion of arrivals who are American-born (.85), minus estimated annual migration of American-born men (n = 995) and women (n = 1,476), 1960–1963.

b. Number minus average annual number of American-born 1960–1963 arrivals, 15–29, who remained in 1996 (men = 287, women = 502).

Notes

1. Laws of Resistance

1. See Renée Kasinsky, *Refugees from Militarism: Draft-Age Americans in Canada* (New Brunswick, N.J.: Transaction Books, 1976).
2. See Chapter 6 and Appendix B, Table B.5.
3. Appendix B, Tables 5 and 6.
4. The "Kennedy List" is discussed in Lawrence Baskir and William Strauss, *Chance and Circumstance: The Draft, the War, and the Vietnam Generation* (New York: Alfred Knopf, 1978). The list itself is in the public domain; see, for example, the Archives of the Toronto Anti-Draft Program in the Thomas Fisher Rare Book Library, Robarts Library, University of Toronto.
5. See Bill Davidson, "Hell, No, We Won't Go: Why Young Americans Are Deserters, Exiles, Fugitives, Conscientious Objectors," *Saturday Evening Post*, 27 January 1968, pp. 21—27.
6. David Meyer, "Tending the Vineyard: Cultivating Political Process Research," *Sociological Forum* 14 (1999): 91. For the political process approach to social movements, see James Rule and Charles Tilly, "Political Process in Revolutionary France, 1830–1832," in John Merriman, ed., *1830 in France* (New York: New Viewpoints, 1975); and Doug McAdam, *Political Process and the Development of Black Insurgency, 1930–1970* (Chicago: University of Chicago Press, 1982).
7. See Jeff Goodwin and James Jasper, "Caught in the Winding, Snarling Vine: The Structural Bias of Political Process Theory," *Sociological Forum* 14 (1999): 27–54.
8. The classic starting point of life-course scholarship in terms of contemporary research is Glen Elder's *Children of the Great Depression: Social Change and Life Experience,* originally published in 1974 by the University of Chicago Press and reissued in 1999 in an enlarged edition under the same title by Westview Press of Boulder, Colorado. For an overview of Elder's development of this perspective, see his "Time, Human Agency, and Social Change: Perspectives on the Life Course," *Social Psychology Quarterly* 57 (1994): 4–15.
9. See John Modell, *Into One's Own: From Youth to Adulthood in the United States, 1920–1975* (Berkeley: University of California Press, 1989).

10. See Karl Ulrich Mayer and Urs Schoepflin, "The State and the Life Course," *Annual Review of Sociology* 15 (1989): 187–209; and Franklin Zimring, *The Changing Legal World of Adolescence* (New York: Oxford University Press, 1982).

11. For sexuality, see Daniel J. Boorstein, *The Americans: The Democratic Experience* (New York: Random House, 1973); for delinquency, see F. Ivan Nye and James F. Short, "Scaling Delinquent Behavior," *American Sociological Review* 22 (1957): 326–332.

12. John Clausen, "Turning Point as a Life Course Concept: Meaning and Measurement." Paper presented at the annual meeting of the American Sociological Association, Washington, D.C.

13. Ian Gotlib and Blair Wheaton, eds., *Stress and Adversity over the Life Course: Trajectories and Turning Points* (New York: Cambridge University Press, 1997).

14. David Surrey, *Choice of Conscience: Vietnam Era Military and Draft Resisters in Canada* (New York: Praeger, 1982).

15. See, for example, Edwin Lemert, *Social Pathology* (New York: McGraw-Hill, 1951).

16. For example, Doug McAdam, *Freedom Summer* (New York: Oxford University Press, 1988); Gerald Marwell, Michael Aiken, and N. J. Demerath III, "The Persistence of Political Attitudes among 1960s Civil Rights Activists," *Public Opinion Quarterly* 51 (1987): 359–375; M. Kent Jennings, "Residues of a Movement: The Aging of the American Protest Generation," *American Political Science Review* 81 (1987): 367–382; James Fendrich, "Keeping the Faith or Pursuing the Good Life: A Study in the Consequences of Participation in the Civil Rights Movement," *American Sociological Review* 42 (1977): 144–157; Jack Whalen and Richard Flacks, "Echoes of Rebellion: The Liberated Generation Grows Up," *Journal of Political and Military Sociology* 12 (1984): 61–78.

17. Sheldon Glueck and Eleanor Glueck, *Unraveling Juvenile Delinquency* (Cambridge, Mass.: Harvard University Press, 1950).

18. Robert Sampson and John Laub, *Crime in the Making* (Cambridge, Mass.: Harvard University Press, 1993).

19. Denis Hogan and Nan Marie Astone, "The Transition to Adulthood," *Annual Review of Sociology* 12 (1986): 109–130.

20. Selective Service System, *Memorandum on Channeling* (Washington, D.C.: Government Printing Office, 1965).

21. Cited in Kasinsky, *Refugees from Militarism,* p. 21.

22. Margaret Atwood, *The Robber Bride* (New York: Bantam Books, 1993).

23. Scott Turow, *The Laws of Our Fathers* (New York: Harper Collins, 1996).

24. John Irving, *A Prayer for Owen Meany* (New York: Ballantine Books, 1989).

25. Pat Conroy, *Beach Music* (New York: Bantam Books, 1995).

26. Jerry Lembcke, *The Spitting Image: Myth, Memory, and the Legacy of Vietnam* (New York: New York University Press, 1998).

27. Todd Gitlin, *The Sixties: Years of Hope, Days of Rage* (New York: Bantam Books, 1993), p. 384.

28. Bernice Neugarten, Joan Moore, and John Lowe, "Age Norms, Age Con-

straints, and Adult Socialization," *American Journal of Sociology* 70 (1965): 710–717.

29. See, for example, Dennis Hogan, "The Variable Order of Events in the Life Course," *American Sociological Review* 43 (1978): 573–586; and David Featherman and Michael Carter, "Discontinuities in Schooling and the Socio-economic Life Cycle," in William Sewell, Robert Hauser, and David Featherman, eds., *Schooling and Achievement in American Society: Studies in Population* (New York: Academic Press, 1984), pp. 133–160.

30. Neil Smelser, "Social and Psychological Dimensions of Collective Behavior," in Ronald Ye-Lin Cheng, ed., *The Sociology of Revolution* (Chicago: Henry Regnery, 1973), pp. 314–318.

31. Lewis Feuer, *The Conflict of Generations: The Character and Significance of Social Movements* (New York: Basic Books, 1969).

32. Neil Smelser, "The Rational and the Ambivalent in the Social Sciences," *American Sociological Review* 63 (1998): 1–16.

33. David Meyer, "Tending the Vineyard: Cultivating Political Process Research," *Sociological Forum* 14 (1999): 81.

34. Charles Tilly, "Wise Quacks," *Sociological Forum* 14 (1999): 60.

35. See John Modell, Frank Furstenberg, and Theodore Hershberg, "Social Change and Transitions to Adulthood in Historical Perspective," *Journal of Family History* 1 (1976): 7–32.

36. Dale Dannefer, "Adult Development and Social Theory: A Paradigmatic Reappraisal," *American Sociological Review* 49 (1984): 100–116.

37. Ronald Rindfuss, C. Gray Swicegood, and Rachel Rosenfeld, "Disorder in the Life Course: How Common and Does It Matter?" *American Sociological Review* 52 (1987): 785–801.

38. Glen Elder, "Time, Human Agency, and Social Change: Perspectives on the Life Course," *Social Psychology Quarterly* 57 (1994): 4–15.

39. For the resource-mobilization model, see Mayer Zald and John McCarthy, eds., *Social Movements in an Organizational Society* (New Brunswick, N.J.: Transaction Books, 1987); for the political-process model, see McAdam, *Political Process.*

40. McAdam, *Political Process and the Development of Black Insurgency,* p. 37.

41. Sidney Tarrow, *Power in Movement: Social Movements, Collective Action and Politics* (Cambridge: Cambridge University Press, 1994), pp. 17–18.

42. Doug McAdam, "Conceptual Origins, Current Problems, Future Directions," in Doug McAdam, John McCarthy, and Mayer Zald, eds., *Comparative Perspectives on Social Movements: Political Opportunities, Mobilizing Structures, and Cultural Framings* (Cambridge: Cambridge University Press, 1996), p. 26.

43. Doug McAdam, John McCarthy, and Mayer Zald, "Introduction: Opportunities, Mobilizing Structures, and Framing Processes–Toward a Synthetic, Comparative Perspective on Social Movements," in McAdam, McCarthy, and Zald, eds., *Comparative Perspectives on Social Movements,* p. 5.

44. Roger Gould, "Multiple Networks and the Mobilization of the Paris Commune, 1871," *American Sociological Review* 56 (1991): 716–729.

45. McAdam, McCarthy, and Zald, "Introduction: Opportunities, Mobilizing Structures, and Framing Processes," p. 8.
46. McAdam, *Political Process*, p. 18.
47. Doug McAdam, "'Initiator' and 'Spin-off Movements': Diffusion Processes in Political Cycles," in Mark Traugott, ed., *Repertoires and Cycles of Collective Action* (Durham: Duke University Press, 1995), p. 224.
48. McAdam, "Conceptual Origins, Current Problems, Future Directions," p. 333.
49. Goodwin and Jasper, "Caught in the Winding, Snarling Vine," p. 39.
50. These include Michael Adams, "American Refugee Study," master's thesis, University of Toronto, 1970; John Cooney and Dana Spitzer, "American Deserters in Sweden and Canada," *Transaction* 6, no. 10 (1969): 53–62; Kenneth Fred Emerick, *War Resisters in Canada* (Knox, Pa.: Pennsylvania Free Press, 1972); Kasinsky, *Refugees from Militarism;* Richard Killmer, Robert Lecky, and Debrah Wiley, *They Can't Go Home Again: The Story of America's Political Refugees* (Philadelphia: Pilgrim Press, 1971); Saul Levine, "Draft Dodgers: Coping with Stress, Adapting to Exile," *American Journal of Orthopsychiatry* 42 (1972): 431–440; David Surrey, *Choice of Conscience: Vietnam Era Draft and Military Resisters in Canada* (New York: Praeger, 1982); Roger Neville Williams, *The New Exiles: American War Resisters in Canada* (New York: Liveright Publishers, 1971).
51. For autobiography, see Douglas Fetherling, *Travels by Night: A Memoir of the Sixties* (Toronto: Lester Publishing, 1994), and James Dickerson, *North to Canada: Men and Women against the Vietnam War* (Westport, Conn.: Praeger, 1999). For a journalistic account, see Alan Haig-Brown, *Hell No, We Won't Go: Vietnam Draft Resisters in Canada* (Vancouver: Raincoast Books, 1996).
52. Jay Scott, "Draft Dodgers: They've Become Canadianized," *Toronto Globe and Mail,* Metro Edition, 18 June 1990, p. B1; see also Robert Fulford, "A Rave Review," *Toronto Life* 27 (1993): 58–65.
53. An interesting example is Florence Bird, who came to Canada in the 1950s when she married John Bird, an Ottawa Press Gallery columnist. Florence Bird was also a journalist and wrote under the pen name Ann Francis. She chaired the Royal Commission on the Status of Women, which played a major role in modifying public attitudes about women's roles in Canada. Bird wrote that "the American role in the war in Vietnam has shocked me deeply; I consider it stupid, unnecessary, cruel, and degrading." However, her opposition to the war went unnoticed. The contributions of American women to Canadian political resistance against the American war in Vietnam have generally been underestimated and insufficiently documented. On Bird's life in Canada, see Florence Bird, *Ann Francis: An Autobiography* (Toronto: Clarke, Irwin, 1974), p. 122. For population trends during the Vietnam war period, see Appendix B, Table B.5.
54. Kasinsky, *Refugees from Militarism.*
55. Elder, "Time, Human Agency, and Social Change," p. 6.
56. Doug McAdam, "Gender as a Mediator of the Activist Experience: The Case of Freedom Summer," *American Journal of Sociology* 5 (1992): 1211–40.

57. Remarks delivered at the National Press Club in Washington, D.C., May 1969. Tape recording, Library of Congress Washington, D.C.

58. For an analysis of the sanctions imposed on those who chose to challenge the selective service laws and the military through the courts, see John Hagan and Ilene Bernstein, "Conflict in Context: The Sanctioning of Draft Resisters, 1963–1976," *Social Problems* 27 (1979): 109–122.

59. Jon Caulfield, *City Form and Everyday Life: Toronto's Gentrification and Critical Urban Practice* (Toronto: University of Toronto Press, 1994).

60. Robert McNamara, *In Retrospect: The Tragedy and Lessons of Vietnam* (New York: Time Books, 1995), p. 269.

61. Ibid., p. 320.

62. The Kleins' story is told in the film documentary *America, Love It or Leave It*. Magic Lantern Communications, 38-77S Pacific Rd., Oakville, Ontario, Canada, L6L 6M4.

2. Opening the Gates

1. "Deserters Will Be Eligible for Status as Immigrants," *Toronto Globe and Mail*, 23 May 1969, p. 1; "Canada to Admit Any U.S. Deserter," *New York Times*, 23 May 1969, p. A5.

2. "United States Citizens Granted Landed Immigrant Status by Specified Ages on Arrival during 1969," National Archives of Canada, RG 76, vol. 692, File 568-3-23—1902.

3. See Renée Kasinsky, *Refugees from Militarism: Draft-Age Americans in Canada* (New Brunswick, N.J.: Transaction Books, 1976).

4. See Margaret Weir and Theda Skocpol, "State Structure and the Possibilities for 'Keynesian' Responses to the Great Depression in Sweden, Britain, and the United States," in P. B. Evans, D. Rueschemeyer, and T. Skocpol, eds., *Bringing the State Back In* (New York: Cambridge University Press, 1985), pp. 107–163; Theda Skocpol and Edwin Amenta, "States and Social Policies," *Annual Review of Sociology* 12 (1986): 131–157; Theda Skocpol, *Protecting Soldiers and Mothers: The Political Origins of Social Policy in the United States* (Cambridge, Mass.: Harvard University Press, Belknap Press, 1992).

5. Nicholas Pedriana and Robin Stryker, "Political Culture Wars 1960s Style: Equal Employment Opportunity—Affirmative Action Law and the Philadelphia Plan," *American Journal of Sociology* 103 (1997):633–691.

6. Skocpol, *Protecting Soldiers and Mothers;* Paul R. Burstein, Marie Bricher, and Rachel L. Einwohner, "Policy Alternatives and Political Change: Work, Family, and Gender on the Congressional Agenda, 1945–1990," *American Sociological Review* 60 (1995): 67–83.

7. Pedriana and Stryker, "Political Culture Wars 1960s Style"; see also David A. Snow, E. Burke Rochford, Jr., Steven K. Worden, and Robert D. Benford, "Frame Alignment Processes, Micromobilization, and Movement Participa-

tion," *American Sociological Review* 51 (1986): 464–481; William Gamson and Andre Modighani, "Media Discourse and Public Opinion on Nuclear Power: A Constructionist Approach," *American Journal of Sociology* 95 (1989): 1–37; Ann Swidler, "Culture in Action," *American Sociological Review* 51 (1986): 273–286; Rhys H. Williams, "Constructing the Public Good: Social Movements and Cultural Resources," *Social Problems* 42 (1995): 124–144.

8. Steven Lukes, *Power: A Radical View* (London: MacMillan, 1974). Lukes's approach builds on earlier work by Peter Bachrach and Morton Baratz, "Two Faces of Power," *American Political Science Review,* 56 (1962): 947–952, and E. E. Schattschneider, *The Semisovereign People: A Realist's View of Democracy in America* (New York: Holt, Rinehart and Winston, 1964).

9. Lukes, *Power,* p. 25.

10. "We'll Treat U.S. Deserters Like Anyone Else, MPs Told," *Toronto Star,* 23 May 1969, p. 2; "Trudeau's Cabinet Divided in 1969," *Toronto Globe and Mail,* 10 February 2000, p. 1.

11. Lukes, *Power,* p. 25.

12. Immigration Department Memo, 2 November 1966, National Archives of Canada, RG 76, vol. 983, File 5660-1, part 1.

13. Tom Kent, *From a Public Purpose: An Experience of Liberal Opposition and Canadian Government* (Montreal: McGill-Queen's University Press, 1988).

14. Document, Appendix B, 26 November 1969, National Archives of Canada, RG 76, vol. 983, File 5660-1.

15. The Canadian immigration law in force at the time, the Immigration Act of 1952, explicitly identified "prohibited classes" that included political subversives, drug users, criminal offenders, prostitutes, homosexuals, mentally or physically defective individuals, chronic alcoholics, and persons "who are . . . or are likely to become public charges." See the *Revised Statutes of Canada,* 1952, vol. 3, chap. 145, pp. 3147–50. The *Manual for Draft-Age Immigrants to Canada* noted in its 1970 fifth edition that "it seems unlikely that anyone would be both acceptable to the [U.S.] army and fall into a prohibited class" (p. 35). *Manual for Draft-Age Immigrants to Canada,* 5th ed. (Toronto: House of Anansi, 1970), revised and edited by Byron Wall.

16. Cited in Kasinsky, *Refugees from Militarism,* p. 63.

17. Tom Kent, interview by author, tape recording, Queen's University, Kingston, Ontario, 22 January 1998.

18. Kent, *From a Public Purpose,* p. 411.

19. See 29 July 1968 revisions to regulations, as reported in 26 November 1969 document. National Archives of Canada, RG 76, vol. 983, File 5660-1.

20. Letter of 17 November 1967 from Tom Kent to M. Cadieux, Under-Secretary of State for External Affairs. National Archives of Canada, RG 76, vol. 983, File 5660-1, part 1.

21. Kent interview.

22. Mitchell Sharpe, interview by author, tape recording, Langevin Block, Ottawa, Ontario, 27 November 1997.

23. Kent interview.
24. See memorandum to the Minister from R. B. Curry, Subject: Briefs on Deserters, 4 March 1969. National Archives of Canada, RG 76, vol. 1112, File 555-38.
25. Kent interview.
26. Quoted in Kasinsky, *Refugees from Militarism,* p. 114.
27. Letter of 9 January 1968 from J. C. Morrison to I. R. Stirling. The instructions in this letter were passed on to district administrators and officers, for example, in a memo on military deserters signed by I. R. Stirling, 12 January 1968. National Archives of Canada, RG 76, vol. 1112, File 555-38.
28. Kent interview.
29. "U.S. Draft Chief Wants to Cut Exodus North," *Toronto Star,* 1 August 1968, p. 21.
30. "U.S. Draft Chief Denies Canada's Help Asked," *Toronto Star,* 2 August 1968, p. 8.
31. Revisions to regulations, 29 July 1968, as reported in 26 November 1969 document. National Archives of Canada, RG 76, vol. 983, File 5660-1. See also Memorandum from Assistant Deputy Minister to the Deputy Minister, 23 May 1969. National Archives of Canada, RG 76, vol. 1112, File 555-38.
32. Ron Haggart, "Underground to Toronto," *Toronto Telegram,* 30 January 1969, p. 8.
33. "Law May Help Deserters," *Toronto Telegram,* 1 February 1969, p. 3.
34. "York U 'Deserters' Sent Back," *Toronto Telegram,* 10 February 1969, p. 9.
35. Memorandum to the Minister, Subject: Canadian Citizens Posing as American Military Deserters, February 11, 1969. National Archives of Canada, RG 76, vol. 1112, File 555-38.
36. "Deserters Refused, Action Termed Proper," *Toronto Globe and Mail,* 18 February 1969, p. 9.
37. "MacEachen Backs Barring U.S. Deserters," *Toronto Star,* 18 February 1969, p. 1.
38. James Ralph Mutchmor, *Mutchmor* (Toronto: Ryerson Press, 1965).
39. John Simpson and Henry MacLeod, "The Politics of Morality in Canada," in Rodney Stark, ed., *Religious Movements: Genesis, Exodus, and Numbers* (New York: Paragon House, 1985).
40. Doug McAdam, "Culture and Social Movements," in Steven Buechler and F. Kurt Cylke, Jr., eds., *Social Movements: Perspectives and Issues* (Mountain View, Calif.: Mayfield Publishing Co., 1997).
41. Resolution Re "Immigration Policy in Relation to Deserters from the American Armed Forces," United Church Board Evangelism Meeting, 20 February 1969, Toronto. National Archives of Canada, RG 66, vol. 725, File 5660-2, part 1.
42. "Who's in Charge Here?" *Toronto Globe and Mail,* 24 February 1969, p. 6.
43. Ibid.
44. On the unique influence of the United Church of Canada, see especially Simpson and MacLeod, "The Politics of Morality in Canada."

45. *Gallup Report,* 23 November 1969.

46. David Surrey, *Choice of Conscience: Vietnam Era Military and Draft Military Resisters in Canada* (New York: Praeger, 1982), p. 116.

47. *Gallup Report,* 21 February 1976.

48. The exact number was 32 percent. See *Gallup Report,* News Release, 23 November 1969.

49. These letters are in the National Archives of Canada, RG 76, vol. 725, file 5560-2, parts 1 and 2.

50. Pierre Berton, *1967: The Last Good Year* (Toronto: Doubleday Canada Ltd, 1997), p. 347.

51. House of Commons, *Debates,* 3 March 1969, "Immigration—Timing of Distinction Deserters and Draft Dodgers," pp. 6166–67; and Memorandum from the Assistant Deputy Minister to the Minister, re: Request for the Production of Instructions Regarding Draft Evaders and Military Deserters, 25 February 1969. National Archives of Canada, RG 76, vol. 1112, File 555-38.

52. House of Commons, *Debates,* 3 March 1969, "Immigration—Timing of Distinction Deserters and Draft Dodgers," pp. 6166–67.

53. Confidential Memorandum to Cabinet, "Admission to Canada of Draft Dodgers and Military Resisters," 12 March 1969. National Archives of Canada, RG 76, vol. 983, File 5660-1, part 5.

54. Letter from Mark MacGuigan to Allan MacEachen, 13 March 1969. National Archives of Canada, RG 76, vol. 725, File 5660-2, part 3.

55. Memorandum from Minister (MacEachen) to Deputy Minister re: United Church Board of Evangelism 20 February 1969. National Archives of Canada, RG 76, vol. 725, file 5660-2, part 1.

56. Report by the Committee on Armed Services, United States Senate, "Treatment of Deserters from Military Service," 21–22 May 1968, p. 44.

57. Memorandum from the Assistant Deputy Minister to the Minister, re: United Church Board of Evangelism, Toronto, 20 February 1969. National Archives of Canada, RG 76, vol. 1112, File 555-38.

58. Draft letter from Allan MacEachen to the Reverend Gordon K. Stewart, 19 March 1969 (note dated 22 March 1969). National Archives of Canada, RG 76, vol. 725, File 5660-2, part 3.

59. Memorandum from Senior Planning Officer to Director General of Operations, "Statement on Draft Dodgers and Military Deserters," 24 March 1969. National Archives of Canada, RG 76, vol. 983, File 5660-1, part 5.

60. Confidential Memorandum, "Draft Dodgers and Deserters," included in briefing documents for Prime Minister's visit to Washington, dated 18 March 1969. National Archives of Canada, RG 76, vol. 983, File 5660-1, part 5.

61. "In the Shadow of the Missile," *Time,* 28 March 1969; "Nixon, Trudeau Confer Here on World Troubles," *Washington Post,* 25 March 1969, p. A10.

62. Pierre Elliott Trudeau's remarks at the National Press Club, Washington, D.C., 25 March 1969, tape recording, Library of Congress, LWO 8217 449.

63. "Off to an Encouraging Start," *Toronto Globe and Mail,* 26 March 1969, p. 6.

64. Allan MacEachen, interview by author, tape recording, Victoria Block, Ottawa, Ontario, 7 January 1998.

65. Memorandum from Assistant Deputy Minister Dymond to Deputy Minister Couillard, [no title], 15 April 1969. See also Memorandum from Assistant Deputy Minister to the Deputy Minister, Subject: Submission on Deserters, 5 April 1969 and Memorandum from Deputy Minister Couillard to Minister MacEachen, Subject: Submission on Deserters, 23 April 1969. National Archives of Canada, RG 76, vol. 983, File 5660-1, part 5.

66. Telegram from R. B. McClure and Ernest E. Long of the United Church of Canada General Council to Prime Minister Pierre Elliott Trudeau. National Archives of Canada, RG 76, vol. 725, File 5660-2, part 5.

67. "The New Church," *Toronto Globe and Mail,* 3 May 1969, p. 6.

68. "No Haven for U.S. Deserters," *Toronto Telegram,* 6 May 1969, p. 6.

69. Stephen Clarkson, "Remove the Barriers to U.S. 'Refugees,'" *Toronto Star,* 7 May 1969, p. 6.

70. Ibid.

71. Among the members were Dalton Camp, Jack Ludwig, Farley Mowat, Robert Fulford, Barbara Frum, June Callwood, Doris Anderson, H. Adelman, W. Kilbourn, Vince Kelly, Stephen Clarkson, Mel Watkins, Charles Templeton, Patrick Watson, Peter Russell, M. Moore, Rev. Gordon Stewart, Jane Jacobs, William Spira, and Allen Linden. See Committee for Fair Immigration Policy, Press Release, 9 March 1969, 11:00 A.M. National Archives of Canada, RG 76, vol. 725, File 5660-2, part 6.

72. [Jack Ludwig,] "Why We Should Not Desert Our Sovereignty," *Toronto Globe and Mail,* 9 May 1969, p. 7.

73. Sharpe interview.

74. Memorandum from the Assistant Deputy Minister to the Deputy Minister, 23 May 1969. National Archives of Canada, RG 76, vol. 1112, File 555-38.

75. Lukes, *Power,* chap. 4.

3. Toronto's American Ghetto

1. Robert Fulford, "Our Newest Minority," *Saturday Night,* November 1968, p. 11.

2. Douglas Fetherling, *Travels by Night: A Memoir of the Sixties* (Toronto: Lester Publishing, 1994), p. 227.

3. Roger Gould, "Multiple Networks and Mobilization in the Paris Commune, 1871," *American Sociological Review* 56 (1991): 716–729.

4. More specifically, Hemingway wrote in a letter, "Christ, I hate to leave Paris for Toronto the City of Churches." Cited by James Lemon, "Toronto among North American Cities," in Victor Russell, ed., *Forging a Consensus: Historical Essays on Toronto* (Toronto: University of Toronto Press, 1984).

5. Cited in Jeffrey Reitz and Janet Lum, "Immigration and Toronto's Stylish New Personality," *Footnotes* 25, no. 3 (March 1997): 1.

6. S. M. Lipset, "Historical Traditions and National Characteristics: A Comparative

Analysis of Canada and the U.S." *Canadian Journal of Sociology* 11 (1986): 113–155, and *Continental Divide: The Values and Institutions of the United States of America and Canada* (Toronto: C. D. Howe Institute, 1989).

7. Arnold Dashefsky, Jan DeAmicis, Bernard Lazerwitz, and Ephraim Tabory, *Americans Abroad: A Comparative Study of Emigrants from the United States* (New York: Plenum, 1992).

8. Cited by Joe Berridge, *Toronto Globe and Mail,* 10 April 1995, p. A13.

9. Myrna Kostash, *Long Way from Home* (Toronto: James Lorimer and Co., 1980), p. 47.

10. John Porter, *The Vertical Mosaic* (Toronto: University of Toronto Press, 1965).

11. Jon Caulfield, *City Form and Everyday Life: Toronto's Gentrification and Critical Urban Practice* (Toronto: University of Toronto Press, 1994).

12. Subsequent praise for the results of these efforts is found, for example, in Arthur Herschman, "Foreign Travel," *Science,* 14 November 1980, 763; Anthony Astrachan, "A City that Works," *Harpers,* December 1974, 14–19; Edmund Futtermayer, "Toronto the New Great City," *Fortune,* September 1974, 126–137.

13. Cited in Berton, *1967: The Last Good Year* (Toronto: Doubleday Canada, 1997), p. 215.

14. Fulford, "Our Newest Minority," p. 12.

15. Robin Mathews, "Opinion: On Draft Dodging and U.S. Imperialism in Canada," *Canadian Dimension,* February–March 1970: 10.

16. *Amex* Archives, State Historical Society of Wisconsin, University of Wisconsin–Madison (henceforth referred to as the State Historical Society of Wisconsin).

17. The referral book that logs this placement service is preserved in the Archives of the Toronto Anti-Draft Program in the Thomas Fisher Rare Book Library, Robarts Library, University of Toronto.

18. See note 2.

19. Fetherling, *Travels by Night,* p. 238.

20. Ibid., p. 113.

21. J. L. Granatstein, *Canadians and Anti-Americanism* (Toronto: HarperCollins, 1996), p. 170.

22. Fetherling, *Travels by Night,* p. 102.

23. Ibid., pp. 130, 135.

24. Oliver Clausen, "Boys without a Country," *New York Times Magazine,* 21 May 1967, p. 97.

25. Fetherling, *Travels by Night,* p. 138.

26. See Berton, *1967: The Last Good Year,* pp. 198, 203.

27. Anastasia Erland, "Mark Satin, Draft Dodger," *Saturday Night,* September 1967, p. 21.

28. Renée Kasinsky, *Refugees from Militarism: Draft-Age Americans in Canada* (New Brunswick, N.J.: Transaction Books, 1976), p. 98. See also Kostash, *Long Way from Home,* pp. 60–61.

29. Erland, "Mark Satin, Draft Dodger," pp. 21–23.

30. A picture of this house is preserved in the Archives of the Toronto Anti-Draft

Program in the Thomas Fisher Rare Book Library, Robarts Library, University of Toronto.

31. Mark Satin, *New Age Options* (Fresno, Calif.: California State University Press, 1991).

32. The archives of TADP contain records of the batches of ten, twenty, thirty, and more copies of the *Manual* that were mailed to the United States during 1968 and 1969. The *Manual* went through six editions and ultimately included a supplement designed to help resisters in Sweden make their way back to North America, to Canada.

33. The following quotes from Phil Mullins are taken from the American Ghetto Oral History Tapes, Multicultural History Society of Ontario, Toronto, Ontario, circa 1978–79 (henceforth referred to as American Ghetto Oral History Tapes).

34. Ron Haggart, "Underground to Toronto," *Toronto Telegram,* 30 January 1969, p. 8.

35. Paul Beiley, "Young Americans in Exile," *Niagara Falls Gazette,* 9 January 1972, p. 1E.

36. Ibid.

37. These tapes are preserved in the Collections of the Ontario Provincial Archives and in the American Ghetto Oral History Tapes.

38. The accounts of The Yellow Ford Truck and Ragnarokr draw extensively from the tapes of Jim Wilson and Phil Mullins, American Ghetto Oral History Tapes.

39. Phil Mullins interview, American Ghetto Oral History Tapes.

40. This account of the Cosmic Egg draws extensively from the Kent Lawrence interview, American Ghetto Oral History Tapes.

41. Michael Ormsby interview, American Ghetto Oral History Tapes.

42. John Phillips interview, American Ghetto Oral History Tapes.

43. See Bill Davidson, "Hell, No, We Won't Go: Why Young Americans are Deserters, Exiles, Fugitives, Conscientious Objectors," *Saturday Evening Post,* 27 January 1968, pp. 21–27.

44. Ibid.

45. Flyer prepared by the Baldwin Street Gallery, 23 Baldwin Street, Toronto, Ontario (n.d.).

46. Stephen Cornell and Douglas Hartmann, *Ethnicity and Race: Making Identities in a Changing World* (Thousand Oaks, Calif.: Pine Forge Press, 1998).

47. Michael Ormsby interview, American Ghetto Oral History Tapes.

48. Lewis Feurer, *The Conflict of Generations: The Character and Significance of Student Movements* (New York: Basic Books, 1969). Scott Young, "Draft Dodgers: A Passive Breed Doing Nothing and Going Nowhere," *Toronto Globe and Mail,* 16 February 1968.

49. "Calm Finally Descends on Baldwin Street: Rock Fans Rock Cruiser after Arrest," *Toronto Daily Star,* 15 September 1969, p. 27.

4. Activism by Exile

1. Doug McAdam, *Freedom Summer* (New York: Oxford University Press, 1988).

2. Douglas McAdam, "The Biographical Consequences of Activism," *American So-*

ciological Review 54 (1989): 745–760, quote on 745; see also Douglas McAdam, "Recruitment to High Risk Activism: The Case of Freedom Summer," *American Journal of Sociology* 92 (1986): 64–90.

3. Ibid., p. 749.

4. Todd Gitlin, *The Sixties: Years of Hope, Days of Rage* (New York: Bantam Books, 1993), p. 384.

5. See Renée Kasinsky, *Refugees from Militarism: Draft-Age Americans in Canada* (New Brunswick, N.J.: Transaction Books, 1976), p. 98.

6. Stanley Kuntler, *Abuse of Power: The New Nixon Tapes* (New York: The Free Press, 1997), p. 17.

7. McAdam, "The Biographical Consequences of Activism."

8. Gitlin, *The Sixties*, p. 66.

9. Kasinsky, *Refugees from Militarism*, p. 134.

10. Doug McAdam, "Gender as a Mediator of the Activist Experience: The Case of Freedom Summer," *American Journal of Sociology* 97 (1992): 1211–1240, quote on 1214.

11. See Mark Granovetter, "The Strength of Weak Ties," *American Journal of Sociology* 78 (1973): 1360–80, and "Economic Action and Social Structure: The Problem of Embeddedness," *American Journal of Sociology* 91 (1985): 481–510.

12. Kasinsky, *Refugees from Militarism*, p. 98.

13. McAdam, *Freedom Summer*, p. 752n. That is, the current political activism of each member of the sample was measured using a scale constructed from the following information gathered in the interviews. First, members received one point for answering "yes" to a question asking whether they were currently involved in any social movement. Then, for all those movements in which they in a subsequent question reported being "actively involved," they received three additional points. Finally, if they were currently working primarily in an activist capacity, they received five more points. The respondent's score on the contemporary activism scale was the sum of these points.

14. McAdam, "Gender as a Mediator of the Activist Experience.

15. Ibid.

16. Doug McAdam, "Specifying the Relationship between Social Ties and Activism," *American Journal of Sociology* 99 (1993): 640–667.

17. I tested this by including main and interaction terms for different-sex siblings in regression analyses. These main and interaction effects were statistically nonsignificant.

18. For two very different discussions of the usefulness of siblings in social mobility research, see Daniel Bertaux, "Social Genealogies Commented on and Compared: An Instrument for Observing Social Mobility Preferences in the 'Long Duree,'" *Current Sociology* 43 (1995): 69–88, and Robert Hauser, "A Note on Two Models of Sibling Resemblance," *American Journal of Sociology* 93 (1988): 1401–23.

19. McAdam, "The Biographical Consequences of Activism"; see also James Fendrich, "Activists Ten Years Later: A Test of Generational Unit Continuity," *Journal of Social Issues* 30 (1974): 95–118, and Michael Maidenburg and Phillip

Meyer, "The Berkeley Rebels Five Years Later: Has Age Mellowed the Pioneer Radicals?" seven-part series, *Detroit Free Press*, 1–7 February 1970.

20. Siblings' income serves in this analysis as an omnibus control for a range of otherwise unmeasured genetic and family socialization variables.

21. The first Canadian immigration department study showed that of thirty-four draft resister and thirty-one military resister files examined, only three had criminal records. The criminal records probably included only minor drug charges. See draft and memo to Minister for use in answering House question number 328, October 1968, National Archives RG 76, vol. 691, File 568-3-23-328. When this issue was raised again two years later, the immigration department reported, "We in the Department have not noticed any new or discernible pattern of offences . . . attributable to U.S. visitors or immigrants." See memo to the Minister, "Subject: U.S. Exiles Turning to Crime," 24 April 1970, National Archives RG 76, vol. 6, File 5660-1.

5. Two Amnesties and a Jailing

1. Personal service contract between Dennis Hayward and Tim Maloney on behalf of the Canadian Coalition of War Objectors, 9 August 1973, in Archives of the Toronto Anti-Draft Program in the Thomas Fisher Rare Book Library, Robarts Library, University of Toronto (hereafter Toronto Anti-Draft Program Archives).

2. A copy of this tape-recorded announcement is preserved in the Toronto Anti-Draft Program Archives.

3. Roger Williams, "The Parley in Montreal," *Amex-Canada*, June 1970, p. 10.

4. A more convincing assessment of the influence of American resisters on student politics in Canada was provided by James Laxer, "The Americanization of the Canadian Student Movement," in Ian Lumsden, ed., *Close the 49th Parallel* (Toronto: University of Toronto Press, 1970), pp. 275–287.

5. *Toronto Star*, 26 October 1970. See Jack Colhoun, "War Resisters in Exile: The Memoirs of *Amex*-Canada," *Amex*, November–December 1977, pp. 21–22.

6. See, for example, Clive Cocking, "How Did the Canadian Mounties Develop Their Unfortunate Habit of Deporting People They Don't Happen to Like?" *Saturday Night*, June 1970, 28–30; and Charles Campbell, "RCMP Harassment of U.S. Deserters: A Three Year History," *Amex*, October–November 1970, 18–19.

7. Todd Gitlin, *The Sixties: Years of Hope, Days of Rage* (New York: Bantam Books, 1993).

8. Tom Bates, *Rads: The 1970 Bombing of the Army Math Center at the University of Wisconsin and Its Aftermath* (New York: Harper Collins, 1992).

9. *Amex*, August–September 1970, 8–9. Ron Lambert, a sociologist at the University of Waterloo with a distinguished record of Canadian scholarship and years of experience in counseling American resisters in southern Ontario, responded in *Amex* by denying that these new immigrants were a threat or menace to Canadian society.

10. "The Ardent Exiles: U.S. Deserters," *Toronto Star*, 17 December 1970, p. 6.

11. Letter from Roger Williams to Jack Colhoun, 30 December 1971, *Amex* Archives, State Historical Society of Wisconsin.

12. A classic picture of this event appeared in the *Toronto Star* on 2 February 1972, p. 7.

13. Ibid.

14. For example, see "Few U.S. Exiles Expected to Return," *Toronto Star*, 18 January 1972, p. 1, and Carolyn Toll, "War Resisters Reject Amnesty," *Chicago Tribune*, 18 January 1972, p. 1.

15. Robert Fulford, "American Exiles Making an Impression on Canadian Culture," *Toronto Star*, 2 February 1972.

16. Bates, *Rads*, p. 353.

17. Valerie Johnson, "An American Tragedy in a Canadian Courtroom," *Saturday Night*, September 1972, p. 22.

18. Ibid., p. 26.

19. Pierre Vallières, *White Niggers of America* (Toronto: McClelland and Stewart, 1971).

20. Johnson, "An American Tragedy," p. 26.

21. Ibid.

22. Lawrence Baskir and William Strauss, *Chance and Circumstance: The Draft, the War, and the Vietnam Generation* (New York: Alfred Knopf, 1978), p. 68.

23. Ibid., p. 107.

24. Aaron Ruvinsky, "Aid Sought for 50,000 Draft Exiles," *Washington Evening Star*, 16 January 1971.

25. Saul Levine, "Draft Dodgers: Coping with Stress, Adapting to Exile," *American Journal of Orthopsychiatry* 42 (1972): 431–440.

26. Ibid., p. 435.

27. "Some U.S. Exiles Turning to Crime," *Toronto Globe and Mail*, 24 April 1970, p. 1.

28. *Toronto Star*, 25 January 1971, p. 1.

29. Levine, "Draft Dodgers," p. 438.

30. Ibid., p. 439.

31. Richard Killmer, Robert Lecky, and Debrah Wiley, *They Can't Go Home Again: The Story of America's Political Refugees* (Philadelphia: Pilgrim Press, 1971).

32. The five were Jean Marchand, Allan MacEachen, Otto Lang, Bryce Mackasey, and Robert Andras. See John Beaufoy, "Immigration Backlog Turns Newcomers into Residents," *Toronto Star*, 2 February 1973.

33. Hugh Winsor, "'Crisis' Caused Arbitrary Cutoff of Immigration Flow, Andras Concedes," *Toronto Globe and Mail*, 6 April 1973, p. 8.

34. Press release, 3 November 1972, Office of the Minister of Manpower and Immigration, Toronto Anti-Draft Program Archives.

35. See the *Amex* press release issued 4 January 1973, entitled "Canada Now Closed to War Resisters Because of New Immigration Rules," *Amex* Archives, State Historical Society of Wisconsin.

36. Notes from Toronto Anti-Draft Program Border Crisis Meeting, 10 December 1972, *Amex* Archives, State Historical Society of Wisconsin.

37. Patrick Buchanan, "The 'Facts' on Exiles," *New York Times,* 20 February 1973, p. 29.

38. Restricted cable, "Draft Dodgers—*New York Times* Article," 21 February 1973, National Archives of Canada, RG76, vol. 6, File 5660–1.

39. Confidential cable from Washington to Ottawa, 21 February 1973, p. 2, National Archives of Canada, RG76, vol. 6, File 5660–1.

40. Ibid., pp. 3, 4.

41. Confidential cable from Ottawa to Washington, D.C., 26 February 1973, pp. 2, 3, National Archives of Canada, RG76, vol. 6, File 5660-1.

42. Confidential letter from Undersecretary of State for External Affairs to Deputy Minister of Department of Manpower and Immigration, 28 February 1973, National Archives of Canada, RG76, vol. 6, File 5660-1.

43. Letter from Carolyn Kline and Carolyn Dingman, Co-chairs of the Quaker Social Concerns Committee of Vancouver, to Prime Minister Trudeau, 8 May 1973, Toronto Anti-Draft Program Archives.

44. Letter from Richard Brown, Toronto Anti-Draft Program, to Andrew Brewin, Member of Parliament, 8 June 1973, Toronto Anti-Draft Program Archives.

45. Press Release, Office of the Minister of Manpower and Immigration, 18 June 1973, Toronto Anti-Draft Program Archives.

46. Minister's Opening Remarks for Committee Stage of Bill C-197 to Amend the Immigration Appeal Board Act, Toronto Anti-Draft Program Archives.

47. Remarks about Immigration Amendments, by Dick Brown, 16 July 1973, Toronto Anti-Draft Program Archives.

48. "United Church Supports Government Olive Branch to Illegal Immigrants," The United Church of Canada, 1 August 1973, Toronto Anti-Draft Program Archives.

49. Colhoun, "War Resisters in Exile," p. 36.

50. Joe Serge, "Deadline September 30 for Illegal Immigrants to Get Status Legalized," *Toronto Star,* 20 July 1973, p. 1.

51. Terrence Belford, "Four Hundred Step Forward Daily, Seek Legal Landed Status," *Toronto Globe and Mail,* 7 September 1973, p. 1.

52. Norman Hartley, "Offer of Landed Status No Trap, Andras Assures Illegal Immigrants," *Toronto Globe and Mail,* 11 September 1973, p. 4.

53. Bill Kovach, "National Drive Seeks Amnesty for Deserters and Draft Evaders," *New York Times,* 28 December 1971, p. 1.

54. Letter from Henry Schwarzschild to Jack Colhoun, 10 February 1972, *Amex* Archives, State Historical Society of Wisconsin.

55. Baskir and Strauss, *Chance and Circumstance,* p. 228.

56. Letter from Henry Schwarzschild to Jack Colhoun, 3 March 1972, *Amex* Archives, State Historical Society of Wisconsin.

57. Letter from Henry Schwarzschild to Dee Knight, 13 March 1972, *Amex* Archives, State Historical Society of Wisconsin.

58. Statement of Henry Schwarzschild before the Senate Committee on Administrative Practice and Procedure, Hearings on Amnesty, 1 March 1972, *Amex* Archives, State Historical Society of Wisconsin.

59. Letter to Sisters and Brothers from Dee Knight, 15 March 1972, *Amex* Archives, State Historical Society of Wisconsin.

60. See Senator George McGovern, "Vietnam Amnesty," *Congressional Record*, 92nd Cong., 1st sess., 19 October 1971, vol. 117, part 28: 3669.

61. Knight interview, July 1998, New York City.

62. Jerry Lembcke, *The Spitting Image: Myth, Memory, and the Legacy of Vietnam* (New York: New York University Press, 1998), p. 67.

63. Address by the Vice-President of the United States, Veterans of Foreign Wars National Convention, Minneapolis, Minnesota, 225 August 1972, *Amex* Archives, State Historical Society of Wisconsin.

64. See Baskir and Strauss, *Chance and Circumstance*, p. 209.

65. William Borders, "U.S. Exiles in Canada See No Amnesty," *New York Times*, 15 November 1972, p. 14.

66. Letter from Jack Colhoun to Henry Schwarzschild, 27 November 1972, *Amex* Archives, State Historical Society of Wisconsin.

67. Anthony Ripley, "Amnesty for Draft Resisters Is Expected to Be Divisive Political Issue for Years," *New York Times*, 30 January 1973, p. 12.

68. Letter from Fritz Efaw to "Comrades," [summer] 1972, *Amex* Archives, State Historical Society of Wisconsin.

69. Letter from Dee Knight to Fritz Efaw, 3 August 1972, *Amex* Archives, State Historical Society of Wisconsin.

70. Knight interview, July 1998, New York City.

71. Letter from Marv [no last name] to Tony Wagner, Dee Knight, and Jack Colhoun, 10 December 1972, *Amex* Archives, State Historical Society of Wisconsin.

72. Letter to "comrades" from Fritz Efaw as President of the Union of American Exiles in Britain, 29 December 1972, *Amex* Archives, State Historical Society of Wisconsin.

73. Colhoun, "War Resisters in Exile," pp. 29–30.

74. Lembcke, *Spitting Image*, p. 68.

75. Belinda Robnett, "African-American Women in the Civil Rights Movement, 1954–1965: Gender, Leadership, and Micromobilization," *American Journal of Sociology* 101 (1996): 1661–93.

76. Letter from Stan Pietlock to Charles Stimac, 25 November 1973, *Amex* Archives, State Historical Society of Wisconsin.

77. Letter from staff to Stan Pietlock, 16 November 1972, *Amex* Archives, State Historical Society of Wisconsin.

78. Sixteen-point agreement, n.d., *Amex* Archives, State Historical Society of Wisconsin.

79. Stan Pietlock, "*Amex* Senior Editor Resigns in Protest over Elitism and American Chauvinsim," manuscript, *Amex* Archives, State Historical Society of Wisconsin.

80. Letter from Stan Pietlock to Charles Stimac, 25 November 1973, *Amex* Archives, State Historical Society of Wisconsin.

81. Report to the "Exile Constituency" from Dee Knight, 15 March 1974, *Amex* Archives, State Historical Society of Wisconsin.

82. Charles Payne, "Men Led, but Women Organized: Movement Participation of Women in the Mississippi Delta," in Vicki Crawford, Jaqueline Rouse, and Barbara Woods, eds., *Women in the Civil Rights Movement* (Brooklyn, N.Y.: Carlson Press, 1990).

83. Letter from Patricia Schroeder to Albert Reynolds, 15 October 1973, and letter from Bella Abzug to Albert Reynolds, 16 October 1973, both in *Amex* Archives, State Historical Society of Wisconsin.

84. Colhoun, "War Resisters in Exile," p. 39.

85. "Ford Wants Draft Dodgers to Come Home," *Toronto Globe and Mail,* 20 August 1974, p. 3.

86. "An Urgent Plea from Exiled War Resisters," *New York Times,* 25 August 1974.

87. Letter to subscribers of *Amex* from the *Amex* staff, 28 August 1974.

88. "Two Years' Service, New Loyalty Oath Ford Amnesty Deal," *Toronto Star,* 16 September 1974, pp. A1–2.

89. "Ford's Amnesty: No Appeal and Pay Is Low," *Toronto Star,* 17 September 1974, p. A3.

90. "A Tough Choice for Exiles," *Toronto Globe and Mail,* 17 September 1974, p. 6.

91. John MacKenzie, "U.S. Officials Prepare Plan for Amnesty," *Washington Post,* 30 August 1974, p. 1.

92. "Saxbe and Schlesinger Meet on Draft-Evader Report," *New York Times,* 30 August 1974, p. 1.

93. "Draft Resister Steve Grossman Speaks at Amnesty Conference: Plans Ten-City Tour in Fourteen Days," National Council for Universal and Unconditional Amnesty, for release 16 November 1974. *Amex* Archives, State Historical Society of Wisconsin.

94. Cited in Colhoun, "War Resisters in Exile," p. 53.

95. "Amnesty Plan Not Working, Resisters Say," *Toronto Star,* 7 October 1974.

96. Ross Munro, "Traps, Loopholes for the Evader in Amnesty Plan," *Toronto Globe and Mail,* 8 November 1974, p. 7.

97. Anthony Ripley, "Draftee Clemency Program Is Assailed," *New York Times,* 22 December 1974, p. 28.

98. Vernon Jordan, "Amnesty Still an Issue," *National Urban League, New York City,* 5 November 1975.

99. "Amnesty Plan Not Working, Resisters Say," *Toronto Star,* 7 October 1974, p. 7.

100. "Draft Dodgers Urged to Boycott Amnesty Extension," *Toronto Star,* 31 January 1975, p. B7.

101. Ross Munro, "Ford's Amnesty: The Last, Best Chance for Draft Evaders?" *Toronto Globe and Mail,* 11 February 1975, p. 7.

102. Jack Colhoun, "Amnesty Program Still a Failure, War Resisters Stress," *Toronto Globe and Mail,* 13 February 1975, p. 7.

103. Paul Montgomery, "End-of-War Rally Brings Out 50,000," *New York Times,* 12 May 1975, p. 1.

104. Knight interview, July 1998, New York City.

105. Fritz Efaw, memo on UAEB Amnesty Actions in November 1974, *Amex* Archives, State Historical Society of Wisconsin.

106. Letter from Fritz Efaw to Jack Colhoun, 4 January 1975, *Amex* Archives, State Historical Society of Wisconsin.

107. For further details of the shift in editorial opinion, see "Editorial and Popular Pressure Tip Ford's Hand," *NCUUA Amnesty Update,* Summer 1975, p. 10, *Amex* Archives, State Historical Society of Wisconsin.

108. Open letter from NCUUA to amnesty supporters, 16 December 1975, *Amex* Archives, State Historical Society of Wisconsin.

109. Letter from Fritz Efaw to Amex-Canada, 30 January 1976, *Amex* Archives, State Historical Society of Wisconsin.

110. Letter from Imma Zigas to Fritz Efaw, 13 February 1976, *Amex* Archives, State Historical Society of Wisconsin.

111. Letter from Senator Philip Hart to Steve Grossman, 16 February 1976, *Amex* Archives, State Historical Society of Wisconsin.

112. Letter from Fritz Efaw to Amex and other groups, 19 March 1976, *Amex* Archives, State Historical Society of Wisconsin.

113. "Jimmy Carter on Vietnam Pardon," Jimmy Carter Presidential Campaign, n.d., *Amex* Archives, State Historical Society of Wisconsin.

114. *Amex* interview with Stuart Eizenstadt, 18 June 1976, *Amex* Archives, State Historical Society of Wisconsin.

115. Colhoun, "War Resisters in Exile," p. 58.

116. Letter from Fritz Efaw to "Comrades" at *Amex,* 19 March 1976, *Amex* Archives, State Historical Society of Wisconsin.

117. Letter from Fritz Efaw to "Comrades" (*Amex*), 22 April 1976, *Amex* Archives, State Historical Society of Wisconsin.

118. Letter from Fritz Efaw to Irma Zigas, 15 June 1976, *Amex* Archives, State Historical Society of Wisconsin.

119. Ibid.

120. Letter from Jack Colhoun to Fritz Efaw, 22 June 1976, *Amex* Archives, State Historical Society of Wisconsin.

121. Knight interview, July 1998, New York City.

122. "Fritz Efaw: A Brief History," Press Release from National Coalition for Universal and Unconditional Amnesty, n.d., *Amex* Archives, State Historical Society of Wisconsin.

123. Knight interview, July 1998, New York City.

124. The following sequence of events is based on "Chronology of Events, NCUUA at the Democratic National Convention, New York City, July 8–15, 1976," from notes prepared by Duane Shank, 26 July 1976, *Amex* Archives, State Historical Society of Wisconsin.

125. Knight interview, July 1998, New York City.

126. Colhoun letter to Efaw, 22 June 1976.

127. "Speech by Disabled Viet Nam Veteran Ron Kovic Seconding the V.P. Nomination of Fritz Efaw," n.d., *Amex* Archives, State Historical Society of Wisconsin.

128. "Speech of Fritz Efaw, Nominee for Vice President," 15 July 1976, *Amex* Archives, State Historical Society of Wisconsin.

129. Colhoun, "War Resisters in Exile," p. 60.

130. Knight interview, July 1998, New York City.

131. See "Amnesty Program: Summer, Fall and Winter," prepared by *Amex* for NCUUA, July 1976, *Amex* Archives, State Historical Society of Wisconsin.

132. "Statement of NCUUA, presented by Fritz Efaw, draft resister nominated for Vice-President at Democratic Convention, July, 1976," Press Conference, Statler Hilton Hotel, New York City, 19 November 1976, *Amex* Archives, State Historical Society of Wisconsin.

133. "Position Paper: Future Directions of NCUUA," June 1977, *Amex* Archives, State Historical Society of Wisconsin.

134. Jack Colhoun, "Still the Back of the Bus: Vietnam Pardon, Stage II," *The Nation,* 14 May 1977.

135. Letter from Jack Colhoun to Sam Brown, 2 March 1977, *Amex* Archives, State Historical Society of Wisconsin.

136. Letter from Sam Brown to Jack Colhoun, 11 March 1977, *Amex* Archives, State Historical Society of Wisconsin.

137. Jack Colhoun, "The Exiles' Role in War Resistance," *Monthly Review,* March 1979, 29–42.

138. Baskir and Strauss, *Chance and Circumstance.*

6. Choosing Canada

1. Jack Colhoun, "War Resisters in Exile: The Memoirs of *Amex*-Canada," *Amex,* November–December 1977, p. 63.

2. This episode of *All in the Family* is available for viewing at the Museum of Television and Radio in New York City.

3. *Amex* Archives, State Historical Society of Wisconsin.

4. Russell Nye, "A Case of Sloppy Journalism," *Washington Post,* 9 February 1972.

5. James Dickerson, *North to Canada: Men and Women against the Vietnam War* (Westport, Conn.: Praeger, 1999).

6. Patrick Buchanan, "The 'Facts' on Exiles," *New York Times,* 20 February 1973, p. 29.

7. See Renée Kasinsky, *Refugees from Militarism: Draft-Age Americans in Canada* (New Brunswick, N.J.: Transaction Books, 1976), Appendix C.

8. Denise Bukowski, "Letter to Chiclets," from an unpublished recollection reprinted with permission of the author, p. 8.

9. Lawrence Baskir and William Strauss, *Chance and Circumstance: The Draft, the War, and the Vietnam Generation* (New York: Alfred Knopf, 1978), pp. 185, 201.

10. The estimate is complicated by the fact that the Canadian census asks respondents about the country of their birth, while immigration statistics are based on the country subjects have come from. I therefor made adjustments in Table B.6 to estimate the numbers of American-born U.S. resisters who arrived from 1967 through 1972. Based on the calculation of American-born arrivals, I then

estimated the number of American-born U.S. resisters who remained in Canada, as indicated in the 1996 Canadian census. The ratios of the third to the second set of columns in Table B.6 yield the proportions of U.S.-born resisters who stayed as of 1996.

11. Bukowski, "Letter to Chiclets," p. 9.

12. Neil Smelser, "The Rational and the Ambivalent in the Social Sciences," *American Sociological Review* 63 (1998): 1–16.

13. In making this point Smelser builds on the work of Donald Levine, *The Flight from Ambiguity: Essays in Social and Cultural Theory* (Chicago: University of Chicago Press, 1985).

14. Albert O. Hirschman, *Exit, Voice, and Loyalty: Responses to Decline in Firms, Organizations, and States* (Cambridge, Mass.: Harvard University Press, 1970), pp. 112–113.

15. Smelser, "The Rational and the Ambivalent," p. 12.

16. Eviatar Zerubavel, *Social Mindscapes: An Invitation to Cognitive Sociology* (Cambridge, Mass.: Harvard University Press, 1997), p. 92.

17. Stephen Cornell and Douglas Hartman, *Ethnicity and Race: Masking Identities in a Changing World* (Thousand Oaks, Calif.: Pine Forge Press, 1998), p. 193.

18. Smelser, "The Rational and the Ambivalent," p. 11.

19. Ibid., p. 6; italics in original.

20. Bukowski, "Letter to Chiclets," p. 3.

Appendix A

1. Leo Goodman, "Snowball Sampling," *Annals of Mathematical Statistics* 32 (1961): 148–170.

2. Douglas Heckathorn, "Respondent-Driven Sampling: A New Approach to the Study of Hidden Populations," *Social Problems* 44 (1997): 174–199.

3. These contacts were provided by Alan Haig-Brown, author of *Hell No, We Won't Go: Vietnam Draft Resisters in Canada* (Vancouver: Raincoast Books, 1996).

4. These contacts were provided by Kirwin Cox, producer of *America, Love or Leave It,* National Film Board, distributed by Magic Lantern Communications Ltd., Oakville, Ontario.

5. The files were those of the Toronto Anti-Draft Program, maintained in the Thomas Fisher Rare Book Library, Robarts Library of the University of Toronto, and *Amex,* maintained in the archives of the State Historical Society of Wisconsin.

6. The American Ghetto, The Multicultural History Society of Ontario, 5 Hoskin Avenue, Toronto, Ontario, M5S 1H7.

7. The RDS system is effective in producing large referral chains because even uncooperative subjects are amenable to social pressure from peers, especially friends, who are directly brought into the sampling methodology. Heckathorn has demonstrated that within several waves most respondent-driven samples provide a good cross-section that incorporates the diversity of the target population.

8. This calendar was adapted from the work of Deborah Freedman, Arland Thornton, Donald Camburn, Duane Alwin, and Linda Young-DeMarco, "The Life History Calendar: A Technique for Collecting Retrospective Data," *Sociological Methodology* 18 (1988): 37–68.

9. Eviatar Zerubavel, *Social Mindscapes: An Invitation to Cognitive Sociology* (Cambridge, Mass.: Harvard University Press, 1997).

10. Ibid., p. 87.

11. See Daniel Bertaux, "Social Genealogies Commented on and Compared: An Instrument for Observing Social Mobility Preferences in the 'Longue Duree'," *Current Sociology* 43 (1995): 69–88.

12. Ibid., p. 75.

13. Ibid., p. 86.

Index